"A beautiful literary debut...part t[...]
lesson in grace and forgiveness, part l[...]
affecting memoirs to come along sin[...]
and Dave Eggers' *A Heartbreaking Work of Staggering Genius*, this
is a brave, lucid, moving account of an ordinary life turned inside
out—and back again." —*The Atlanta Journal-Constitution*

"Moran honestly depicts his life in all its pain and beauty,
poignantly chronicling his journey from boy to man."
—*National Catholic Reporter*

"Martin Moran not only writes unflinchingly about the sexual
abuse of a child, he expands it into a meditation on suffering, despair, forgiveness, redemption, and the mysterious workings of
grace. He elevates the confessional to the level of art."
—Michael Cunningham, author of *The Hours*

"Powerfully lays bare the largely accidental work of forgetting and
the long march back to memory." —*Out*

"A beautiful book. Martin Moran is a graceful, witty, perceptive
writer, remarkably brave, free of self-pity.... [B]ecause he refuses
simplification for the sake of judgment and yet insists on the ne-
cessity of rendering judgment, *The Tricky Part* is fully human, un-
settling and wise." —Tony Kushner, author of *Angels in America*

"Bravely compassionate, unflinchingly honest, and ultimately,
hopeful." —*The Boulder Daily Camera*

"Martin Moran has written a story about difficult, painful and
deeply personal events with uncommon generosity and decency.
The story is shocking, even brutal, but I felt cleansed at its end.
He has found compassion where I would have thought there was
none." —Terrence McNally, Tony Award–winning author of
Frankie and Johnny in the Clair de Lune

"Chronicles [a] complex journey.... Moran is an adept storyteller who's disarmingly honest." —*People*

"Martin Moran has written an account of a childhood at once conventional and nearly unfathomable. A deep, tempered spirit shines through every page, by turns understated and dazzling, wildly comic and gut wrenching."
—Nick Flynn, author of *Another Bullshit Night in Suck City*

"A poignant and provocative memoir that delves behind the titillating headlines to reveal what's really at stake when children are sexually abused by authority figures." —*Booklist*

"A tender, searingly honest, and heartbreaking account of the legacy of sexual violation. Moran bravely unveils the tricky part: the paradoxical worlds of longing and shame, the erotic and the reviled, the profane and the sacred all living in one act, one man, one life.... [A] literary and spiritual exorcism."
—Eve Ensler, author of *The Vagina Monologues*

"*The Tricky Part* is that rare, triumphant thing—a book so bravely remembered and so fully imagined as to be capable of rendering a life in all of its moral complexity."
—Richard McCann, author of *Mother of Sorrows*

"In documenting his troubling childhood relationship with a much older man, [Martin Moran] eschews ready sensationalism and—instead—bravely articulates the complexities that color even the most taboo relationships. And he accomplishes it all with a prose style that is rich, immediate and constantly surprising. His is a book both haunting and profound."
—Doug Wright, winner of the 2004 Pulitzer Prize for Drama for *I Am My Own Wife*

Martin Moran

THE TRICKY PART

Martin Moran grew up in Denver and attended Stanford University and the American Conservatory Theater in San Francisco. He lives in New York City, where he makes his living as an actor and writer. He has appeared in many Broadway and Off-Broadway plays, including *Titanic*, *Cabaret*, *Bells Are Ringing*, *Floyd Collins*, and *The Cider House Rules*. He won a 2004 Obie Award for his one-man play, *The Tricky Part*, which he continues to perform all over the country. For more information, visit www.thetrickypartbook.com.

THE TRICKY PART

A Boy's Story of Sexual Trespass

A Man's Journey to Forgiveness

Martin Moran

ANCHOR BOOKS
A Division of Random House, Inc.
New York

FIRST ANCHOR BOOKS EDITION, MAY 2006

Copyright © 2005 by Martin Moran

All rights reserved. Published in the United States by Anchor Books, a division of Random House, Inc., New York, and in Canada by Random House of Canada Limited, Toronto. Originally published in slightly different form in hardcover in the United States by Beacon Press, in 2005.

Anchor Books and colophon are registered trademarks of Random House, Inc.

The poem "Ever Present" is reprinted with kind permission of the author, Robert Irwin. "My Ideal," words by Leo Robin, music by Richard A. Whiting and Newell Chase. Copyright © 1930 (renewed 1957) by Famous Music Corporation. International copyright secured. All rights reserved. Reprinted by permission. "Fire and Rain," words and music by James Taylor. Copyright © 1960, 1970 (renewed 1997, 1998) EMI Blackwood Music Inc. All rights reserved. International copyright secured. Reprinted by permission.

Most of the names and some identifying details in this work have been altered for the sake of clarity and to ensure the privacy of individuals.

Library of Congress Cataloging-in-Publication Data
Moran, Martin, 1959–
    The tricky part : a boy's story of sexual trespass, a man's journey to forgiveness /
Martin Moran.
        p. cm.
    Originally published: Boston, Mass. : Beacon Press, c2005.
    1. Moran, Martin, 1959– —Childhood and youth. 2. Actors—United States—Biography.
3. Sexually abused teenagers—United States—Biography. 4. Child sexual abuse by clergy—
United States. 5. Catholic Church—United States—Clergy—Sexual behavior. I. Title.
PN2287.M6993A3 2006
792.02'8092—dc22
[B]
                2005057046

Anchor ISBN-10: 0-307-27653-8
Anchor ISBN-13: 978-0-307-27653-7

www.anchorbooks.com

Printed in the United States of America
10 9 8 7 6 5 4 3 2 1

For
Henry Stram

And for my parents,
Martin and Carol

I HAVE LEARNT THAT THE PLACE WHERE THOU
ART FOUND UNVEILED IS GIRT ROUND WITH
THE COINCIDENCE OF CONTRADICTORIES, AND
THIS IS THE WALL OF PARADISE WHEREIN THOU
DOST ABIDE.

Nicholas of Cusa,
The Vision of God

Contents

Prelude

AT THE END of the second-floor hall of a small Catholic school, a sixth-grade boy stood transfixed in front of a wooden statue of Saint Sebastian. He'd passed it for years but lately found he was drawn to stop and study the three-dimensional story, the pierced flesh, the life-size proof that you've got to go through hell to be a saint. The boy tried to imagine the soldiers of the Imperial Guard and the events that might have brought them to this moment, stringing their bows, taking aim at their compatriot. And Sebastian? He looked so beautiful, the boy thought, with his rock-star hair and melancholy face. How is it that he stood there tied to a tree, plugged with arrows, and took it with such grace? The martyr's plight, his swimmer's body, his loincloth drooping from hip to wounded hip, gave the boy a deep, unlocatable twinge.

One day, the principal came upon him staring at the statue.

"It was a gift," she said, her little buzz of a voice startling the boy. "From an alum who lived in Italy. Beautiful, isn't it?"

He nodded but then looked back at the saint and whispered, "No."

"Why do you say that?" the nun asked, untangling the magnifying glass from her crucifix, both of which dangled from silver chains around her neck.

The boy grimaced and pointed to a waxy trickle of blood running along the sinews of Sebastian's left calf.

"Oh, don't worry, dear, he's not in his body here. He's already flying back up to our Lord." She reached up to clear a cobweb from the arrow stuck in Sebastian's thigh.

"How do you know?"

"Oh, we don't know," she said. "We believe."

For a moment they stood side by side, nun and pupil, gazing up at the suffering soldier.

"Come along, mustn't be late," the sister said as she turned and hurried away, leaving the boy alone to ponder this thing. The being bound, but flying.

Book I

FALLING

I

MARCH 28, 2002. It's Holy Thursday. That's Catholic for three days before Easter, and I'm in Las Vegas. I've come from my home in New York City to visit my father. We're at Vons, a fluorescent grocery store roughly the size of Manhattan, waiting in line to pay for pork chops. There's a bank of slot machines near the exit clanging away, and I find, as I do each time I come to this desert city, that I'm in shock to think it's here Dad's retired and will likely die.

There, on a rack in the checkout line, on the cover of *Time* magazine, is a gray and ominous drawing of the back of a bishop and these words: *Can the Catholic Church Save Itself?* The headlines of the scandal are everywhere at the moment. It's an uprising, the body of Mother Church erupting with such force that the shock waves are reverberating, at long last, all the way up to her head. Cardinal Law will resign before the year is out. I reach for a copy of the magazine.

"Jesus, that's been goin' on for a thousand years," my father says, jutting a finger at *Time*. "Did I ever tell you what happened to your aunt when she was little?"

"No, Dad."

"Father Murray, the basement of St. Bede's. I don't know what went on, but thank God the janitor happened by. I never knew anything about it until your aunt refused to let Murray say your grandmother's funeral mass."

I say to my dad, "Wow," but nothing else, because suddenly I'm riveted by a photo, page twenty-eight, of Father Kos and a Dallas boy, age twelve, who killed himself at twenty-one. I know the story of Kos and his altar boys; I'd cut every clip of it from the papers in '98 and stuck them in the thick file I keep under my desk. I'd read about the young men who'd gone to court and were awarded millions and the promise of a public apology from the Archdiocese of Dallas. I can recall the *New York Times* photo of them, handsome and courageous in their suits and ties, sitting at a table, along with one stricken mother who was there on behalf of her deceased son. I'd seen all this but I'd never, until this moment, seen the face—God, the face—of the boy who shot himself dead. His tiny-toothed smile, the light in his eyes, are absolutely haunting. He's in altar-boy frocks, all white, and the arm of the man with the Roman collar is slung behind his slim shoulders.

"Do you want me to buy that for you?" my father asks. I look into his kind old face and wonder, again, what it would mean, what it would be like, to tell him the story.

"No thanks, Dad, I'll get it."

This story that will not let me go.

April 1, 2002. Easter Monday. I've left my dad in Vegas and I'm in Los Angeles to visit my goddaughter; maybe pick up some acting work. I'm headed south, or possibly east, in the haze of the Hollywood Freeway when my cell phone gives three bleeps. A message. *Maybe a job.* One hand firmly on the wheel, I press voicemail, put the thing to my ear.

Marty, it's Bob C— (I hit the brake. The SUV behind me honks). *I got your letter saying you'd be traveling West. I'd dearly love to see you. I'm at the Veterans Hospital in LA. Here's my number. . . .*

I take the next exit and come to a stop in the glare of a 7-Eleven parking lot, stunned that he's alive, that my letter actually found him.

I'd lost all track of Bob. I'd spoken to him once, by phone, nine years before when I was on a visit to Denver, my hometown. I'd sat,

I remember, on the edge of my mother's bed, next to the phone, possessed suddenly by the idea of contacting him. My fingers had trembled as I dialed the number I'd just searched for and found. I was shocked when he picked up right away. We had a curt conversation: *It does no good to dwell on the past,* he'd said. *I've made my peace with God. I hope you do too.* Then he'd given me his address, saying that I should write. Numb, I'd jotted it down on the back of a housepainter's business card that was sitting on my mother's nightstand and stuck it in my wallet. Where it remained until, a few weeks before taking this trip West, gripped again with the idea of finding him, I called once more. *Disconnected. No address. No further information.* He must be dead, I figured, or moved long ago. I'd waited too many years. I mailed a note anyway with a *Please Forward* to the old address—some little town in California. I never imagined I'd hear from him, let alone that we'd ever be in the same place at the same time.

I pick up my cell and half dial him, hang up. Half dial, hang up. *Come on,* I tell myself, *do it. Just do it.* He answers on the second ring:

"Hello."

The pitch, the tenor of his voice enters my body like a lance. *Him,* after all these years. Him, reduced to a little human hum across a wireless. Very businesslike, we arrange to meet.

Thursday, April 4, 2002, the morning of the meeting.

My old high school friend, Jodi, prints out directions from her house in North Hollywood to the Veterans' Complex off Sepulveda Boulevard. "Good luck, Mart," she says. "Wring his friggin' neck for me."

Jodi is quick to fury on this subject, which always sets me to wondering about anger. My own anger, whatever, wherever it is, feels lost or buried somehow in complicity, I think. As if having wanted, allowed, has squelched any right I have to wrath or innocence. I remember when I first told Jodi all that happened, she looked at me with such pity that I blurted: "Hey, doll, *I'm OK.* It's not like the guy murdered me, calm down." "I'm so sorry that happened to you," she said, and I watched as she glanced across the room at her child, and the worry that flashed over her face told me I'd lived her idea of a parent's nightmare. And then I think of another friend who, when I shared the story said, "Oh, my . . . weren't you a lucky little boy." When he said it, I laughed like a lunatic.

It's a gorgeous day.

Bob's instructions take me to a red-roofed convalescent home. I park the car. I get out and walk past the well-kept lawns and palm trees. A pretty place for mending, I think.

I ask for C—, please?

Crisp and smiling, the nurse points to the elevator. "Second floor, dear."

"Thank you."

First I step into the men's room for a pee, for a breath. I stand in a stall and take from my pocket two double-A batteries. I'd meant to do this in the car. Forgot. So, standing there in front of a toilet, I snap them into my little tape recorder like a lousy spy. I don't really know why I'm doing this. It's as if I'm afraid that without a record I'll forget everything or never believe any of it actually happened. As I snap the batteries in, I'm thinking: *This is rude. Maybe illegal, immoral . . . fuck it.* I stick the recorder in my jacket pocket and catch myself in the mirror above the sink and break into a crazy grin.

The corridor is long, hospital-white. There are two to a room. I check the names, scrawled in black marker, tucked beneath plastic next to each door. Dazed-looking vets are everywhere. Some walking silently, wheeling IVs. Some staring out the window. The long hair, the age, say Vietnam. As I walk I rehearse lines in my head, afraid I'll go blank when I see him.

Do you remember the last time I saw you?

Bob, who was it, exactly, who sent you to prison?

And then the door is open and I'm thinking there must be a mistake because it's his name there but I don't recognize either person in the room.

In the far bed, a dark-skinned man is coughing up what appears to be part of his lunch. In the nearer bed, sitting up, is a plump person with a mop of white hair who looks to be someone's grand-mother. My first thought is: *Are there women vets here?* There must be, I figure, but wait, it *is* a man and he—like everyone else—is wearing a rose-colored frock, prison-like, with faint numbers sten-ciled above the breast pocket. He's holding a plastic fork, poking at broccoli. Slowly, the face revolves toward the door, blinks once.

"Are you Marty?"

I nod. His voice, no question.

"I never would have recognized you," he says, and in that in-stant, like a shift from blurred to sharp, I get him. Exactly. Under the mop of grandmother hair I apprehend the features of the vig-orous, thirty-year-old man I once knew. *This is him,* the guy who taught me about Buckminster Fuller and geodesic domes. This is the guy who took me glacier sliding. It was the summer after sev-enth grade, on a raft trip. He led a group of us campers into some Wyoming peaks and we came across a huge glacier and he said to all the boys: "OK, OK, climb up and slide down!" Everyone was terrified. Nobody moved, and Bob whispered into my ear: "I *know* you can do it." And I just turned and climbed and climbed. It must have been a quarter-mile long, this thing. I got to the top and tied my jacket around my butt and all the other guys linked arms at the bottom of the glacier to keep me from slamming into the rocks. It was insane. I screamed the whole way down and they caught me! I was king for a day. Brave, for once. This is the guy who woke me late one night at the mountain ranch and said: "Hey, come with me, Marty, you gotta see this." He grabbed a lantern and took me to the barn. The vet had come in the middle of the night to help deliver a calf. Bob and the vet had their arms all up in there because the cow was in trouble and suddenly this rickety-legged creature covered with goop and blood came out. Lying there on the barn floor . . . *alive!* And Bob turned to me and smiled and I felt so lucky to be there, to see something so real.

"I don't want to interrupt your lunch," I tell him.

"No, no. It's OK."

He keeps blinking at me through these large, gold-framed glasses. I think of moving in to shake his hand but that seems ridiculous and we're in a freeze like, what? Victim facing perpetrator? Or like estranged ex's. Ex-altar boy, ex-almost seminarian, ex-friends? enemies? lovers? I don't know. Definitions fail, bleed one into the other. I watch him lay his fork on a paper napkin and I ask,

"How are you?"

"You're catching me at a pretty down time." His eyes are green, he's looking right at me but there's not a glimmer in there and I think: *Jeez, the light's been bludgeoned out of this guy or maybe he's on something—antipain, antidepressant.*

"What happened?" I point to his right foot, which is enormous, wrapped in white gauze up to the knee like the limb of a mummy.

"Oh, bad infection. They had to amputate a little."

"Wow, sorry."

"Ah, well," he says. "Stepped on a stupid screw in the driveway. Life." He shrugs, chuckles. "I've got diabetes. You remember how I liked my Coca-Cola."

"Yep. I do." I glance toward the hall, wanting to move outside, somewhere private.

"You look good," he says. "Your dad had quite a belly by your age."

I'm thrown at his mention, his memory, of my father, who he met, I think, maybe twice. I start chattering.

"Well, I'm an actor and the work's very physical, keeps me fit." In my skull I feel the buzz of words and how they're utterly weightless and how it's our bodies that are grave somehow, communicating, catching up. For my bones the whole experience isn't thirty years away but three feet.

"I see," he says. "You work in the theater, then?"

"Yeah. Uh-huh. Some TV. Plays and musicals sometimes. I sing and . . ." *Christ, Marty,* I think, *why not just give him an uptune and a ballad? Lord, he's got just the lost, ugly mug you'd expect in a news item on pedophiles — pasty pale, geeky glasses.* "It's always eight shows a week, very rigorous . . ." This sharp lament moves through me as I think how much the course of my days has been affected by this broken being in front of me. "But Broadway pays pretty well, when you can get it."

I watch him push, with an index finger, his glasses up the bridge of his nose, then scoop his bangs to the right. The gesture (*exactly* as I remember it) sends a tremble through my chest. It's as if I'm forty-two and twelve at once.

"Are you in New York?"

"Yes, I've been in Manhattan twenty years now." This sentence, somehow, gives me a sense of center, of pride. "I live there with my . . . my boyfriend, Henry. We've been together for seventeen years." I want him to know, I realize, that I'm all right, that I've found success, stability. "Do you remember the last time we saw each other?"

"I do," he whispers, dropping his head, tripling his chin. "You were, what? Fifteen? You drove all the way to my place in Sunshine Canyon without a license. We sat by my empty fireplace and you told me you were ashamed that we'd ever met and that you never wanted to see me again."

I'm stunned and, oddly, flattered that he remembers it—the scene, my words—exactly as I do. It seems to say that it, that I, meant a lot to him. Is that what I've come for? I wonder. To see if I'm as vivid for him as he's been for me? That I wasn't just another little boy, an easy target, who gave it up to him?

"That tore my heart out," he says. "I curled into a shell that night after you left, for nearly two months."

He's speaking the truth, it seems. Or is he playing me? The confusion feels familiar. I finger the button of my recorder but don't push. I'm afraid it will click too loudly.

"Did you know, Bob, that this weekend will be thirty years exactly since we first actually met? April 7, 1972."

"Oh, I'm not aware." He shakes his head so that his hair falls back into his eyes. "Dates are fuzzy. I couldn't say the exact—"

"Oh, I can," I tell him. The man in the other bed coughs. He is watching a TV fixed high on the wall. I'm concerned he might hear me, and then I try not to care: "It was three months after my twelfth birthday. Except for my head, I didn't have a hair on my body. I didn't know a thing, barely what a wet dream might be."

"Let's go outside," he says, scooting across the bed toward his wheelchair. "Let's go outside."

2

A PHOTOGRAPH HANGS in my study of a boy standing in a kayak at the edge of a pond, holding an oar triumphantly over his head. He's wearing a shy, crooked smile, a Speedo swimsuit, and a lifejacket. He's a tiny twelve, this boy, and no matter how many times I look at him, I'm astonished that it's actually me. The me of thirty-plus years ago, spring of 1972.

The picture was taken up in the Colorado Rockies about two hours west of Denver, the town where I grew up. We lived, two parents and four kids, down in an alphabetical neighborhood —Grape-Glencoe-Holly-Hudson-Ivy-Ivanhoe—rows of identical houses known as Virginia Vale. In 1960, when my Dad and Mom bought the place, nineteen-grand got you a single-story shoebox-shaped house with an unfinished basement and a square chunk of dirt to call your own. The feature that distinguished one home from another was the color of brick. Red, yellow, gray, and the occasional orange. And every other house had a big porch, the houses between, a little porch. We had a big porch. Red brick.

We lived in Virginia Vale but, somehow, what seemed most important was that we belonged to Christ the King, our church and school up the hill. And I felt a great deal of pride (which is a sin) about my school. Once they asked me to cover the phone when the office nun got ill. I just happened to be passing by on my way to the multipurpose room and, always anxious to please, I was thrilled to take her seat for a few minutes. Pretty soon the phone rang. I picked it up.

Hello, Christ the King.

I was in heaven.

Or, later, when I was on student council and had to dial out into the worldly world for bank balances or Styrofoam cups:

Hi, this is Christ the King calling . . .

Usually there'd be a pause on the line and I'd experience, right inside my breast, a little burst of glee.

Most of the kids in my neighborhood went to public school. McMean or Fallis Elementary. I kid you not. *Edwina Fallis* Elementary. She was a beloved kindergarten instructor. Still, I just think it's one thing when your school is named after a dead teacher and another when it's named for the Risen Savior.

Every classroom at Christ the King had, hanging from the front wall, a clock and a crucifix. And every day, during math or spelling, I would stare up and watch the hands ticking past the numbers, while Jesus's remained nailed at quarter to three. They were stuck there on the yellow brick like an odd couple that seemed, somehow, to be dueling. My eye would bounce back and forth: Time . . . Eternity, Earth versus Heaven. It was like watching *Now* spin toward the hour of death.

Sister Agatha was our third-grade teacher. She was a heavy woman, in every sense of the word. She wasn't much taller than us nine-year-olds. She was shaped like a box. A black box. A moving cube of church. She was, among the many nuns in my life, the most intense. Often, before we'd go off to the restroom, Sister would turn, face the front wall, and raise her cloaked arms in the shape of a V, as if pleading to be beamed up. With one hand she indicated the hour and with the other our near naked Lord. "We line up by one but we live by the other," she would proclaim in her crackly voice. Crackly because there was always something like grief or cheese caught in her throat. Sometimes in the midst of a lesson, especially if she was annoyed with you, she would gesture up to the cross then look at you and blurt out: "He died to set you free!" And I'd think, *Free from what? From where?*

There was a brief moment one afternoon (I was little, first grade) when I thought I'd cracked a piece of the Catholic code. It was when the bell rang, as usual, at 2:45 to release us for the day. Alleluia! I grabbed my satchel and as I did I glanced up to realize that the clock and Jesus told the exact same time and I thought, *That's it*. But, right away, I knew whatever it was He'd done it was supposed to mean more than just getting to leave here, being set free to go home. Nothing could be that simple, could it?

Sister Agatha had a very particular method for teaching cursive. She'd put on 45 records of simple songs for each different letter of the alphabet—"Farmer in the Dell" for *W*, or "Three Blind Mice" for *G*.

"OK children, letter *G*. Remember the tail; every letter has a tail so they can connect, make meaning." She'd plop on the record; we'd clutch our number 2 pencils as she sang, "Three blind mice . . . *tail*. See how they run . . . *connect!*" One afternoon late in the year, right in the middle of drawing letter *G,* she just froze, staring at her chalk. We sat there until, finally, Carol Buell went to the office to get someone. They came and took Sister out into the hall and we never saw her again.

Christ the King or CK, as we called it, was situated on a little hill at Eighth and Fairfax, sandwiched between Holy Ghost to the west and Most Precious Blood (a rougher neighborhood) to the east. Little Catholic fiefdoms all over town, fiefdoms of the soul, concerned, of course, with matters of the *hereafter*. That's something you get from the time you're tiny: *After* is what you're shooting for. *After* is what counts. *Here* is basically a problem. We made a mistake, we fell, and we're stuck *here* in this unreliable flesh, struggling to earn our way toward a bodiless eternity in a very nice place with all the saints.

And, lucky you, you learn this, that there's a huge army of the Good and the Dead just waiting to be called upon, prayed to, because they've been through the earthly wringer and *released*. They're part of the oxygen. Their stories are everywhere, stained into chapel windows, pressed into books and calendars, like Catholic celebrities, sacred movie stars. There's a saint for every day and a patron for every profession. Cecilia for music, Luke for doctors, Genesius for prostitutes and actors. You've got Jude for desperate causes and there's even Saint Claire of Assisi, who saw visions on the wall of her cell, of events unfolding far, far away. She's the patron saint of television. It got so you recognized the saints' hairdos or their particular wounds. Sad Saint Lucy with her eyeballs on a plate, or the virgin Agatha with her breasts on a platter, or Saint Denis, carrying his own head down from Mont Martre. Halloween is nothing to a kid from Catholic school. Everywhere you look, there's blood and gore and metaphor.

Sister Agatha was passionate about the saints. I remember how annoyed she was on the feast of Saint Martin when I replied to her inquiry that I didn't know much about him.

"If you're lucky enough to share a name with a saint," she said, "then you should know their feast day. Agatha's, for example, is the fifth of February." Sister picked up a piece of chalk and wrote on the board in beautiful, curvy letters: *AGATHA*. "It means 'good girl' in Greek. She was the first, the very first virgin martyr of the church." Sister touched her chest, leaving a smudge of white over her heart.

She made me stand and read Saint Martin's story aloud from *Miniature Stories of the Saints.* When I opened to the proper page there was a dreamy drawing of him: long brown hair, handsome face with dark eyes gazing up toward . . . up. I knew right away that if he lived here-now instead of Rome-then, he would have been captain of the team and picked me right away.

The book told how he was a soldier who met a freezing beggar in the street one day. Having nothing but the cloak on his back to offer the poor man, Martin took his sword and chopped his cape and gave half of it to the beggar, who, lucky for Martin, turned out to be God.

That day during recess, Ricky Flynn cornered me. "Give me half of your Mars bar."

"No," I responded.

"Come on," he said. "I'm the beggar, you be the saint."

I didn't see how, with his mean eyes and snotty nose, Ricky's could be the face of God, but that's the tricky part. So I ripped my candy in half and Ricky just laughed with his mouth full. "Thanks, Saint Martin." I felt stupid and mad and more unsaintly than ever. You see, we're supposed be like them, the saints, but they're all holy and dead and it's hard to know where to begin.

One day we third graders were having a silent study period, waiting for the hands to reach 2:45. I should have been reading but I was dreaming about Wesley, the neighbor boy who occasionally babysat my older sister and me. I didn't know why but I longed to sit next to Wesley as next to a fire on a winter's night. But he always remained alone and silent at the end of our living room couch, studying his geometry while I sat on the floor doodling his name in my workbook. It seems that during my daydream I stuck my hands in my front pockets. Suddenly, Sister Agatha was in front of my desk.

"Stop that," she whispered, or hissed, really, as if she'd transformed into the serpent of Eden she talked of incessantly. I sat up straight, my hands still caught in my corduroys. "Do you need to make a trip to the toilet?"

"No."

"Then stop it." She pointed to my pockets. Mortified, I pulled my hands out and folded them on top of *Phonics for Fun*. She was trembling. Or that's how my mind's eye, my body, remembers it: this hallowed nun quaking at my offense. "That's nothing down there," she said "to be toying with." I didn't know why, but I knew well, my body was fit to blame.

She walked to the front of the class and clapped three times—her signal that it was time for another lesson about how we're bad.

"Children, if the devil has his way, we'll never reach our greatest desire: *Union with God in the life everlasting.*" She straightened her little round glasses and looked right at me. "There's a war inside of us, children, because the Kingdom of God dwells within but so does our sin. There's not a lot of room in there"—she placed a hand on her stomach—"and they are both going at it, white knight and black, angel and devil, tangling us up. And if"—she raised a finger—"*if* you allow . . ." She stepped toward me and the bell rang. She never finished.

3

IT WAS A hot afternoon in June, soon after I'd made it through third grade, and my new friend, Nathan, knocked at the back door.

"Mart. Get your swim trunks. Let's walk to the JCC."

"OK," I said, glad to follow him anywhere.

Nathan and his family lived just across the chain-link fence, in the yellow-brick house kitty-corner behind us. I didn't know much about them until one day I started seeing Nathan in his backyard taking care of his gerbil, Moxie. Nathan was tall for his age and had the longest, blackest hair I'd ever seen on a boy. I first learned his name when his mother yelled, *"Nathan,* get your butt in here!" Her voice shook the pussy willows surrounding our incinerator. He asked me over one afternoon to watch *Creature Feature.* I found out he was a year older than I and went to shul as well as a school. Everyone—his three big brothers and sister—talked at once and loudly. His father was a wrestling coach and was always grabbing Nathan's brothers and pinning them to the floor. It was a war zone of affection. I didn't see Nathan often but whenever I did, he always showed up out of the blue, with a definite plan.

"Come on," he said, standing on our patio that bright June day, straightening his cool wire-framed glasses. "This is a day for swimming."

"OK."

I followed, picking up what I could of his overflowing confidence. Past Flamingo, a right on Forest, we hopped barefoot down the broiling pavement past the rectangle houses, big porch, little porch, big, all the way to the Jewish Community Center.

I remember how the light shimmered on the water. This was the biggest and best pool around, shallow to deep packed with horseplay and high-pitched laughter. This was no place for laps, just splashing under the mile-high sky, pink backs smeared with Coppertone.

Eyes red, fingers shriveled, Nathan yanked my foot from under water, leapt up and out of the pool, calling, "Follow me."

Magic words. I trailed his lanky frame up a back stairwell, stepping into his wide, wet footprints. We dripped our way down a long hall, feet-flops echoing along the polished tiles. As we reached the end of the yellow-colored hall, I smelled smoke. Nathan pushed open a door and—my God—it was a foreign country. A sprawling room filled with dozens of dads. They were seated around card tables or perched in fat lounge chairs watching the ball game.

"That was a bullshit penalty!" one man roared, sticking a cigar back into his mouth.

Some concentrated on books and newspapers. They were all naked. Naked as could be. Except some had on white socks and brown sandals, the kind Jesus used to wear. I was astounded. I'd never really seen bare grown-ups. Somehow, in my world, people emerged from separate compartments, scrubbed and fully clothed. The men had towels around their necks and were moving slowly in and out of steamy doors, chatting. This must be what they meant, I thought, by *Community Center.* Or by *Jewish.*

I panicked, thinking I didn't belong here. Not allowed. That we'd wandered into something definitely venial, possibly mortal. But Nathan, with his usual assuredness, plunged right through the bare bodies. I followed, head down.

There was Nathan's dad, sitting on a small stool with a crossword folded over his lap. I clenched, preparing for him to yell like he did at home. Nathan's dad looked up, his gray eyes flashing.

"Hi, sweethearts," he said, quiet as could be. "What's doing?"

Nathan borrowed his dad's towel and sat down on his knee to help with the puzzle. I wandered through the smoky sweat, lost in a forest of men. Who knew the human physique had so many shapes and shades? Or that human hair grew in such places and patterns? I heard splashing on the other side of a swinging door. I went in.

It was a huge chamber filled with showers, the kind I'd seen once when I visited the local public high school. There was only one grown-up in the room. A guy around eighteen or nineteen, I figured. He stood at the last shower opposite the door, rinsing shampoo from his curly brown hair. White suds made their way down his neck and chest. I recognized him. He was the lifeguard who blew the whistle when we ran too fast to the deep end. He was wearing red trunks with the cross on them. Not the crucifix, but the little white cross that meant he'd save you if you were hurt or drowning. He glanced my way. He had the whitest teeth you ever saw.

I turned on the nearest shower, next to the door. The warm water soothed my neck, ran down my spine. I loved that feeling. It's what lured me out of bed on school mornings before 8:30 Mass. I watched the water glide down my stomach and jump off the drawstrings of my baggy trunks, scattering and flowing away. It had been another funny day with Nathan. Whenever I was with him, such grown-up things seemed to happen.

I looked up and saw the lifeguard taking off his red trunks. He began wringing them in the shower, his wide back tilted, twisting with the effort. He was bright white where his suit had just been, the rest of him dark with summer. He turned then and, in an instant, I froze under the hot water. My insides tangled, tightened as the space between him and me filled up with something that made my heart race.

Would I look like that in ten years? I wondered. A perfect triangle of hair below my belly? Everything . . . larger? I turned away and tightened my strings. I stared at the yellow tile, imagining ways I might begin to drown under a shower.

I twisted back around, I couldn't keep, I couldn't stop, looking at his . . . him.

I heard voices—Sister Agatha's, Sister Joan's—tell me this was wrong, rude. Or worse, this was my will acting up. Involuntarily curious, like Eve. I knew I should turn away but, heavenly God, he was beautiful. I watched the water slide across his skin and I could swear I was recollecting something I already knew. I recognized something in his shape; I felt some infinite hope in his particular curves.

He turned off the water and reached to grab his towel from a nearby hook. He shot me a look. I lowered my eyes to the drain, then peeked again. He dried his hair in a way that said he had no idea how nude he was, and then he wrapped the towel around his hips and walked my way. I dropped my eyes again to the swirl of water. I felt him, long-limbed and easy, right next to me. He paused and I looked up. His eyes were brown. And kind. He nodded— a polite farewell—as he reached for the handle of the door, and when he'd gone all I felt at the pit of my stomach was the weight of it. All I could see, stretched from now to forever, was the terrible trouble I was in.

4

FOR AS LONG as I could remember, since kindergarten at least, mornings were trouble. I often woke sick to my stomach. As I got older, I used to sneak out to the side of the house to barf right before car pool came to pick us up for school. I'd plant my feet in the snow near the naked rosebush, press my forehead against the brick, and get it out. If I could time it right, if I got past these early moments of the day without anyone hearing, it'd be OK. None of the questions. *What's wrong with you? Sick again?* I had no explanations. Only embarrassment. At first, everyone figured it was the flu or a bad bit of food. But then it happened too often. I couldn't skip school. Not again. Mom and everyone else lost patience. But if I could keep it a secret, get it over with quietly, then I could go to school, get on with the day. Every day a test, a chance to please. A chance to bring home As—the marks that held power, it seemed, to brighten the gloom. To make Mom smile. I'd lean into the brick and what wanted out so badly squeezed its way up the back of my throat. It spilled and burned right through the snow, a yellow hole down to the dirt. I'd wipe my mouth, tuck in my shirt, hurry along to grab my books before car pool honked. Hurry along, wondering what in the world was wrong with my body.

There was a statue of the Virgin Mary outside school. She was blinding white up on her pedestal, her arms lovingly outstretched, her wrists cocked in this odd way that always made me think she was directing traffic. You could sit on the steps, not far from Mary, and look west to see the whole front range of the Rockies, from Pike's Peak in the south to Long's in the north and all the mountains in between, standing jagged and mighty over our Disturbed Region. That's what Father Elser—our priest and sometimes science teacher—told us Denver is called in geologic terms. A *Disturbed Region*. Because of all the tectonic accidents and violent collisions that create such beauty. He told us that a rock, a mountain, may look at rest, but they most certainly are not. Everything is filled with ceaseless subatomic motion. Often, in the mornings before Mass, I would stop and chat with Mary or with the godly view, the way you do with mountains and statues because you sense that somewhere behind the stillness, behind the scenes, they are alive somehow and keeping an eye on things.

One morning I was sitting out on the steps getting air, staring west, when Paula Plank appeared and gave me a kiss. She'd been running. She was out of breath and late, like me, but she stopped and stood still at the bottom of the stairs.

"Hi," she said.

"Hi."

Her cheeks were flushed, two splotches of red spreading over freckles. We locked eyes for a second, blue on blue, twinkle to twinkle. She said not another word, though I thought I heard her brand-new breasts whisper *morning* from beneath her plaid uniform. She reached out and gave me a kiss—a chocolate kiss—and ran.

I watched her go; the pleats of her skirt swirling, her plump calves scrambling up the steps. When she reached the side door of our church, the bells began clanging across the clear sky. She turned to wave and beckon me, then slipped inside. I stood there in my navy blue jacket and gray wool pants, and pondered Paula's gift. It sat like a big silver teardrop in the palm of my hand. And out of the top of it, like a tiny plume of smoke, flowed a ribbon on which was printed in light blue letters: *kisses kisses kisses*.

I should have told Paula: *No, thanks*. It was Lent and I'd given up chocolate. "Virtue grows through deliberate acts," Sister Christine had said on the day we wrote on a secret piece of paper what we'd chosen to sacrifice for the five and a half weeks leading up to Easter. "Pray for grace, you'll get the help you need."

But the kiss was so sweetly, so quickly, given. It would have been rude to refuse. *Put it away, save it for Easter, tally up your virtue*, I thought. I glanced toward our square yellow-brick school, toward the rectory, the convent. Not a witness in sight. Inside, at Mass, they were reciting the Creed by now. *We believe in one God, the Father, the Almighty, Maker of Heaven and Earth, of all that is seen and unseen.* I peeled back the foil. I took a bite. There was a loud bang. I popped to my feet and shoved what was left of Paula's gift into my pocket. I turned to see it was the screen door. The slamming of the convent door, and there was Sister Christine, hiking up her habit, dancing down the steps.

Sister Christine was our sixth-grade teacher. I loved her. You know how there always seems to be one nun in the bunch who's different, cool. That was her, Sister Christine. She had a twelve-string guitar and a bucktoothed grin that made you want to sing. She was a tall, handsome woman with reddish brows and, I think, red hair—though that was another mystery that remained just beyond the veil. She still wore hers while most of the other nuns had taken them off. I asked her why once and she said, "I wear my veil as a constant statement of a deeper reality." She was full of sayings. During class she'd often repeat, "Remember, it's through discipline that the transcendent enters our lives." She'd grown up on a ranch north of town and you could see it in her mighty stride. She marched straight for church, swinging her guitar case. Her rosary beads clacked against her thigh. I chewed fast and held still on the steps. She came to a halt and turned her head.

"Marty," she called out. "You're late."

"I know. Sorry."

She took a quick glance toward church, then walked over to the top of the steps.

"Lord, it's so clear today." She caught my eye. She was one of those adults who, when they looked at you, really *looked*. I ran my tongue around my teeth and swallowed, hoping to erase any trace of my transgression. "Marty? Are you sick again?"

"I'm OK. How are you?"

"Fine. Just . . . not sleeping well." She moved down a couple steps toward me and propped her guitar case up, held the neck of it. "Have you been practicing your tunes?"

"Yep."

Sister was the first person in the world who ever said she thought I might be musical. That's how it started. Now I was studying with her twice a week, during recess, just the two of us chatting on a pair of stools, me learning chords on my cruddy little guitar. *Tie me kangaroo down sport, tie me kangaroo down.* I was always glad to be with her and not out on the playground, worrying about which sort of ball might hit me in the head.

"Marty, you need to get a better instrument. A real guitar. They're not that expensive. Why don't you find a way to earn a little extra money?"

"A job?"

"You're at the age where that might be really good for you." She gazed again toward the mountains. "Hard to believe Lent's already here. Everything's going to bloom soon. What did you give up, Marty?"

"Chocolate." I looked down at my loafers.

"That's a tough one."

I nodded.

"Our Lord spent forty days and forty nights in the desert with no food or drink. And all for *us*."

"Why *us?*"

"We're blessed."

"He must've nibbled *something*."

"Nope."

"How do you know?"

"It's written."

"Forty days. Why so long?"

"Lent is good practice for when you grow up and have even greater appetites to curb." She looked right into my dark, chocolate-stained soul. "These actions," she said, "are part of our redemption."

"I know."

"A way of buying back what was lost."

"Sister . . . what did we lose?"

"Oh . . ." She stared far away over the treetops. "Our true place of rest. Our home with God." She picked up her guitar. "We just have to keep winning our grace."

My stomach growled: grace drowning in Hershey's.

"Come on. Hurry up, or we lose." She started toward Mass, then stopped suddenly and turned back to look at me.

"One day your soul shall be released, Marty."

"I don't think so."

"No, faith. You're a good boy. You'll be released."

"From what?"

She glanced down at her sensible shoes. Her eyes had the most sorrowful look. A look that made me want to squeeze her hand or give her a kiss.

"From loneliness," she said. "From being alone."

We both stared toward Mount Evans. One stately cloud, all marbled and bright, slid slowly north. She nudged me in the arm with her big elbow.

"Look at those hills!" she cried. *"Nil Sine Numine."*

"What prayer is that?"

"Not a prayer, exactly. It's our Colorado state motto: 'Nothing without Providence.'" She snatched up her guitar and stepped swiftly. "Come along . . . can't keep still. Time to move."

5

SISTER'S SUGGESTION THAT I find a way to earn money gave particular motion to the motion of things.

I got a job. And the most astonishing thing about becoming a *Denver Post* paperboy, besides ringing people's doorbells and taking their cash, was that suddenly I was friends with George Doyle. Chubby, mean, paperboy. The neighborhood menace. Though he was Catholic and lived just around the corner, chances of us ever being chums were slim. He was public (McMean) and two years and most of puberty ahead of me. His idea of fun was dropping a lit M-80 firecracker into the corner mailbox. *Bang!* So I was astonished when, at our paperboy marketing powwows, he seemed to take a shine to me. He gave me advice and I gave him extra rubber bands. It was the bond of capitalism.

He used to call me Marsh, short for Martian.

"Marsh," he bellowed one day, "*that's* your mistake. Don't ever collect from the Weinstocks on Friday night. Jewish people won't touch money after sundown. It's a Sabbath thing. *Tip death.* As for the Catholics, shoot for cocktail hour. Any day."

It was the Monday after Easter. A sunny day, the paper, slim. I flung the headlines onto the lawns of my patrons, happy to think how I'd become the final link between world events and the residents of Kearny Street. When I finished I zoomed over to George's place, dropped my bike on their dried-up grass, ducked under their sickly weeping willow, and walked up to the porch. I felt queasy every time I came to fetch George but these nerves, I figured, were a small price to pay for the cachet of hanging out with a bona fide bully.

I knocked on the screen door and immediately there were heavy steps. I prayed it wasn't his dad. Tall and terrifying, he was chairman of the local NRA; had guns hanging all over the house like precious paintings. I'd gone hunting with him and George one Sunday in March. With Mr. Doyle's coaching and a telescoped gun, I shot a gray jackrabbit right in the neck. Mr. Doyle congratulated me, one of the few times I'd heard him talk and the only time I'd seen his tight, crooked smile. He grinned as we walked through the tumbleweeds to examine the splattered body of the bunny. The rabbit's eyes were open, frozen in a terrible question aimed at me. "Well done," Mr. Doyle had said, nudging the belly of the rabbit with his boot. I felt sick. Worst of all, we just turned and walked away. Left it lying there, flies dancing around its bloody head. An act against all hunting rules. Now, whenever Mr. Doyle saw me he'd ask: "Wanna go hunting?"

"Who's there?" came a high-pitched voice.

I was relieved it was Minnie, the live-in housekeeper.

"It's me, Marty."

"Oh. Oh . . . come in, hon."

She swung the door open, big smile on her face because, well, because it was me: the boy from Christ the King. She had a rag in one hand and a spray bottle of Parsons ammonia in the other. Minnie loved Parsons. Said it was the one true cleanser, like Catholic was the one true church.

"George ain't home yet," she said. "He's running late on his route . . . trouble at school. Again." Tough as a tank, dressed like a Howard Johnson's hostess; Minnie scooted to the fridge and took out a quart of milk. "That boy'll be the death of me." She slapped down a glass, then leaned against the turquoise-colored oven and clipped the Parsons to her belt, where it hung like a gun.

"Did you have a good Easter?"

"Yep."

"How's school?"

"OK."

"Who said Mass this morning?"

"Father Elser."

"Oh, now . . . he's a saint."

I nodded, thinking, *God, if she only knew what a surly saint.*

Father Elser, our priest, was German by way of Ireland and all shriveled from years as some kind of prisoner of some kind of war somewhere. It was all sad and vague but one thing was clear: whatever happened to him, it was our fault. He was always angry about something.

On Holy Thursday the week before, he'd stormed into our sixth-grade class in the middle of reading lab and sent Sister Christine and all the girls to the multipurpose room. His face was red, the veins in his neck sticking out.

"Vich one of you boys stole wine from the sacristy?"

I had that reflexive moment where I felt sure I'd done it, started to raise my hand, but we all knew it was Ricky Flynn. He'd tried every trespass on the list. Ricky didn't fess up so we all got the usual twenty Hail Marys. Then, instead of storming out, Father walked slowly to the blackboard and picked up a piece of chalk. We watched as he scribbled:

The Sacred Seed of God.

Through his thick tongue, he spoke.

"Ven you grow from a boy to a man, Got gives you the seed of life. In each drop there are a thousand hopeful Catholics. After the sacrament of marriage in the sacred act of intercourse they will race to find the egg inside a woman. The fastest one will penetrate the egg, be born and baptized into the one true church. This will happen in Got's own time."

It was stunning to hear him speak of this. To hear that human beings are inside of seeds inside of us. His good gray eye (the other was glass) wandered across our frozen faces.

"Your genitalia are for procreation. Do not abuse. If you do, you abuse Got. A mortal sin." With that he dropped his chalk and marched out the door.

"You want some more milk, hon?"

"No thanks, Minnie."

There was the sound of a key in the front door. Minnie stiffened. George dropped his coat on the hall floor and headed for the fridge.

"School called. They said you ditched third period."

George glanced around and gave Minnie a filthy look. She fondled her trigger.

"Wait until your father comes home."

"He doesn't give a shit."

"George!" she cried, moving toward the basement door. "Dinner's at six," she said as she disappeared down the steps.

"Come on, Marsh!"

We jumped on our bikes and flew past the shoebox-shaped houses and out onto the dirt trails that twisted their way along Cherry Creek. Plump as he was, George was poetry on a bike, leaping off jumps and zooming down the paths like a jackrabbit. I nearly killed myself trying to keep up. I'd cracked my head open twice already, gotten stitches and scars. I wore them like merit badges, proof of being a boy. We zigzagged through the elms and aspens, their branches scribbled against the sky. Buds were everywhere but the leaves hadn't burst yet. We'd just turned the clocks forward and you could feel, folded in that extra hour of light, the promise of summer. Of schools closing and pools opening. The late afternoon sun was strong, poised high above the Rockies, like a blazing whole note.

Finally, worn out, we dropped our bikes and slid down the steep path right to the creek's edge.

"You got to lean into it," George said, all out of breath. "You're afraid of everything."

"Am not."

"Are too."

He threw a punch toward my stomach. I flinched.

"See," he said. "See how you are?"

"What?"

"*Nervous.*"

I leaned back and watched the muddy creek, picked up a rock and threw it as far as I could. It smacked into a tree on the other bank.

"Hey, George? Where's all this water go?"

"Joins the Platte, the Missouri, the Mississippi . . . dumps into the Gulf of Mexico, I think."

"Wow, all that way?" I stared at the current. "It's like Virginia Vale is connected to the whole planet by Cherry Creek."

"Don't get weird," he said.

I turned and watched the rise and fall of the purple lettering— *Led Zeppelin* —written across George's big chest. His black T-shirt was too small, *Zeppelin* stretched to the limit. His blond hair was damp, curled at the ends with trickles of sweat. He had brown fuzz on his lip; it had gotten thick lately. He told me how he was planning to use his new razor soon. I was waiting for all of that. The hair sprouting and body spurts described in the back of my Scout book (page 273). I was awaiting the big dream, the trigger, wondering if maybe then I'd get big. And strong. And sure.

George grabbed a fistful of dirt, hurled it into the creek, and right out of the blue asked: "Hey, Marsh, was that counselor, Bob, at St. Malo the summer you were there?"

St. Malo was the boys' camp up in the Rockies run by the Archdiocese of Denver. Most of the counselors there were, or were thinking about becoming, seminarians—men training for the priesthood. It was a gorgeous place. My dad had gone there, my cousins.

"Who?" I asked.

"Remember that guy, Father Mac's assistant. Bob? He was always taking pictures of us, yelling about the right way to do pushups?"

I did remember. An image popped into my head of him standing with Father Mac at Chapel. Tall guy with dark-framed glasses.
He had combat boots but always wore penny loafers with dimes in
them to dinner. But I remembered him especially because he told
the most amazing campfire stories about jungle ghosts and war in
Vietnam. He'd been a soldier there and brought back weird gongs
and drums, which he used, at just the right moment, in his stories
(*Bang!*) to scare the shit out of us. Even the older campers would
scream. After lights-out he'd come around the bunks to make sure
we weren't too frightened to sleep. "Are you OK?" he'd whisper,
pressing a piece of butterscotch into your hand or leaving a Jolly
Rancher perched on your tummy.

"You mean the guy with the ghost stories, right? Who slept in
the dorm?" I asked George.

"Yeah."

"He was cool."

"Well, he knows my dad from down the Veterans' Club." George
dug a rock from the sand. "He's starting a boys' camp of his own
up on a mountain ranch. He's fixing it up, wants help this weekend. He's paying ten bucks. Want to go?"

"A ranch. Wow. But, I'd have to find someone to cover my route.
And 8:30 Mass on Sunday—it's my turn to serve."

"Well, try."

I told George I would, I'd try. The picture in my head of me on
a ranch in the Rockies had already set my heart racing.

6

THE FOLLOWING FRIDAY, right after school, I sat in our kitchen. Waiting.

The earth trembled. I ran to the window to see what had happened. A huge truck had come to a halt in our driveway. I noticed the fat tires, the way the tread spilled off the concrete and onto dad's lawn. God, there'll be ruts of ruined grass, I thought. Dad'll be furious.

A man, taller than I remembered him at Malo, hopped out of the cab and marched toward the house. He had on the penny loafers.

"Mom! He's here." I grabbed my pack off the hall bench, set it near the door.

My home has never known such weight, I think. Mom must feel it, too; she sits so still at the end of the kitchen table. It's like there's a moose standing there, leaning against our stove. His genial smile, his green eyes are trained on Mom. One of his legs is crossed over the other, easy like. Both big hands are propped up beside him near the front burners, his thumb covering the *W* of Westinghouse. His red flannel is unbuttoned enough to reveal the clean, white T-shirt that covers his chest and the little hairs that creep over the collar like an advancing army of daddy longlegs. He has a brown belt, faded Levis. Stuck in the loafers are the shiny dimes. His heft is leaving prints in the linoleum, I think, tracks through the kitchen like the ruts his truck is leaving on the lawn.

He's larger than the images I have stored in my head from camp two summers before. I can't believe he's in my kitchen. Except for when he whispered *goodnight* and left candy, he spoke to me only once that summer after fourth grade when I spent two weeks at Malo. It was when I walked by his room and he invited me in to see the photos tacked to the wall over his tiny bed and dresser. Black-and-white pictures of mountain ponds and aspen trees. And smiling campers standing next to mountain ponds and aspen trees. "Are you a photographer?" I asked. "Among other things," he replied. He was the only counselor who slept in the dorm. Father Mac wanted him to keep a close eye on things, he said.

Mom's squinting at him. Her nail file midair, motionless.

"When do you think your camp will open?"

"I hope by the third week in June." His voice is velvety. He shifts, uncrosses and recrosses his long legs. I think the kitchen will shift with him, tilt to the south. "We have a lot of work yet to do on the main dining hall." He shoots me a look as if, in this instant, I've become his recruit, one of the *we.* "Plastering and painting." There's a ring of keys dangling from his belt. I try to count them. He's got more than the janitor at school has. Fifteen, twenty, maybe. How many doors can there be in one life? How many locks?

"How many boys do you expect to attend?" Mom looks so small, hunched at the table, asking her questions. I notice (perhaps for the first time ever) how shy she can be. Shy or preoccupied or both.

"I'm not sure yet. I'm just getting out the fliers. But I don't want more than fifteen or so a week. This way we can work together, build community. There'll be the usual—archery and horseback and fishing and so on." He pushes, with an index finger, his glasses up the bridge of his nose and scoops his bangs to the right. "But, more importantly, I want the boys to experience life on a working ranch. That's my idea. A real introduction to husbandry."

"What's the nearest town?"

"Allenspark."

"So you can get whatever you might need there."

"Yes. And there's Estes Park too. There are stores and two churches nearby, so we've got all bases covered." He smiles. Mom nods.

I glance out the window. Paul Newcomb and his little brother Eric, and Bobby and Michael Foster, have pulled up on their bikes. Stopped at the end of our driveway. They're pointing at the bails of hay piled in the open bed of the truck; the wooden-handled tools leaning against the yellow tailgate. There's rope and boxes and machinery and all sorts of ranch stuff and it's all in a rig in *my* yard and they're wondering, I know, what's up. What they're missing. And I feel the rush of it. An adventure has pulled right up to my door. He's come for *me*. I hope they hang around long enough to watch us drive away. I move to the hall and pick up my pack.

"Where is the place, exactly?"

"Up the Saint Vrain, about three quarters of an hour. Not far from Meeker Lodge. You know that area?" Bob's hand brushes, scratches quickly, near the buttons of his fly, where his jeans are most full and faded.

"Not so much. When will you have him back? I think he's got homework."

"Mom . . ."

"Around sundown Sunday. Is that good?"

The word *sundown* sings through my head as we walk out front and I give a slight nod to my silent neighbors. *Sundown . . . that's ranch talk*, I think.

Mom stands in the doorway, nail file motionless at her side.

Bob ignites the huge engine, fights with the stick shift, and the truck moves backward. The boys on their bikes scatter like minnows. The tires curve out over the grass. He doesn't seem to notice. I hope the marks don't go too deep, that they'll disappear before Dad gets home.

"Let's get George," he says.

I turn to see the boys frozen on their bikes as Virginia Vale trembles under the weight of what Bob owns. I watch how they gawk as he takes the left turn, swinging us wide around the corner.

7

I WAS RIDING on a cloud, five feet off the ground in the cab of his six-wheeled International Harvester. Already, I couldn't wait to tell the guys at school about this. Me in a big yellow truck. Me, on my way to do a job. I could feel the hum of engine rise through the soles of my boots and up my legs. I was in the middle, George at the open window, and Bob, counselor Bob in his red flannel and Levis, was at the wheel. The wind, smelling of brushwood, swept through the cab. A chance thrill, I was thinking. This is a chance thrill! Or, as Sister Christine would say, *Nil Sine Numine.*

Everything, at the very last second, just fell into place. Jay Jones said he'd cover my route and Father Elser got someone else to serve Sunday Mass and Mom said yes and it was Friday and I was free, free to go. We passed the Coors plant, its stacks sending up beer-colored smoke, and climbed west, up into the rocky arms of Clear Creek Canyon. James Taylor was on the radio.

Lord knows when the cold wind blows . . .

"Have you ever driven a tractor?" Bob asked. "Or milked a cow?"

"Nope." I shook my head and his teeth flashed white.

"Well, I'll teach you. I'll bet you're a quick learner."

I shrugged and felt pride or something leak through the heat of my cheeks. The luck of being included.

We were up far and high now, near timberline, with snowcapped peaks rising up on all sides. The road was barely a road, more like two tracks of mud through a meadow. The sun had disappeared, but the light of day still lingered.

"Watch your knee, kiddo," he said.

I closed my legs and watched his forearm, these marbled blue veins, shift the stick rising from the center of the floor. The truck lurched through the slippery ditches. We moved past a three-way fork in the road and clattered over a cattle guard. There was a wooden sign with a white arrow:

"That's the way to Bright Raven," Bob said.

"Who came up with that? That's no name for a ranch," George said.

"Why not?" asked Bob.

"Ravens are black. And they're scavengers."

"Not white ones."

"No such thing."

"Keep your eyes peeled. If you spot one, it's good luck." Bob winked at me.

"Bull," said George.

We rounded a clump of blue spruce and suddenly he hit the brakes, cut the engine.

"What's wrong?" George asked.

Bob put a finger to his lips. "Shhhhhh . . ."

He was staring at the clearing ahead. Something was out there— a mob of brown. Then my eye caught a clue—antlers. A ton of them, not eighty or ninety yards away.

"Deer," I whispered.

"Wapiti," Bob said. "Wild elk."

Their long necks were bent to the ground; they were eating. A little one with crooked legs kept pushing its head into the belly of its mother, searching for the place to suck.

"See the bull at the far end?" Bob said. "Look at that rack. He's the king. Bet he's mounted every doe in the crowd."

I looked at Bob looking at the elk. He belongs here, I thought. He knows about the wilderness. At St. Malo he used to camp out in a real tepee; he used to lead the hard hikes up Long's Peak. I didn't know him then, he was too important. I just couldn't believe I was sitting next to him now.

George nudged me. "Look, two are fighting."

We watched two of them butt heads, their hooves kicking up clumps of soil.

"Nah, they're just playing," said Bob and, reaching his arm up with a sigh, he let his right hand fall to my nape. His fingers began to brush up and down over the fuzz there, sort of inadvertently, but his hand was talking some story, direct from my neck down into the middle of things. Warmth was rising at the center of me and the elk were grazing and the sky going lavender and I let my head fall back, press into the curve of his palm. Something was in there, a bottomless mystery, a long way to tumble. Maybe a friend.

And suddenly his hand split to start the engine and we roared ahead as a hundred black and terrified eyes snapped around to see a yellow truck with three humans—or who knows what they saw or thought—and in that instant they ran for their lives, a stampede of fur leaping across the meadow until all the elk disappeared.

Sorry, I wanted to say. *Sorry we made you go.*

Bob shifted and the stick smacked my knee.

"Sorry," we both said.

When we got to the ranch, we did real chores. We milked the two cows by hand and fed hay to the horses. Bob made spaghetti for dinner and then he led the way down a trail that ran alongside the brook and ended up at the A-frame cabin across the meadow. That's where we'd sleep best, he said, in the loft there.

"Turn on the flashlight," George snapped. "It's pitch black."

"Your eyes will adjust," said Bob.

The sky was amazing, packed with stars. I looked up and saw the upside-down *W.* My favorite constellation. I'd learned it in Scouts. "Look, Cassiopeia. I've never seen it so bright!"

"Where?" George asked.

I pointed.

Bob said, "Good eye, kid. Caseeoh-pay-ee-ah." Then he explained. "She was the ancient queen of Ethiopia, you know. She made the mistake of looking at Medusa's head and was turned to stone. But then the gods forgave her, split her into pieces, and hung her in the sky."

"Fuck. They call *that* forgiveness?" George said.

Bob laughed. "Well, you gotta pay for breaking the rules." He put down his pack and stepped to the side of the path to pee. He undid the buttons of his fly and looked up. "There's a million stories up there, you know. The stars can guide you. Save your life." His piss hit the ground. "Before we went to Nam, my brother and me, we learned to read the sky like a map." He turned and I could see his eyes on me through the dark. Then his teeth as he smiled and said, "Hey, I'll give you a book on celestial navigation."

I nodded.

"A shooting star!" George cried.

I looked up and just caught it, and blinked, wondering if it really happened.

"That star died a thousand, maybe a million years ago," said Bob.

"That's *bull,* Bob," George said.

"No, it's true. It takes years for light to travel. It's all . . . already happened."

When we got to the cabin, Bob stayed downstairs to build a fire and George and I grabbed our sleeping bags and crawled up the ladder to the loft to get ready for bed. It was cold and dimly lit up there and George said, "Ah, Marsh, you don't need those dumb pj's, man. The more naked you are, the warmer. That's how blood and feathers work, like the Indians did it. Didn't they teach you that in pansy scouts?"

I looked down at George's pink moon of a face poking out of his sleeping bag. "How do you know what the Indians did?"

"Everyone knows, dummy."

I dropped my pajamas and slithered into my down sack. The nylon smelled like campfire, icy against my skin. "Brrrr." I tightened the drawstring to my neck. "Hey George? What's Bob *do?* Was he ever a seminarian?"

"Dunno. He quit, I guess. Does construction. Carpentry."

Wind shook the slatted ceiling.

"He's cool, isn't he? I never *knew* there were so many con-stellations. You know what? He's gonna give me a book about it. George? Did you really see Pegasus when he pointed to it? George?"

He was conked.

I was wide-awake. A truck, driving a tractor, milking a cow. I mean, what a day. *I'll wear my boots to school on Monday,* I thought. *All muddy. See if Sister Christine or any of the guys notice. I'm a rancher now.*

The rungs of the ladder creaked. It was Bob, climbing. He burped as his head popped up over the floor.

"Hey," he said.

"Hey," I whispered. I thought the noise would wake George. It didn't. He was snoring.

Bob set down a can of Coke and a lantern that had been hooked around his wrist, and then he pulled himself the rest of the way up into the loft. He stood, stooped, really, because he was too big for the place, then picked up the lantern and hooked it to a nail. It swung gently, hissing. A moth was tangled in a cobweb near the nail, its little shadow shifting in the light.

He hunched over me.

"George is down for the count, eh?"

I nodded, amazed at how warm my bag had become, how fast my blood was doing its work. George was right about the Indians.

I watched as Bob finished off his Coke and started taking things out of his pocket. The ring of keys. Loose change. A leather wallet. He placed everything just so on top of a battered dresser. He tugged his T-shirt over his belly. I looked out the one small window—a box of sparks.

Bob's belt buckle hit the floor.

His chest was filled with brown hair growing right down to the stripes of his Fruit of the Looms hanging there from bony hips. Like the loincloth carved on the Saint Sebastian outside Sister Joan's of-fice. He took off his glasses and placed them on the dresser. There were dark smudges under his eyes. I hadn't noticed them until now.

They made him look sad, the same look Sister Christine had when she talked of paradise. A look that made you want to help.

I sat up and whispered, "My teeth, I forgot to brush. My mom's really strict about it. I better go down."

"One night off won't ruin you," he said, arranging his sleeping bag so that our zippers touched. "You got to break the routine now and again."

I could smell the sweat of him. His calves were right next to me. White and huge, they made me think of a Sunday roast. He reached up and with a sudden flick of his arm the lantern was out. Then he rummaged through a drawer. I lay back down and watched him move like a ghost in the million-year-old light. His briefs glowed in the dark and the whole floor bounced when he walked. He un-snapped his Breitling—the watch he told me his grandfather had given him, the one he wore in Vietnam. It sparkled as he laid it next to his bed.

"Here's an extra pillow. Lift up."

"OK."

He slithered into his bag.

We listened for a time to George's steady snore, to the wind and the branches outside.

"Tomorrow's supposed to be good weather. We'll get an early start."

His fingers found my neck and started their talking. I held ab-solutely still but there was the one little muscle that dared to in-sist. Like a current running through me I didn't even own, it rose, willful, curious. And my heart was going crazy, like it wanted out. I was still as a mountain but full of motion.

He fumbled around the edge of my bag, looking for the zipper. He tugged it quickly downward. A stream of cold air ran from my shoulder to my hip, right past a thousand years of what I knew was taboo. He reached over and with large hands, scooped me into his bag. I remained limp. My body seemed to know, to *want* whatever this was but I didn't want to help. Not one bit. I needed to save some part of me for looking Sister Christine in the eye. I couldn't

hear for all the blood pounding in my head but I knew that someone, somewhere, was saying: *Stop.*

He turned me on my side so that my back was to him, then
wrapped his arms around me, tenderly, tightly. My head fit right
under his chin, the hair on his chest tickled my shoulder blades and
I simply could not believe the *size* of him, all the surface of him
—endless skin on skin, like I was being swallowed into another
planet.

He reached down to slip off my underwear. I let him. As my
shorts slid past my knees, suddenly into my mind came a picture
that hung from the chalkboard in Father Elser's science class: a
color-coded chart of all the layers of the earth from crust to core,
and it was the liquid core I was thinking of—the orange ball of fire
hidden under a million layers because it's too much, too dangerous. The secret urge buried at the center of everything, the force
that pushes up the trees and the mountains too and I wondered,
*How did I slip here so fast? To the secret at the center of bodies. The center
of him.*

God, oh God, is this you?

He pressed against me as though he'd found all he ever wanted.
I was it and I was terrified, amazed to be the one, as if I was a mag-
net and he stuck on me. My whole body humming with . . . *touch,* a
force mightier than family or church or anything I'd ever found in
a book. This must be it, I thought, the grown-up world, the way
it is. With a swift move of his hand, he placed himself, just so, between my legs. A part of my mind, the part asking: *What in the
world is he doing?* was looking on now, as though observing us from
overhead, as if observing a collision that I was in and I knew there'd
be damage. Real trouble. *Come on now!* I thought. *One word, one
scream, one virtuous move and you could change the course of everything.
Couldn't you? Choose to wake George, startle Bob. Stop the accident.* But
I didn't. I allowed. It was as though he was touching me into being and I was dying to find out who I was.

One of his arms circled my chest as with his other hand he
cupped himself between the very top of my thighs. The smell of

Johnson's Baby Lotion filled the room as he slid himself, back and forth, along my legs. I heard a tiny cry, a flutter through his throat as he squeezed the air out of my lungs. *This must be what a man does with a woman and what does that make me?* He squished me again, gave another soft cry, and suddenly there was warm liquid on my legs. *My God,* I thought. *What is it?* It smelled like swimming at the JCC. *Oh, wait . . . no, it must be . . . thousands of souls searching for an egg. What has he done? This guy is a murderer. What a mess, a massacre.* I wanted to call down to the drowning Catholics, *I know this isn't what you expected. Sorry. I'm sorry.*

His hands were fast all over, plucking and playing with me, and there was a wave at the center of me, rising. A motion that threatened to burst, to split me open, and I panicked, thinking I might spill piss everywhere.

"No!" I whispered, trying to move his hand away, but he insisted, and then nothing in heaven or on earth could stop it now, up from the core of me coming. My first, my very own seed splitting up and out and swimming away down my belly. What happened? Did it really happen? Over in a second, like the shooting star. I tried to steady my breath, to lie as still as I could.

After a while he moved his hand away and shifted so we were both on our backs. I turned my face away into the scratchy pillow and right there next to my nose, his precious Breitling was glowing. Hands ticking past the numbers: *11:49,* and the date, *7 April 72,* burned into my brain. Every second hereafter I'd be different. I was twelve years, three months, and fourteen days old. This was the end of? . . . the beginning of? . . . over in a second. Nothing like the scout book, page 273—*Nocturnal Emission*—said it would be. In a dream all my own. A dream with a girl.

I tucked myself back into my bag. He was silent; George snored. I brushed my fingers across my stomach, over the evidence, wondering at the blame stuck there, at how fast you can fall. I looked toward the window, to the stars and space beyond, and tried to strike a deal.

God, please . . . this has to be just ours. Top Secret.

8

"YOU'LL BLOW UP *the house...!*"

Mom is screaming, her teeth yellow and decayed, her face and hair all white. Dad's on his knees wearing his dark suit with a red tie. He slides a long, lit match into a hidden hole under the furnace. Mom roars, "Stop!"

Dad doesn't listen.

"It's the pile-up light," he says quietly. Always quiet. "The pilot light for heaven's..."

BOOM!

Everything explodes orange and then I'm alone in my dream watching myself sleep on the cement floor in the basement. I'm curled next to the big, silver furnace. No pajamas, only my underwear, a loincloth. Jesus-style.

The furnace has a mouth — slits for air — like teeth. If I sit up I can see through, down to its stomach, to the blue gas fire inside.

Mom's slippers scratch overhead, like rats scattering across the kitchen floor. She'll never guess that I'm not in my bed, that I'm way down here....

"Rise and shine," came a voice.

Boom!

A deep voice, trespassing, *rattling around in the furnace, rattling in my dream....*

"Let's rustle up some breakfast."

Like mosquitoes, the words buzzed, needled their way into my ear.

"Guys...?"

I opened my eyes. Pale light spilled through a small window. Daybreak. There was an insistent thudding. I realized it wasn't from the world but my own heartbeat. I shut my eyes again. *Sleep, sleep. Back to the basement....*

A large thump startled my eyes open.

"Chow and chores. Let's go."

The air was cold and full of the smell of cedar, of the jumble of what was me and what wasn't. A lump to my left was snoring and I turned to see George's red nose poking out of his bag and then it all came to me. Landed on my chest. I was in the loft of the A-frame cabin. On Bright Raven Ranch. His ranch, near Estes Park.

Another thump.

"C'mon, guys."

And that was him, down the ladder, down below. He was... moving furniture? Stacking firewood, maybe? Whatever it was it banged against the wall, shook the floor.

George stirred and spoke.

"Too early. Shit... too *cold*."

"Guys awake?"

"We're coming," George grumbled.

"I'll be out front," said the voice from below.

The cabin door opened, then closed, squeaking like the hinges of a haunted house.

"Fuck," George said, sitting up. "Maybe he's got French toast." I kept still and watched puffs of his breath float and evaporate toward the ceiling. "Why so fucking early?" He pulled his red sweater over his head. Clumps of his blond hair stuck straight up as if in protest, or shock. "I hope he's got something good." Then he stood, yawning, and rubbed his eyes with tight, pink fists. "C'mon, Martian." He pulled on his long johns and pants, his two pair of socks, and disappeared down the creaking ladder. I listened as he fumbled for his coat, stepped out, and closed the door.

Not a bird. Not a peep. One Martian on Mars. Even the wind was holding its breath; everything hushed as on a holy day.

I wiggled my toes, then slowly sat up. The smell of pine and smoke—scout trips trapped in the feathers—rose from my bag. My stomach wasn't right, nauseous, and the skin of it was pinched and sticky. I looked toward my navel for reasons.

I found evidence.

Touched it.

Flaky glue, dried-up seeds.

I was naked, and in a panic scrambled to find my underwear, cover my tracks. I felt a wild wave of dread, thinking that if I didn't find them, someone else would or already had, and there'd be no end to the questions. My arms dug, searched crazily until suddenly I saw them balled up next to his pillow. I couldn't imagine why, but his silver Brietling was wrapped around them, like a joke, like a ribbon around a gift. I snatched up my briefs, letting the watch drop, and hurriedly slid them on.

I sat still to stare at the time, at the fat, stupid watch on the filthy floor. The sliver of silver ticked off the seconds, jerking its way around the blue face, number to number. It seemed odd somehow that it worked, beat, independent of him. The new date was there. Things had gone right ahead and flipped to the 8th of April. Strange he'd left it behind like that, like this. He guarded it with his life, so he said, because it'd given him luck in the jungle. He'd come home alive. I lifted it up for a moment. It was surprisingly hefty, thick, like him.

I looked around at the rust-stained mattress, the battered dresser, the splintered ceiling. What was snug looked ugly now, and unreal, as if I'd woken into someone's movie, into the scene set in the attic, the scene of the crime.

I dropped the watch, slid out of my bag, and slowly got into my long johns and bell-bottom jeans, buttoned up my favorite blue flannel shirt. I stood but was dizzy, had to keep stooping, stopping for air.

I went for my socks, all scrunched up and burr-filled on the floor. I shook them out, started to put one on, and there was my pink foot hovering over it—his precious watch. I raised my knee. I raised it to smash the fucking thing. But instead, my body bent and I scooped it into my pocket. I took a breath and imagined him reaching toward me as I handed it over. I could see his green eyes lit with gratitude, his hand tousling my hair. I could hear his warmest voice saying: "Thanks, kiddo."

I zipped up my jacket and stepped outside. There was a frail mist over the meadow. The sun hadn't appeared but was sending the idea of light, blue and unreal. Instead of standing in an actual place, in real time, it seemed as though I'd entered into a hallucination of a Saturday morning somewhere. The air was mountain-immaculate and rushed, frigid, into my lungs. I sank to the porch to tie my boots.

Patches of old snow dotted the clearing and glowed in the dim light. George was kicking at one, sending shaves of muddy ice every which way.

"My fingers are freezing," he muttered. I saw he was missing a glove.

Bob or whoever or whatever he might be, for at that moment he was registering as some strange mammal in Levis and red jacket, was bent over the tractor working with a wrench, yanking at wires. Occasionally he—it—cupped a hand to his mouth to blow on fingers.

"The fucking thing won't start," George informed me, rolling his eyes.

I fiddled with my boots and kept glancing toward the man in the jeans on the tractor, wondering when, if, he'd look my way. Wondering if his eyes would tell me that I was actual, there, or if this was a dream and I was as unreal to him as he was to me. I pulled at my red laces until I had two perfect bows.

"Let's just walk to the dining hall," George growled.

"Nah . . . this should do it," declared the figure in the faded jeans. He smiled—*why this grin?*—as he tossed his wrench into a toolbox. "All fixed." There was a clatter of metal as the wrench landed, a pealing clank across the valley, and just then, almost as if Bob planned it, cued it; a slice of light peeked over Twin Sisters—the peaks to our east. The meadow caught fire and everything, except for the pointed shadows of the conifer trees, turned golden. The rays were like trumpets, pure and glad. Glad, I thought, because the day was new and didn't yet know. Once the sun climbed high enough to see, surely there'd be thunder.

Bob jumped into the driver's seat, the only seat, and, after a few tries, the engine came to life.

"C'mon, fellas."

I stood unsteadily and took one step toward the tractor. The smell of diesel cut across the thin air. Acrid. A wave of nausea. I stopped like a stone, feet stuck in the dirt, fear gripping my ribs.

"Earth to Martian," said George. I looked into his pink, pudgy face, wondering what he could know of any of this. He'd never let himself be the girl.

"Come on," said the guy on the tractor.

There was an empty, crumpled can of Coke near my foot. *His trash.* My eyes were stuck on the red and white, on the twisted cursive of *Coca-Cola.* It reminded me of the world: McDonald's —Saturday with dad, cheeseburgers and grass clippings in the back of the Plymouth. Field Day, when Father Jack provided soda pop. I could still run the three-legged with Mark Groshek... couldn't I?

"Hey, are you coming?"

My feet obeyed, jumped onto the axle of the tractor and found balance next to George. I stood not five inches behind our counselor, staring at the frayed rubber band that dug its way around the back of his skull. This, God knows why, remains the sharpest image from the fog of that morning: standing on the red tractor, staring at the back of his head. At strands of his fine, filthy hair tangled into the band, which was attached over his ears, holding his nerdy glasses in place. Hair that trembled on account of the engine. I studied his bald patch, the flaky skin on the crown of his head, as if I could see inside, find the answer to the question repeating in my own brain: *Who is he? Who is he?*

His long legs worked the pedals, his right arm struggled with the gearshift as George and I perched between the giant tires. My eyes drifted to the bulging black tread, fantastically large tires, taller than I was. "Shit!" George cried, as off we went and there was nothing, not a thing to do but grab tight to Bob. Hold him fast to keep from falling.

George's face was pinched and yellow under the fluorescent light of the kitchen. I watched as he took his tongue, piled high with oatmeal, and stuck it out toward Bob, who turned from the stove just in time to see George spit the goop back into his bowl.

"Yuck."

Bob said nothing, but I saw how the muscle of his jaw jumped as he clenched his teeth, how his hand tightened around the wooden spoon. I felt my own jaw move as, little liar without a morsel in my mouth, I chewed with the primness of the teacher's pet. I felt it, cursed it—this eternal wish to please, the habit of Catholic school courtesy creeping right up, straightening my spine. Even now. Even this morning. George looked brilliant to me across the table, with his slumped shoulders and his mean tongue. I looked down into my bowl of mush, wishing for some of what he had. Whatever it was.

The two Holsteins stood at the ready. One stamped a hoof; the other let out a fart as we put Vaseline on our hands. Bob set the pails and stools for George and me and showed us again how to squeeze the teats. I sat and reached for the contraption, the pink, dangling nipples. The udder looked like an overblown rubber glove, about to burst.

"Start right at the top and slide down," he said. "Just like you did last evening. You know how it works." He was hovering over my left shoulder, his voice greasy as the teats. He still hadn't looked at me.

Squirts of milk ricocheted and bubbled up inside our buckets. The sweet smell cut clean through the dank odors of the barn. It was amazing to see, to smell, the source. Amazing to me that this massive mother, this wall of big bones and smooth hide, allowed me to sit by and pinch milk from her. I expected her to kick me, to ask for someone older or more experienced, but there was no protest, except for the gentle sway of her tail, which caught me a few times in the face.

"Rest your head against her haunch," Bob said. "Her tail won't get you there."

I pressed the side of my face to her rump and kept squeezing as gently and firmly as I could. I felt calmer, glad for the work, for the results. Glad for her animal patience. Now and then her muscles twitched against my cheek. I wanted to sink right into her, mother cow, and thank her just for being. For accepting.

Bob took over when our hands wore out and then we poured the milk into tall, silver canisters. "We'll have cream with our lunch," he said, easily lifting the heavy cans into a cooler.

The few chickens and two horses were noisy and glad at the sight of us, with our pellets and hay. We spread their fodder and watched as they squawked and whinnied and chewed. I leaned on the fence and looked up past the main house to where the clearing ended and the peaks began. The warm light was bathing everything—the yellow grass, the red storybook barn. The bright sunshine reflected off the granite faces of the mountains and off the high glaciers of snow. I looked around at the cloudless, cheerful sky and felt astonished. Astonished, I think, that everything was simply going on. Impossibly beautiful and ordinary. I scanned the edge of the woods, waiting. For what, I wasn't sure. I had this feeling that our secret must have seeped into the trees, into the air, and at any moment a terrible storm or a squad of men in blue uniforms or black cassocks would emerge to arrest him, us, time. But nothing. The trees stood there as if they were in the same trance as I, swaying slightly in the breeze. The sun climbed and the snow melted and the animals ate and pissed and I felt relieved. And betrayed.

George was sent off to paint the dining tables and Bob asked me to help him mend a section of fence next to the barn. He handed me a pair of work gloves made for a ranch hand like his, like him. Three times my size. I had to make a fist to keep them from sliding off.

"Stretch this around the post over there." He handed me two strands of wire, then raised his gloved hand, pointed. "Pull tight."

I dragged and stretched the barbed wire around the wooden pole and yanked it. I was glad for a next move, a duty. I watched him place nails in his mouth, wrapping his lips around them so the sharp ends were out, like silver fangs. He looped the wire through a metal bracket and I wondered if this was when we might see each other. Now that we were alone. If this was when he might say something about it. But he didn't look up, wouldn't look over. It was as if he was concealed under a dark cloud, or we both were. He threw off his jacket, then raised his hand and took one fang out. His eyes were crystal green, glued to the task. His combat boots sloshed and sank into the midday mud as he picked up his hammer and placed the nail where he wanted it. His arm began to swing, his muscles trembling with each blow. The nail went in, and then another, and another, the smack of it echoing across the ranch. Sweat glistened on his forehead; his glasses slid down the bridge of his nose.

"Let it go," he suddenly commanded as he slumped against the fence post to catch his breath. I dropped the wires and watched his eyes go toward the patch of aspen tucked beside the barn. I gazed there, too, at the close-knit grove of trees, slim and smooth and elegant, just beginning to bud.

"What does your father do?" he asked.

"He's a writer. For the *News*." My voice sounded weak, my words slow across the vapor.

"Oh ... a writer," Bob sang, as though impressed.

In the noon light, the bark of the aspen had the color and texture of human skin.

"Are you close?"

I glanced over and saw that he was still staring toward the trees. The shadows were there under his glasses, under his eyes. Like smudges of misery. There was something wrong with him, I thought, and he knew it. Knew there were people who'd kill him if they saw what he was.

"I dunno ... guess so," I said, tapping the fence post with my boot.

"George said you're top of your class at Christ the King."

"No. My friend Mark Groshek is."

"But you're close to the top."

I shrugged.

"I'll bet you can do anything you set your mind to. I can tell. You're a champ."

I felt my face heat up. His praise was like food I didn't know how to refuse.

"I mean it," he said. "You're special."

We were quiet a long while, listening to nothing, to everything. I studied the black scars on the aspen where branches had broken away or where someone had taken a knife and carved initials. On one trunk, right under the gouged shape of a heart, I thought I saw *RC + JC*. I wondered if that could be him, Robert C—. Him and ... Jesus?

"With some work, this'll be a great place," Bob said, looking out toward the meadow's end. "One great boys' camp." He lifted a hand and pointed. "The archery range is going to be just over there."

I took off my gloves and draped them over the post. I put my hand in my front pocket and walked toward him. He didn't move or look at me. My nose came even with his bottom rib, not far above his brown leather belt. He'd missed a loop. I gazed up at his ear, at the lobe of flesh, the ridges of pink circling in toward his brain. It

looked like something belonging to an animal, something you'd
study at the zoo. I wanted to say something that would go in there.
I had no idea what.

I was standing close enough to hear him breathe, but he seemed
so far away. In a movie, in a dream. I couldn't put together that he
was the same person who'd held me the night before. He was naked,
wasn't he? Head to toe. And I was, too. He'd left sperm on me. And
now we were standing out in broad day and he was over there and
I was here. There are his whiskers. A shadow. Thicker today than
before, when they scratched the back of my neck. That happened.
It happened.

He was pretending, it seemed, to study something out there in
the meadow. Making plans for his ranch, maybe?—Bright Raven
Summer Camp. I reached out and, though I didn't mean to, I made
a sound like a scratch of the throat and he looked, not at me but
at my outstretched hand. He stayed quiet, gazing at the contents of
my cupped palm.

"Oh," he finally uttered, like a little kid coming to. He removed
one glove and carefully lifted the watch. He put it to his ear for a
moment, then onto his wrist, and picked up his hammer.

I stepped back to my post and slid on the giant gloves and a voice
came to me from the dark. It came to me from some part of my
mind I'd never met, and it said: *It's OK. This is how it is.*

"Hey, buddy, pull the third line there around the middle," he
said. "Yank tight."

And I did. I followed instructions and pulled as tight as I could
and the chores and the day proceeded. I helped rake the stalls of
the barn and clear a path from behind the dining hall toward the
archery range. He gave us peanut butter sandwiches and fresh milk
and we worked and worked until the sun slid behind the mountain
and never once did the voice leave me. It came from inside like a
stab but I understood that it was here to help. There was something
good in this, I thought. Good that I learn the truth of how it is.

And the day grew cold and the stars came out and the man in

the Levis pointed again at the heavens, at the Milky Way and the Big Dipper and the guiding North Star. At all the fiery constellations. And this time George found Pegasus and that made him so happy he laughed. The man's voice was sweet and tired from all our work. The moon was just rising above the mountain as we walked the trail along the creek to the porch of the cabin, took off our boots, climbed up the creaking ladder. All the same as before but all different for knowing.

There was the undressing, the keys out of the pocket and placed with the can of Coke on the beat-up bureau. There was a fart from George and a joke from Bob and the crawling into bags. Me in the center again. There was the taking off of the watch, the swapping of pillows, the wait for George's sleeping, the wait to find out if the man would dare. If I would.

The lantern went out.

George's dumb, innocent snore began and there came the reach of a hand, the touch of his fingers, out from behind the dark cloud. Warm and ready to talk. And the voice inside whispered: *Go, if you want. You can't help it. It's the way it is. . . .*

And my loneliness took me on the six-inch trip over to Bob's bag. This time I helped, a little. I scooted with my legs, slid myself over toward the heat of him and he was all there, come out of hiding. There were no words in the dark, no eyes, just the flesh getting to it. The please, the pleasure, the longing to be talked to, back to the tight curve of his stomach, the coils of grown-up hair below his navel. I was back at the center touching the source of things, him rising out of his cotton briefs, pulsing, I thought, *for me.* Better than a gold star or straight As. I was in, I was holding fast. I was forgiven.

And the wind was skipping off the roof, stirring protest through the pines, and the silent moon and stars sent down their dim, dying light. He moved his head down to my belly—*how strange*—until his lips, warm and wet, were there on me. Then he took me into his mouth. God, so this happens, too? My God . . . *so be it.* I pushed into the dark; pushed, thinking that *this* is what I prayed for all day long. Relief. And thanks be to God, if He was anywhere anymore to be thanked, the explosion came, it came and I was split right there into a million pieces, hung so far away that I vanished. I pushed and pushed and stifled the cry, spoke the prayer: *Swallow me, Oh God, Swallow me away from here....*

9

WE LEFT THE ranch late Sunday afternoon, the end of that weekend. The truck roared its way down Saint Vrain Canyon. The road followed the creek's lead, twisting its way east, back toward the city. The radio played what it could catch, snatches of static and Cat Stevens. I was in the middle again, George at the window, Bob at the wheel. The three of us were quiet.

We stopped at the Arby's in Boulder. Bob treated us to a shake and a sandwich.

"Thanks for everything guys, we got a lot accomplished."

He passed the fries. His eyes were gone again. Gone all day behind the cloud.

We passed the green sign that tells you: WELCOME. YOU'RE ONE MILE HIGH. The street lamps were just coming on.

George was dropped off first. Then Bob drove around the block toward my street. I watched the squares of light go by—the glow from my neighbors' kitchen windows. The McCoys, the Tynans, the Pecks. I had the strangest feeling that I'd been to the other side of the world and back again and that my house might not be there anymore.

We stopped at the corner of Exposition. There was no traffic, but Bob didn't make the turn. We just sat, engine idling. I spotted Mrs. Lachada, stocky in her housecoat, kneeling in her front yard, digging. She was a crazy gardener. I'd help her sometimes with chores. Led Zeppelin was on the radio. *There's a lady who's sure all that glit-*

ters is gold. . . . He reached over and clicked off the music. The silence pressed me close to the passenger door.

"George smokes dope, you know," he said.

"What?"

"He has a rough time without a mom. That's why he needs good people, like you." He was gripping the wheel as if we were speeding. "Do you?"

"What?"

"Smoke dope?"

"No." I grabbed my knapsack from the floor and stuck it on my lap. My eyes moved to the sticker on Mrs. Lachada's station wagon: AMERICA, LOVE IT OR LEAVE IT. She'd stuck it there after she lost her son in Vietnam.

"Good. I'm glad you don't. I hope you never do, because you've got talent coming out your ears."

He shoved the stick and made the turn. I wrapped my fingers around the door handle. We passed all the silent, rectangle houses. The Fosters' house, the Starmans'. . . .

"This is it," I said. I glanced at the kitchen window; relieved no one was looking out.

"Thanks again for your help."

I nodded and pushed open the door.

"Marty?"

I stopped.

"I'm glad George invited you. I hope you'll come work again, soon."

The cab rocked gently.

"Marty?"

I turned but couldn't find his face. He was staring at the dash, and the glow of instruments made his cheeks green, his eyes empty sockets.

"Our friendship—it's different, you know. Because it's—"

I took a quick look at the house. No movement there but the flickering blue light from the den window. *Wonderful World of Dis-*

ney or *Mission Impossible,* that's where they must be. Sunday-night television. Dad on the floor, curled around his vodka tonic, smoking his filterless Philips. Mom on the couch, adding up household receipts. Little brother, sisters. I'll say a quick hi, take out the trash (my Sunday chore) and go straight to my room.

"In another time and place," he whispered, "what we shared is good. It's all right. Everything's OK. You know why?"

I stared ahead toward the sign near the corner: CHILDREN AT PLAY.

"Because there's love, you know? And, it's between us."

I looked at his drooping, unshaven cheek and something like hate took hold of me. I hated that he used the word *love,* and I had a sudden sense he'd said all this before to someone else. To others. And I realized that he was scared of what I might do and I felt a mean rush of power and for an instant then, our eyes met as he reached over to take my shoulder. But before he could touch me I was out of the truck and moving toward the house, toward the flickering blue light. I could hear the engine stuck there, idling, but I didn't look back. I kept walking. I opened the yellow front door of my house and there came from the den a deep, commanding voice. The one you'd hear every Sunday after the fireworks of *Disney* were finished, just before the top-secret assignment self-destructs: "Your mission, Mr. Phelps, should you choose to accept it . . ."

"I'm home."

And I heard the truck pulling away, and then the sizzling sound of fire as I entered the room and found my family gathered, staring at the Magnavox, where the secret agent's impossible mission was going up in smoke.

10

MY LITTLE BROTHER, David, was still asleep, his breath steady in the bunk overhead.

The sun had just appeared, ricocheting around the window-well and through the dirt-stained glass of our basement window, throwing light across the lemon-colored walls, the orange shag carpet. The colors were Mom's, her scheme for the boys' room: blinding cheer. I lay there with a storm in my chest and began to do for myself what he'd taught me over the weekend.

"Boys!" my mother yelled down. "Breakfast. Car pool will be here soon!" I stopped to listen as she closed the door at the top of the stairs, as her slippers slid across the linoleum. I closed my eyes —there was the lifeguard at the JCC, his red swim trunks . . . then Bob, the buttons on his faded Levis. The explosion came fast, rising through me like a mushroom cloud, blowing my head off.

"You'll be late."

"OK, Mom. OK!" I shouted.

Every morning at Mass, Father says: "Lamb of God, you take away the sins of the world." I'd knelt and whispered my faults— made-up and real—through the fuzzy screen of the confessional. I'd bowed my head, prayed my Hail Marys, asked forgiveness for fibs, for swiping quarters from Mom's purse. I'd asked for the stains to be washed away. But what happened, what did you do, when the sin was so big it was *you?*

Lamb of God you take away the sins of the world, have mercy . . .

My brother stirred in the bunk above, crawled down the ladder, and left the room. I listened as he climbed the basement steps, then I sat up, slipped off my briefs, and wiped my stomach. I knew it all along, didn't I? That there might be this, a Bob in the world, a body that would betray me. *Lamb of God, you take away the sins of the world . . . please, take this body.*

I knocked softly on the door of Dad's john. Never did that. It was his corner, his private orbit. He opened the door, a gust of steam.

"Dad?"

"Pull up a seat, tiger."

I sat, cross-legged, on the toilet.

He was at the gray sink, wrapped in his red-checkered robe. He was putting cream on his face. The room smelled of Old Spice. I watched him scrape at his cheek, then over the summit of his Adam's apple.

"Dad?"

"Damn," he whispered as a little star of blood blossomed on his throat. Quick, he dropped the razor, snatched his lighter from the pocket of his robe. There was the flick of flame and suddenly, balanced between his fingers, a tight white cigarette. No filter for this guy, up to the mouth, a direct hot hit. Threads of white drifted from his nose. Dragon smoke streamed from his lips and bounced off the reflection of his bushy brow. He looked into the glass, into his half-shaven, grown-up whiskers, and saw something far away, it seemed. Something he didn't like. He set his cigarette down carefully on the edge of the sink, where there were two brown marks burned permanently into the porcelain. Marks I'd touch sometimes when he was gone, to see if they were still hot. He grabbed a piece of toilet paper and pressed it to where he was bleeding, then lifted and touched the Philip Morris to his lips again. The tip glowed orange as he took a deep drag. He turned his face toward me and formed an *O* with his lips, as though he was going to sing to me. Or kiss the air. His mouth puckered, then pulsed like a hungry trout, and from deep within his burning lungs, ring after perfect ring of smoke signals appeared, lined up like a flock of birds. As they glided over, I reached out to grasp them. They scattered.

"Dad?"

"Yeah?"

He coughed horribly then and Mom yelled that it was Pop-Tarts, and car pool any minute. I ran to get dressed.

11

INTO MY SIXTH-GRADE classroom I took: Mud from the ranch. Brown leather boots clomping across the linoleum. Shit-kicking weights on the end of my legs, making me master of myself. I'm two inches bigger in these things. Even without them, I'm taller now. Superior. In the space of one weekend at the foot of a mountain, I've been thrust up, eyeing things now from a new height. Adult territory.

I bend to fix the thick, red shoelace, straighten the blue cuff of my polyester pants. No one else in my class wears footgear like this. That's just fine. No one else knows of these things. They weren't chosen to walk in the muck of a real barn. They didn't have the luck, the fate, the sweet devil-joy come their way. I'm different, always have been, knew it all along.

Just fine. Fine with me.

What happened, what I did, what I am, stands between me and everybody else in the whole fucking world. Every body. Except one.

And the boots are my own keepsake. They're like the pledge—*just between us*—tied around my feet. And a ring of mud around each sole to recall the trail I've gone down. Down to the pleasure, to the wet earth smell, to the hidden world of skin on skin. The muck sticks. It's our glue.

But, strangely, when I think of *it,* it's not exactly him I'm thinking of. It's more the *force,* the thing that's been revealed. That's most of what I'm feeling, thinking of. The orange ball of fire at the center of it all. I've seen it, this grown-up truth. Contacted it. And none of you sorry sixth graders can imagine where I've been. How big and real it was, is. The flesh of it. None of you teachers or parents or priests with all your rules and books can possibly imagine what's humming right now in my chest, heating up my thighs. The power of it. The hum of a holy spirit, the holy hum of sex, come to enter my life, fill the void. At long last the burning question has a solid answer. *Touch.*

Our sixth-grade class is the last room at the north end of the hall on the second floor. Windows run along the west wall, opposite the clock and the crucifix. I look outside. The mountains are there, distant and clear. They are out there calling and calling and I want to go, up into the wild. I want to live as an animal. A savage. How can anything in these books be real? Anything from these churchified, city mouths? I've stumbled upon the one, the only thing that is *real.* Everything up till now has been a lie, hasn't it? My body is all on fire with the truth.

I turn away from the windows and up to the cross. The crucified, nearly naked corpus. He looks at me differently now and I want to tell him—*How dare You,* and I want to pull off his little loincloth, Mr. Son of Man, and ask him a thing or two about gods on earth. The kind with dicks.

Sister Christine asks us to rise. She gives directions about the reading lab, about concentration, but her voice is garbled by the hum of molecules dancing between bodies, bouncing around the fluorescent lights. The gigantic chords ringing in my head muffle her words. I've tried twice and our eyes have met and she doesn't seem to see someone other, someone different. It's all easier than I thought; to make what happened seem like it didn't. To hold it down in a corner inside and act just the same. It's someone else's story, all *that,* someone else's body. Or, if it really is my story, well then I can hold it quietly within while I tell the stupid world another tale. The tale of the golden one. The altar boy. The tale they want to hear, the one that will protect me.

—

At fleeting moments I want to scream, to burst forth with the news of what I discovered. Or what discovered me. I don't want to confess, but to boast. *You see, the thing I'd been waiting for, it happened!* But it passes as quickly as it comes, replaced by the sharp stab in the gut. *Shut the fuck up.* The stab that's already becoming familiar.

It's late at night, early in the morning, when I'm all alone. That's when I begin to feel the weight of worry. The shame like a blade sharpening itself against the core of me. *Bury it. Bury it. Dig deep and bury it.*

At recess Tuesday, my first lesson since the ranch, I strum defiantly. *A hundred miles, a hundred miles, I can hear the whistle blow a hundred miles . . .*

"Your fingering is strong. You practiced over the weekend, didn't you?"

Her auburn brows are raised, such pleasure in her face. She couldn't possibly imagine, could she? The chords that have been plucked over the weekend, the music I'm strung out on. And I have not the least problem. I look her in the eye with an easy smile and say, "Yes, Sister. I practiced."

It's so much easier than I think it will be.

Lying.

12

A FEW MORNINGS LATER, I was sitting on the floor, on the gritty beige carpet of our front hall. Car pool was due any minute but I was moving slowly, lacing my boots. Dad stood at the hall mirror, wrestling with his tie. His blue tie with the tiny yellow typewriters all over it. His fingers fluttered around his throat, his hands racing the clock. Like everyone in the world, he was due at a desk.

My eyes drifted up past the gold-framed poem my mom had nailed to the wall—*Go placidly amid the noise and haste*—to the crucifix hanging just left of the front door. A classic, foot-tall wooden Jesus.

"We should take that down," I said.

Dad glanced at me for a second, his shaggy eyebrows taut, each rising to a sharp point—devilishly handsome. "Christ?"

"No. The palms," I said. "They're dead."

"Burn them."

I looked up at the hairy fronds drooping around Jesus's neck, dried and yellow like a ratty old scarf. I'd stuck them there myself nearly three weeks earlier, on Palm Sunday, the day we remember Jesus's triumphant mule ride into Jerusalem. The Sunday before the Holy Thursday he's betrayed and it all comes tumbling down.

Three weeks, forever ago.

"Damn," Dad whispered. I looked over. His lengths had gone wrong. Again.

"Why don't you use a clip-on?" I asked. "It's easier."

"Clips are for kids. Didn't you get a real tie this year, for your confirmation?"

"No." I yanked at my red laces. "Fake."

Dad dropped his head and examined how close the tips of his tie came to his zipper fly, considering, it seemed, whether to start all over. His necktie hung flat over his white shirt, then bowed way out, following the bulge of his belly. This paunch was new, sudden, as if one night he'd sneaked out and swallowed a basketball. The one that sat unused in the garage. His slim, Korean Conflict days were gone. Slumped there, head hanging, he looked like a big Winnie-the-Pooh. A friendly stuffed thing that wouldn't go anywhere without being carried. I looked into the mirror where his bald spot glowed. A pink moon amid a dark sky. He lifted his face suddenly, and the reflection of his eyes caught mine in the mirror.

"Since when do you wear your hiking boots to school?"

I felt my face go hot. "Since now," I said, tying a double knot. "Since I went to the ranch."

"That guy's camp?"

"Yeah."

Dad pulled apart his tie.

"Your great aunt arrives today."

"Who?" I stood and stuffed my bologna sandwich into the top of my knapsack.

"Your Aunt Marion." I stepped over and both of us were in the mirror—junior and senior. His English Leather wafted over and attached itself to my clothes; the smell of him, I knew, would stick with me all day. "She'll be at Grandma's the next few weeks."

I studied the gentle father in the glass. His pale lips, his watery blue eyes, his large ears. I'd been doing this lately, spying on his face, searching for a familiar feature. A piece of chin or cheek or bone that hinted at our relation. That I belonged to him. I had a growing feeling there'd been a mistake, that I'd come from somewhere else. I suspected he felt it, too. That he wondered what, other than his son, I might be.

"Has she been here before?" I asked.

"No. She's not allowed to travel." Dad's hands kept busy, the hair on his knuckles a blur. We both stared into the glass, two pale Martys caught in the same square frame, like a photo of fellow strangers.

"Why?"

"She's cloistered."

"What's wrong?"

"Nothing's *wrong*. She's cloistered. She's a contemplative." He slid the knot tight to his Adam's apple. A tiny Band-Aid stuck on his throat crinkled, looked as if it might fall. "She's a Maryknoll nun . . . like a monk. She prays full-time."

"All day?"

"Pretty much." He began to button his collar. "She's a good person to have on our team," he said, as though we were gathering forces, gearing up for the big game against God. "Maryknoll's let her out to celebrate her fiftieth jubilee with us."

He grabbed his car keys off the hook next to the mirror and moved past the crucifix toward the door. The dead fronds wiggled as if they were waving goodbye. "Why don't you change shoes," he said as he stepped outside.

That day, during recess, I found my older sister, Chris.

"What do you think a lady monk would look like?" I asked.

"I don't know. Like a nun, I guess."

"I wonder if she'll look like Grandma? Or maybe like you or me. Imagine her in an airplane, flying in her habit, belted into her seat like everyone else."

My sister smiled. A screechy voice rose from the volleyball court. "Chris . . . come on!"

"Aunt Marion's the older sister? Right?" I asked.

"Yeah."

"How old?"

"Dad said she was born around 1900."

"So she's seventy-two."

Chris nodded, fixing the barrette in her long blond hair.

"Six of my life would fit into her one."

"Guess so," Chris said, running back to her game.

Eighth period, the chalkboard was jammed with geology.

Mountains have complex internal structures formed by folding, faulting, volcanic activity, igneous intrusion, and metamorphism.

Between 80 million and 40 million years ago, the LARAMIDE OROGENY *raised the Rocky Mountains.*
> *Tertiary sediments.*
> *Paleozoic and Mesozoic strata.*
> *Intrusive igneous rocks.*
> *Precambrian structures.*
> *Tectonic plates.*

"Everyone look out the window toward Mount Evans," Mr. Johnson said as he pointed west.

It's warm out, I'll deliver my papers fast, I thought.

"What's the elevation?" Silence. "Who knows?"

"Fourteen thousand two hundred and..." Carol Buell began.

"Sixty four," he said, writing the number on the board. "Based on what you read in chapter eleven, what are *some* of the elements, Mr. Flynn, that might have formed this great mountain, one of the tallest in our state?"

"Well, umm..."

He always called on people he thought hadn't read the assignment.

I stared at the far-off crown of snow on top of Evans. *She stays hidden,* I thought. *A secret life.* A picture kept coming into my head: An old, pale nun in a locked closet. Nothing there but a wooden cross, a prayer book, and a candle. *What must she know, talking to*

God all day? What must she see that others wouldn't? What would she look like come out of the closet, all the way to Denver? I couldn't get her, my idea of her, out of my mind. I decided that when I finished my paper route, instead of meeting George at the bike trails, I'd go straight to Grandma's house.

"Mr. Moran?" I turned from the mountain to find Mr. Johnson's eyes on me. "Are you with us?"

"Yes."

"Why don't you define *orogeny* for the class."

I dropped my bike on Grandma's manicured lawn and went straight into the house.

They were in the kitchen. I could hear their voices, then Grandma's laughter and the tinkling of silver against plates. I put my hand on the swinging door but didn't push.

"This one's from London," Grandma said.

There was a response, too quiet to understand, a confidential whisper drifting through the door along with the smell of roast. I moved my ear closer and slid my hand down the white wood. My fingers left a trail of inky prints. I licked the side of my hand, wiped them away, then opened the door a crack.

Grandma was seated at the table, facing my direction, looking as immaculate as her kitchen. She'd been to the beauty parlor for sure. Her white hair was swept up in neat waves, like a collection of snowdrifts. She wore a silk blouse, a string of pearls. She reached over and pulled her Queen Elizabeth cozy off the teapot. I pushed the door slightly and my great aunt came into view.

She sat at the head of the table, tiny shoulders hunched, profile to me. She was a lot smaller than Grandma, or seemed to be under her veil and mound of dark drapes. She wore silver glasses. Her face wasn't as ghostly white as I'd imagined it would be. The flesh of her cheek and hands was pink and seemed to glow amid all the black of her. She was old school, you could see that right off, not like most of the nuns at school who'd begun wearing skirts, showing a bit of calf. Grandma had a lot to say about the liberal changes, the lack of Latin, since Vatican II. "If you want skirts and guitar music you can go see those queer people in the park," she'd said to me more than once. I wondered if she discussed such things with her sister. Grandma stood and picked up the pot.

"Don't go to any more trouble, Jo, dear," Marion said as she smiled and held out her cup and saucer. I liked hearing Grandma's nickname—short for Josephine. Grown-ups used it, and it fit somehow. Jo, the boss. Marion stirred sugar into her tea, her crooked fingers clutching the spoon. She looked like she'd dropped from another time, totally out of place next to the multislice platinum toaster. I wondered what someone who knew nothing of nuns would make of the old lady in the costume, stirring powder into her brew. I felt I was peeking into a fairy tale, The Old Saint and the Society Woman.

I knocked softly.

"Grandma?"

"Yes?"

I stepped in. Marion placed her cup in its saucer and sprang effortlessly to her feet. Because she stooped slightly, the large cross around her neck dangled over the dark, flat front of her. With one hand she stopped, then pressed the silver crucifix over her belly as she stared at me through thick lenses.

"This is Marty junior," Grandma said as she stood and cleared some dishes to the sink.

"Of course," said Marion, her gaze steady. "I've heard a lot about you." I held tight to the door, wondering how much and from whom.

"Well, come in, for heaven's sake. Say your hellos," said Grandma.

I clomped across the polished floor. I couldn't see but felt the look Grandma shot toward my feet. She *would* notice; she was finicky about such things. She'd expressed her horror at my bell-bottom jeans more than once.

"Why are you wearing those Frankenstein boots?" she asked.

I shrugged. Marion reached out and took both my hands.

"*How are you?*"

I didn't hear her question so much as experience it—three words sailing across space and settling into the center of me. I mumbled a response—something polite.

"You look like your father," she said.

I lowered my head and looked at the tangle of our fingers. Her hands were soft and clean. I should have washed, I thought. I had the black print of the world's news all over me. She wore a ring that held, in a small silver circle, the letters *PX*.

"Can you sit a minute?" she asked.

Her eyes, moist and hazel-colored, beamed at me from behind her spectacles as if I was seeing her through a magnifying glass while she studied me under a microscope. Her gaze, like her words, entered. Warm.

"Sure," I said.

She let go of my hands and reached down to lift her habit. As she sat, a breeze brushed by me, smelling of cotton and soap.

"You've got a paper business, your grandmother said."

"I deliver the *Post*." I took a seat across from her. "I cover Kearny and Krameria."

"Pennies in your pocket."

"Ninety dollars a month."

"Good Lord!" She tucked a wisp of white hair back under her veil. "You'll pay your own way to Notre Dame."

"First I want to get a minibike," I blurted, which startled me because I hadn't told a soul my plan, except George. She looked confused and I figured that maybe they'd been invented since she'd been closed in. "It's like a small motorcycle."

"No son of mine," Grandma interjected, turning off the faucet and drying her hands. "Those things are for police and hoodlums."

"I'm sure he'll do what's best for him," Marion said, picking up her tea.

Grandma walked over and squeezed the back of my neck. "Don't keep your great aunt too long, Mr. Bell-bottoms. She just got off a plane. And Monsignor Mulcahey's coming to dinner."

"I'll be fine," said Marion.

"Yes, I know. You're always fine," Grandma said as she sailed out the door.

Marion's eyes seemed full of delight. "You'd better grab one before I eat them all," she said, sliding a plate of Grandma's butter cookies in my direction.

"Did you come on a 747?" I took a cookie.

"A what?"

"One of those huge planes?"

"What I saw of it, yes, it was very large. Lots and lots of people. Honestly, I had my eyes closed most of the trip, saying my Rosary —the Glorious Mysteries."

"Were you nervous?"

"Well, yes, a little. The Lord's Will be done, of course, but . . ." She shrugged and chuckled, then slid a piece of cookie into her mouth. I spied a few teeth, small and yellowed. "Have you flown?"

"Just on my bicycle."

She laughed again. "Well, it is a miracle. I'm not accustomed to leaving the ground, I must say. When I did travel it was usually by train, or by boat."

"Ocean boat?"

"Yes."

"I've never done that either."

"I wager you will one day. I traveled across the Pacific to the Philippines, through the South China Sea, when I was in the missions. That was years and years ago. I taught in a girls' school outside Manila, and in Seattle too, before I was called to the contemplative life." Marion leaned forward to take another bite of a cookie. Some powdered sugar landed on her chest, like a mess of stars across the night.

"Is it strange?" I asked.

"What?"

"To be here."

"It's a great comfort to see family. To meet you."

"I've never met someone from a cloister or—" I studied her wrinkled face. It was framed by her veil in the shape of a square. "What
are you called?"

"A cloistered Maryknoll sister."

"It must be really quiet there?"

She nodded.

"Do you miss people?"

"There are people. Nineteen of us right now." She took a sip of
tea and looked toward the window. Toward Grandma's rosebushes.

"But you're alone, praying all day?"

"We garden and cook and have periods when we speak."

"But you're not allowed out?"

"Except for medical attention or very special occasions—like
this." She opened both her palms toward me, the way they do in
statues, and smiled.

"But how can you be away from everything like that?" I'm not
sure why and I didn't know if it was right, but I felt I could ask her
this thing. She pushed her glasses up to the bridge of her large nose
and looked away.

"It's a question asked often, dear. My mother asked me the same
thing from the beginning. It was painful for her. When she was
able to visit, we had to speak through a wrought-iron grill. She often cried. 'I'm not "cut off," Mother,' I would tell her. 'I am *with*
you.' We don't all need to be in the rush of the world, Marty. Sitting quietly in one place, it's possible to travel the universe . . . to,
perhaps, know God."

I nodded. Something about her, no, not her, but the *idea* of her,
frightened me. I couldn't help feeling that there must be something
wrong with her, or weird about her, to want to do such a thing. I
knew that, in part, I'd ridden my bike here simply to see what a
locked-up woman come out of hiding looked like. Sitting with her,
she seemed very sane.

"It's a *radical* life, Marty." She pursed her lips; the way Grandma did sometimes, so that they were in the shape of a heart, moist and red. "God went all the way for me and I wanted to go all the way for him, that's all. When the call came, I knew it was mine."

"The call from the cloister?"

"Not from but *to*. A call, you know, to God."

"Really?"

"You were confirmed this year, weren't you?"

"Just last month."

"Sealed with the gift of the Holy Spirit."

"I guess," I said, looking down at my boots. "Accipe signaculum doni Spiritus Sancti."

"You know the Latin?"

"Only because the Bishop said it over and over."

I remembered well the evening Mass, my confirmation, my grand-father (my sponsor) silent in the pew beside me. "You've reached the age of discretion," the bishop said to me and my sixth-grade classmates. He stood on the altar in his golden robes, seven feet tall with the red miter on his head. "You are soldiers of Christ." "Accipe signaculum doni Spiritus Sancti," he intoned over and over as he smeared oil on each of our foreheads. He reminded us that we are all inclined to evil and that this—confirmation with holy chrism— was like getting an injection to guard against the devil. As if the devil were measles and confirmation, our vaccine. "Do you reject Satan?" he asked us.

"I do."

"And all his works?"

"I do."

"And all his empty promises?"

"I do," we all said, repeating the words spoken for us when we were baptized as infants. Now we were old enough to speak for our-selves, and I had to wonder: *What works? What empty promises?* I re-member when the bishop laid his warm hand on me and smeared his oily thumb across my forehead; I shut my eyes tightly. I *wanted,*

I was ready, to feel *something*. A rush of heat, a shield of protection, a wave of Holy Ghost—something right and good and powerful entering me. Then I'd understand just how to reject Satan; I'd understand the knots in my stomach, and where to fit in, how to be good. I bowed my head until it touched the pew in front of me, flesh to wood, and asked for help. I felt nothing but the cold varnish against my skull.

Marion tapped the table with one finger. "Marty, you'll *know*. This is an important time in your life. So much will start happening for you. You listen and you'll find it, you'll have a calling, too. A vocation. Something fine."

I could smell the roast and see the silver glint of sun on the edge of the toaster and the round shape of Grandma's cookies on the white plate and the crooked, wrinkled fingers of Marion's right hand as she reached for her tea, and it seemed as if I was looking at a strange and brilliant segment of my life, a photo of a moment I'd always remember—the moment when I could feel adulthood rising up inside of me like a light. And I could feel how I was neither stranger nor child to this great aunt of mine and that it was something good to be sitting with her.

"You're a fine student, Marty. That's what I hear."

"In some things."

"What do you enjoy, dear?"

"English. And Great Books Club. We just read *To Kill a Mockingbird*."

"Is that a good book?"

"The best I've ever read since *Johnny Tremain*. Or maybe *The Call of the Wild*. And I like music. I'm taking guitar with Sister Christine."

"Music too?"

I nodded.

"Like your Great Uncle Ted. He led the boy's choir at Fordham. He was a Jesuit. Very musical."

"Grandma's brother?"

"My brother, too. He died some years ago." Marion brushed her pinky across the white cotton tablecloth, collecting cookie crumbs into a small pile. "What do you dream of being?"

I shrugged.

"Irritating old aunt question." She smiled at me and took up her tea again. "You've had some thoughts, I dare say."

"Mmmm, a lawyer, maybe. Like grandpa. Or . . . a writer, like dad."

"A writer," she repeated. Her eyes brightened, or they seemed to, and the me that came here to please perked right up.

"I like to make rhymes!

> When you get in trouble at Christ the King School,
> Sister David Ann makes you sit on a stool.
> You may think you're someone cool,
> But caught in a corner, you're just a fool."

"That's just the beginning of a dumb one," I added, my hands fluttering. "I make 'em up all the time."

"It's good. Do you have a favorite poet?"

I told her the only one I knew off the top of my head:

"Robert Frost."

"Oh yes, our own Mr. Frost." Marion closed her eyes:

> "Companionless, unsatisfied, forlorn,
> I sit here in this lonely tower, and look
> Upon the lake below me, and the hills
> That swoon with heat, and see as in a vision
> All my past life unroll itself before me. . . .

"Before me," she repeated, and opened her eyes. "It's slipping away. I memorize my favorites. I recite them sometimes for the sisters, at recreation . . . it's been too long. Do you know Longfellow?"

I shook my head. "He doesn't rhyme."

"Not in this poem."

"It sounds so sad."

Marion laughed. "The poems I like best seem to be the sad ones." Her gaze went out the window. "A writer," she repeated. I followed her eyes out toward the thick, green bushes. A few buds, tight and pink, looked ready to burst. Marion seemed to be looking for the sky, for the space, to consider my future.

"Or a rancher," I said, my eyes lost in the clouds above the Rockies. The moment it fell out of my mouth, the word, the idea, felt foolish. "I mean . . . I mean a real rancher. I just started learning about animals and what they need and how to take care of them and hay and . . ." I kept my eyes west but I knew she was looking at me now and I felt, I knew, I was testing things. I spoke in a whisper. "I love being away from the city, away from *here,* from everyone, up where it's quiet and smells different." We both remained silent; there was just the drip and sizzle of Grandma's roast. "I have a friend who has a ranch. He's turning it into a camp for boys. I went there to help him." I laid my hands flat on the table and looked at them. "He called and wants me to come again. He thinks I'm a great worker."

"I'm sure you are."

"He was one of the counselors at St. Malo. Father Mac's assistant. He was a seminarian, I think. Now he's not sure what he'll do, except for making the ranch a good summer camp."

"Your friend studied for the priesthood?" A flicker came into her eyes, as I knew it would.

"I guess, for a short time." (It occurred to me that I didn't know what was true about him, but I wanted Marion, my family, everyone to be impressed with his credentials.) "He was a soldier, too. In Vietnam." My voice got louder and higher, as if, suddenly, I was on the witness stand defending him. "But he knows about so many different things. How to fix machines and take care of animals and how to make things grow. Real things you don't learn from books."

"What's your friend's name?"

"Robert," I said quietly, as if it was the answer to a dare.

"Pardon?"

His name got swallowed, I felt sure, down into the folds of her robe. I scooted forward, sat up. My face hot again, my body being, doing things, without permission. "Bob," I said, a little louder.

"Might he return to the seminary?"

"I don't think so. He's doing other things."

"Well, it's a real gift from God to have such a friend." How could all of this exist in one place at one time? Her eyes and robes? My body? His name? "I imagine you would be a beautiful priest, Marty."

These words out of her mouth were so powerful. I felt an explosion in my chest, a fiery mixture of pleasure and embarrassment, which threatened, suddenly, to make me cry. Pleased like crazy that she could see this possibility in me and embarrassed at the thought I'd been performing again, busy all this time charming her, angling for just this blessing: to be seen as a little priest-to-be, a man of God. I said nothing, studied my feet again.

"You must have thought about it," she said.

"Well, yes. Sometimes. When I was younger I did but now it's . . ."

"Younger? But you're only twelve."

"And four months."

She finished her tea. Her cup trembled slightly as she placed it in the saucer. "You'll know your calling when the time comes."

I stood and stuck my dirty hands in my pockets. She remained seated. We looked at one another and she smiled.

"I'll be back," I said, turning to go.

"Marty?"

I stopped mid-kitchen and spun around.

"He's not disappointed in you, you know."

"What?"

"To God, the darkest depths of the human heart are as clear as the pages of a book lying open in the sunlight." Her eyes danced over to mine.

—

"This'll look sharp," Dad said, holding up my new necktie. It was red and it was real. He stood behind me at the hall mirror in a crisp blue suit, in a cloud of English Leather. "Pretend that my hands are yours and watch how you tie it." His grin in the glass told me he liked this—a knot for his son, a clear task amid the puzzle of being a parent. He bent his knees slightly and slid his arms through mine. I looked down at his hairy knuckles fumbling with the bright cloth. "No, look up in the mirror," he said. "Watch the reflection of what I do, otherwise you'll get it all backwards." His belly was against my back, my head nearly touching his chin. It made me think of sledding in Evergreen, of the time he slid his arms under mine to guide us through the snow. The few moments like this, close ones, made me wonder who he was, how I could know him more.

I thought of the quiet evening we sat next to each other on the back patio. I often thought of it. A cool evening the summer before, after we'd mowed the lawn. The grass looked as close cropped as the crew cuts we'd both gotten that morning from Ken the Barber. Dad had just come outside after taking a shower. He wore a fresh white button-down shirt, khakis, brown loafers. He held the first vodka tonic of the evening in his hand and surveyed what was his. A rectangle of parched land transformed into a green carpet. The just-cut smell of it perfumed the air. The sprinkler was on, I remember, hissing its rhythm, turning in jerky circles like some crazy creature chasing its tail. All was in order. A few of Mom and Dad's friends were due for a simple, late dinner—burgers and potato salad out on the patio. This was for him, I believe, the best moment of the summer weeks. Saturday dusk, a day off from the desk, his labor in the field accomplished, his shower taken, first drink poured. Perhaps these were even among the best moments of his life—before the divorce, before the lawn yellowed, before we all grew and split. "Did you put the clippers back in the garage, tiger?" he asked, his voice as hushed as the light.

"Yeah." I was sitting on the edge of the patio, my bare feet buried in the grass as I kept an eye on the hose. It was my job to move it every fifteen minutes. Dad came over and sat near me. He set his drink down between us, not far from his left hip. Ice tinkled against the glass, sending a gentle chime out across the neighboring yards. He shook a Philip Morris from the pack in his front pocket and lit it. A deft, one-handed dance. "You smoke a lot," I told him.

"Oh, well." He looked at the little stick in his hand and grinned. "It's like holding a bit of your own death." He chuckled and, figuring it was another of his Irish jokes, I did, too. The sprinkler hissed. A few stars appeared. I looked over at the four-o'clocks. They were open for their second performance of the day, bright pink and taller than I against the brick outside my parents' bedroom window. They were my favorite flowers, the way they could tell time and show off.

"Is there something you'd die for?"

The question seemed to just fall from his mouth. A lost thought. I wasn't sure I'd heard him right or if he was even talking to me. I turned to him. His gaze was out over his lawn, out toward the pussy willows along the back fence.

"What?" I asked

"Is there something you'd die for?"

His bushy brows were raised, his blue eyes on me now. I was waiting for the pun, for the wry smile, but his face stayed serious.

"Die for?"

"Yes."

I was eleven then, there was only living ahead as far as I could see. I watched Dad take another drag from his cigarette, blow smoke toward the darkening sky. The stillness seemed to tell me that this was an important moment, just between us. He glanced at me again. I had no words, and shrugged, sure that I was failing a test, that I lacked something essential.

"Well, that's too bad," he said. "You've got to wonder what makes life worth it if there's nothing you're willing to die for."

He picked up his drink and jiggled the cubes, sending more chimes across the night.

"What about you, Dad? What would you die for?" I wanted to know the right answer. I wanted to know the heart of him.

He was silent. I looked for more stars poking through the purple sky; figured he was thinking how he'd put it. What he'd say about family or God or maybe ... about me? He lifted his glass to his lips and held it there without drinking. I studied the muscles and tan of his arm, the way the smooth skin disappeared under the rolled, white sleeve of his shirt, disappeared down under with all the rest that was buttoned up and hidden. I scooted close and glanced at his face, thinking I might tell him what my classmate Maura said the night he came to pick me up at Great Books: "That's your dad?" she whispered in my ear. "God ... he's to die for." I stayed quiet. He took a sip before he spoke.

"Tell you the truth," he said. "I haven't the foggiest." Then he chuckled and raised his glass, as if to toast his patch of grass.

"OK, loop this fat part of the tie over this, then tuck under, pull through, and tighten. Got it?"

"Dad?"

"Yeah?" He began undoing the knot.

"Do you think Aunt Marion will like this poem? It's not so, you know, literary. She likes Longfellow and Yeats and—"

"Don't worry. You're the one she asked to be on the altar for her Mass. Now, watch in the mirror." He started looping the tie again. "That's what matters, not that you've got the exact right poem. I'm sure she'll like it. It's sweet." (I'd chosen Shel Silverstein's *The Giving Tree,* a story about a tree that gives everything to a boy throughout its life until finally the tree's just a stump for him to sit on when he's old. A tearjerk tale of codependence.) He guided my hands until I got it right, till we both had knots up to the lumps in our throats. He moved to stand next to me, facing the glass. "It begins," he said, his face gone serious, his shoulders thrown back. "Now you'll know what it's like to have a noose around your neck."

The him in the mirror wasn't smiling. I turned to await the lep-
rechaun grin, but the man just stood there, staring ahead, like a
private awaiting his orders.

Monsignor Mulcahey signaled for me to rise from my pew. "The
first reading will be offered by Sister Theodore's great nephew,"
he said, using Marion's chosen Maryknoll name: *Theodore*—gift
of God.

   My heart was thumping. I scanned the faces of my family as I set
the pages on the pulpit. My uncles, aunts, and cousins. They looked
so pleased and proud and sure that I was up to this. It was a strange
and wonderful feeling that I, the boy with a secret tucked beneath
his skin, under his new suit, could stand as the one chosen to deliver. I heard the rhythm of my heart in my ears, fiddled with my
tie. If they only knew who I really was, it'd be over. Yet here I stood.
Things will start happening for you, she'd said. *Vocation is given like a
gift.* I looked down at the neat column of stanzas, the simple draw-
ings. She'd pulled me aside at my uncle's house after dinner, before
dessert. *I want you on the altar at my Mass,* she'd said. *You choose what
to read. Something that rhymes, if you want.* She was in the front pew
now, in her best habit, navy blue. I glanced at her for just a second.
She was beaming. I began to read. Why, even with these nerves,
even with this fear that they'll see I'm a phony, did it feel so right
to be standing in front of them? Reciting? Something inside my
wild body, a force, a remembrance, lifted my chin, fueled my voice.
The sound trembled in my chest and filled the chapel. It was the
sure tongue of a grown-up I didn't yet know. It was the sense, for
an instant, that everything, even me, was good.

Two weeks later, I returned home on a Sunday evening after spending my second weekend at Bright Raven Ranch. This time it was
just him and me. We'd stopped again at Arby's in Boulder. He'd
bought me a roast beef sandwich and thanked me for my good
work. When we got to my house, he dropped me at the curb. This
time he didn't wait, he drove right off. I stood in the front yard,

staring at the red brick, at the square of light in the kitchen window. A heavy sickness came into my stomach—an argument, a rip, a chunk of me gone off in the front seat of a truck. And the sickness, I knew, was my own. My own doing. I walked slowly to the door and reached for the knob, assembled my face.

"Hi, Mom."

She was at the kitchen table, filing her nails. It was late, *Mission Impossible* already over.

"A letter came for you," she said without looking up.

I set my pack on the hall bench. "A letter?" I took off my muddy boots, set them on the rubber mat, and walked into the kitchen. "From who?"

"*Whom,* you mean."

"From whom?"

She pointed her file toward the little black-and-white Zenith. On top of it sat a small white envelope. Written on the front in beautiful, blue cursive it said: *Master Martin Moran, Jr.* It looked like holy script. I picked it up.

"At first we thought it was for your father."

Cloistered Maryknoll Sisters, it said, in the upper-left corner. *Ossining, New York.*

"It's from her."

Mom nodded. "How was your weekend?" she asked.

"Busy. We did a lot of work." I tucked the letter into my pocket, next to the five Bob had slipped me.

"Don't forget to take out the garbage."

I took my pack downstairs to my room, sat on the bed, and opened the letter.

Dearest Marty,

I hope this finds you well and happy, and I hope that you find time to write. (Send me one of your rhymes!) Today a tall iris opened at the very end of our garden, surprising us all with its vivid color and beauty. I thought of you.

13

WE FOUND WAYS to be alone. It seemed to just happen, no parental impediments, no questions asked. Sometimes he picked me up in the truck. Other times in his cream-colored VW Bug. He didn't come into the house; he just honked the horn.

That first summer, instead of going to St. Malo, I spent two weeks at his ranch-camp cutting hay, shooting arrows, and sneaking off for sex with him. There was a ragtag collection of nine or ten other campers there. It was strangely disorganized but we enjoyed taking care of the few horses and goats, the two milk cows, and spending time fixing things up, going for climbs. Sometimes I wondered if he was involved with any of the other boys. It seemed not. It seemed to me that I was the only one. Most of the kids appeared to be troubled cases. The depressed and the delinquent. Kids he'd rounded up, kids he meant to help—a boy from Michigan whose dad hated him, two brothers from Nebraska whose parents were splitting. A loner from Longmont.

When summer was over and winter came, it wasn't just off to the ranch that we sneaked. There was an apartment in Boulder belonging to someone I never saw; there was a garage in Arvada, a little log cabin in the woods outside Nederland. An old lady owned it, he told me. Someone among the many Bob had charmed, someone I'd never meet.

I remember waking there once in a big feather bed, a huge comforter covering us, the cabin surrounded by blinding sunlight reflected off two feet of fresh snow. I had braces on my teeth by then, and little patches of hair on my body. Bob was still asleep. I slipped off my headgear and set it on the nightstand. (The orthodontist and my mother had told me I must wear it religiously or I'd always be bucktoothed and no one would take me seriously when I grew up. So at night, after our sex, I'd slide it into my mouth and strap it around my head before going to sleep.)

I hopped naked out of the warm bed to build a fire in the wood-stove. It was freezing. Bob woke and threw on a pair of sweatpants. We began arguing about how best to place the kindling and the newspaper. "I learned this in Scouts," I told him. "Wrap the paper tight, stack the kindling loosely." He disagreed—paper loose, he said, kindling packed tight. Suddenly our hands were tangled inside the soot-covered stove, each of us struggling to get his way. I remember how ridiculous it seemed, how odd it felt, to be bickering, first thing in the morning. Like an old married couple. Or like two little kids. And Bob stood there, three feet taller, twenty years older, pouting like a child because I told him he was stupid and angry because I got my way. In the quiet tension of that morning, as the fire warmed the cabin and he cooked our breakfast, I remember him asking me, "Why do you always just lay there, like a fish?"

"What do you mean?" (I knew and didn't know what he was referring to and instantly felt embarrassed.)

"Most of the time you just lay there, like you're not interested. Except that I know you are."

I just shrugged my shoulders and ate the rest of my oatmeal. He let it drop. I thought of it often, slowly figuring out that what he was telling me was that he was frustrated with our sex, that I wasn't a good lover.

In fact, I did lie there like a fish. I needed to feel that what was going on, no matter how much pleasure I found in it, was being done *to* me. I meant to hide, hold back, the want. I didn't want to let him, or my self, know that I owned any part, any desire, when it came to sex. He—it—was all happening *to me.* I had to hang on to that thought. For survival.

—

Sometimes, many weeks, even a couple of months, went by without hearing from him, and I'd think, *Good.* Good, he's forgotten, and so have I, and it won't happen again. I won't let it. But a letter would arrive or, more often, a phone call announcing a project, offering an invitation, and I'd be ready and wanting. "I've bought some land of my own in Sunshine Canyon," he said one day on the phone. "I'm going to build a house on it. Why don't you come this weekend and help me get started."

"All right."

His whiskers were thick, almost a beard. It had been long since I'd seen him, two months, maybe. I remember the ache that night, sitting next to him in the truck. The pure want, the physical feeling of missing him. Of missing the pleasure of touch. Of having been shot up with him and now, most definitely, hooked.

We stopped at the garage in Arvada on the way to Boulder. It was an auto-repair shop of some sort. It was after hours and no one was there. Bob had a key, said he worked there sometimes. Who knew? His doings, his life, his past, were all so vague. (I still told people he'd once been a seminarian, though by now I knew that not to be true. How or why he'd ever been hired at Malo, I didn't know.) There were cars, two or three of them, jacked up on the silver columns of hydraulic lifts, wheels off, engines dismantled. The smell of oil and electrical wire lurked everywhere. Bob said he had to gather some tools, and I went to the toilet to pee.

The next thing I knew he was standing behind me. I remember feeling embarrassed, for an instant, that he'd just walked into the john while I was standing there peeing. But the embarrassment vanished quickly. There was little in the world, I think, that could shock me by then. Or so it seemed. Something had changed: my reticence was gone and my want, fierce. His fingers on me were a drug, electric, and I remember how I reached behind and grabbed him, squeezed him with both hands, then cupped my palms around the mound of his penis. Like finding the root of a tree right below the faded cotton of his jeans. Like rediscovering, holding on to, my own secret. Nothing timid now. I was admitting, holding, the shape of my very own desire. And I could tell this surprised him. I wasn't being a cold fish now; I'd show him. We moved, tumbled to a bench. There were greasy work boots and sneakers lined up below us in neat little pairs. I studied the stains and shoe-strings, thinking: *Yes, it's happening again.* There'd always been one small part of me that wondered, each time I was planning to see him, if perhaps *this* would be the time it stopped. This time it wouldn't happen and we'd simply be friends, do normal things. We wouldn't end up naked and out of control. But it always, always happened. I could never, didn't know how to, stop it. It was hap-pening again and this time I *knew* how much I wanted it. This night, head dangling over the dirty work boots of the absent me-chanics, I felt any reservations I might still possess melt away. Ut-terly. And I wanted, I tried, to please him. I gave him what he desired. He spit and I entered him for the very first time and I squeezed him for dear life, for all the many weeks I'd grown older and hadn't seen him. I fucked him. And after, as he rolled tools into a rag and I tied my boots, I felt more lost than ever. Riddled with shame, terrified that there was no going back now. Ever. *Seventh grade and my fate is sealed,* I thought. *I'll never be other than* this.

Once, I convinced my scoutmaster that, instead of going to one of the usual scout campgrounds, we should pitch our tents on the land of a friend of mine who was building a house near Nederland. "It's near a creek," I told him. "In a beautiful canyon. Some great climbs around there."

He finally agreed, and one Friday night Troop 63 packed into two station wagons and went to make camp about a quarter mile downcreek from Bob's house. We built a fire and roasted our wee-nies and said our goodnights, because we were going to get up early for a real climb. Mr. Welton, our scoutmaster, was big on hikes. His favorite piece of equipment was his pedometer, which was at-tached to his belt. He kept close watch on it whenever we went off on our adventures. His rule was that it wasn't a real hike unless we'd trekked at least ten miles.

That Friday night, after everyone else had fallen asleep, I slipped out of the tent I shared with my fellow scout and good friend, Mark, and made my way through the bushes to the creek. There was an old rope that I knew of, tied to two trees on opposite banks and suspended about two feet above the water. I knelt down and wrapped my hands, then my ankles, around the rope and shimmied across. It felt unbelievably exciting to me. The whoosh of the water just below my dangling head. *One false move and I could drown,* I dramatically thought. I felt like crazy Romeo risking his life, climbing the wall to get to his lover.

In short order I reached the other side and found the path that ran along the highway to Bob's place. I stepped through the side door of his house (he'd given me instructions by phone earlier that day) and straight to his bed. The secrecy, the adventure of it, was fantastic. It gave me such a feeling of pleasure and power. As if this secrecy was becoming the fuel of my life. My secret weapon. My hidden fire. And part of the game, the fun, was no one finding out. Second-class scout and cocksucker, straight-A altar boy and slut.

I slept with Bob until first light and, like Romeo upon hearing the lark, I squiggled out of bed, shimmied back across the river and into my sleeping bag. Mark was sound asleep. I remember feeling thrilled when I got back to my tent. I lay in my bag listening to the birds, grinning at my own daring. My cunning. I had a whole other life that no one knew of. My own private universe, my own merit badge for sex. A warm, buzzing secret at the base of my stomach. I'd hold tight to it, even if it killed me.

That day, Mr. Welton kept goading me. I was tired and lagging behind. He looked at me, "Come on, what's wrong with you?" And then, looking at his pedometer: "We have miles yet to go."

Late one Friday night toward the end of seventh grade (it was always Fridays—after school) we were in the truck making our way up the canyon toward his still-unfinished house. We planned to work there all weekend. I dozed against the passenger door. Bob and I had already stopped to have sex at the garage in Arvada and now I was sinking into that familiar haze of regret, the indefinable and bottomless sadness that always followed the explosion of physical pleasure. I remember glancing out the window and seeing a yellow sign, a warning to climb to safety in case of heavy rain. And soon after, Bob hit the brakes hard and let out a terrible sigh. I sat up quickly.

Standing in the middle of the road, not twenty yards ahead, was a woman with a long white coat. She wore high heels. She looked like an upscale secretary or PTA mom, utterly out of place standing alone on a dark mountain road. She stared at us, frozen in the headlights, a strangely glamorous ghost. Bob put on the hazard lights and slowly pulled up to the right and stopped not far behind her green Toyota. The woman stayed where she was in the center of the road and I watched as she wrapped her arms around herself and lowered her head.

"Stay put," Bob said, as he climbed out of the truck.

As he approached her I saw what the matter was. On the left edge of the road, not far from her car, was a deer lying on its side, breathing heavily. I could see its brown fur and the white part if its belly rising and falling rapidly. There was a patch of blood spreading around its head, black as oil.

Bob spoke to the woman for a moment, both of them looking at each other and then over to the animal. Bob took her arm and walked her toward her car. I knew the voice he must have been using, the gentle one. It looked as though he was trying to convince her to get in but she shook her head and leaned against the driver-side door of the Toyota, her hand over her mouth. Bob stepped over and took a quick look at the deer. One eye of the poor creature was visible to me, wet and shining in the beam of our headlights. Bob walked briskly to my side of the truck and motioned for me to roll down the window.

"Open the glove compartment."

I pressed the silver button and the lid fell open. Bob reached in, took out a pair of work gloves, and slid them into his back pocket. He reached in again and found a chammy cloth. Wrapped inside it was a handgun. From a little cardboard box he then took two bullets, slid them into the pistol's chamber. It all happened so quickly —a weird dream. He walked over, knelt down in the road, and put his hand on the deer's neck, leaned over its face. His lips moved. I wondered if he was talking to himself or the animal. The deer's nostrils were moist, widening and shrinking with each breath. Bob stood suddenly, pointed the gun, and fired. The shot echoed up and down the canyon. That was it. After checking the animal's neck again, for a pulse, I supposed, Bob grabbed the gloves from his pocket, put them on, and dragged the small thing to the runoff ditch on the opposite side of the road, leaving a long streak of blood across the tarmac. He spoke to the lady for a moment, touching her arm once with his gloved hand. She nodded and got into her car. Bob hopped in the cab, took out the extra bullet, and put it and the gun away.

We followed the lady for a couple of miles until she slowed, put her hand out the window to wave, and turned off the main road. "I told her to call the highway patrol," Bob said. "To pick up the animal."

We drove for a while in silence, picking up speed as we came to a clearing, where there were houses along the creek. "We can start work on the railing for the deck tomorrow, until the roofing supplies come." Bob sounded calm; we were getting close to his two acres, his half-finished, two-story house, the first real thing he'd ever owned, so he said. And he was obsessed with making it perfect—skylights and fireplaces and a great deck stretching out over the creek.

"What kind of gun was that?"

"A nothing, small caliber."

I kept thinking about it, that it had been there all along in the compartment in front of me and how quickly he'd grabbed and used it. How awful and merciful it was. And I kept wondering what he might have said to himself or to the deer before he killed it. Something private, something I shouldn't ask.

"Did you kill people in Vietnam?"

A puff of air came out his nose, a sort of snort. It was a mile or more before he said anything.

"They gave medals for it."

When we walked in the house, the first thing we did, even before putting the groceries away, was fall into each other's arms. On the plywood floor, next to his half-finished fireplace, we had sex. I fucked him again. We held one another tightly and all the while I knew, I could feel more than ever, the terrible sadness. We were far away from each other. He was somewhere I wasn't and I was somewhere he wasn't. Our bodies were touching, groping for relief, but our thoughts, our spirits, were utterly separate. In our sex, I realized, we never made eye contact, never, ever, kissed. And this night, I began to understand in some way how we were using each other. To forget. To get out. Maybe he was trying to forget the war or the deer or the day. And I was busy trying to obliterate the very thing I was doing with him. What I was becoming. It felt dreadful and exciting and so terribly truthful, all at once. *Hold on tight, this is life. It's really hard, so hold tight to whatever you can.* I felt I understood that his holding me had not a thing to do with me. That each of us was for the other a collection of parts. Not a whole. Not at all.

It was over quickly and we went quickly to bed.

I began to be aware of other boys, at least two who I knew were also sleeping with him—Kip and Steve. They were slim and blond and blue-eyed, like me. They were great guys, warm and smart and somehow vulnerable. Like me, I guess. He once referred to us as his Three Musketeers. There was a Saturday morning at Bob's house that I remember still with a kind of awe and tenderness. I was talking with Kip in Bob's kitchen as we made breakfast. We'd both come up to work for the weekend. Kip had just put strips of bacon in the pan, was turning up the flame. I was slicing oranges. We were talking quietly because Bob was still up in bed. Unusual for him; he was an early bird.

Suddenly, there came the sound of Bob's voice calling for Kip. Kip paused a moment, his fork hovering over the crackling bacon. He turned to me and, with the slightest smile, said: "Would you cook this a minute?"

"Sure."

He went upstairs and I slowly flipped the bacon. Very soon— I don't remember how long but the bacon wasn't yet done—Kip was back. He walked up silently and took the fork from me. Just then, Bob called my name. "Marty?" It felt terribly awkward. I held still. Then Kip turned to me with this comical grin and said: "You go get in the frying pan, I'll finish the bacon." And we burst out laughing. Two thirteen-year-olds howling at his joke, this absurd situation. I remember thinking how smart and funny this guy Kip was. How he seemed calmly resigned, philosophical, about what was happening. And how amazing it was to laugh at what we both knew was going on but didn't dare speak of. That we were part of some secret club; a little blond, blue-eyed bordello. Kip was like some kind of sunshine that morning. His humor gave me hope. Hope that we'd get through this thing we'd gotten ourselves into, that it might not be as fatal as I often felt it was. That, in the end, we'd be OK. We finished giggling and I turned to go upstairs to Bob's room. Fifteen minutes later the three of us were at the breakfast table discussing what work needed to be done that day.

Mr. McGruder, our seventh-grade sociology teacher, in a rare attempt to bring history alive, asked us to write an essay about a personal hero. "We've talked of Hercules, and General Patton. Let's hear your idea of a real hero. Someone in your life." We were given a week and were told we'd read them aloud to the class. I composed an essay entitled "My Friend Bob." In it I discussed how my hero knew the names of plants along mountain trails. How he built a camp on a ranch so that young men could learn about the land and animals. About real stuff you'd never get from a book. I said how he was strong and had taught me to be strong and never to smoke and that he had served our country in Vietnam. On the afternoon when I stood to read my work, I remember how my scalp and then my entire body tingled. It was magical, surreal, to glance up at the faces of my classmates as I told them of my friend. My living hero. The telling turned me giddy. I was daring to speak the name of a love and I felt ten feet tall.

When class wrapped up that day, Lisa DeAngelis came over to me as I was about to leave the cloakroom. She hardly ever spoke to anyone but her two perfect, beautiful best friends—Jen and Marie. I was stunned when she reached out her hand and stopped me.

"I liked your essay," she said.

"Thanks," I replied as I pulled on my parka. "Thanks."

I watched as she reached for her ski cap and coat. Her bright blond hair fell below her waist, nearly, neatly, to her tailbone. "Didn't the guy you wrote about," she continued, "didn't he used to be a counselor? At St. Malo?" She turned toward me and slid the blue cap over her lustrous head, tidied her hair over her little ears.

"Yeah, that's where I met him."

She leaned forward and unveiled her perfect teeth. "My older brother said he's a *queer*."

She walked away, the swish of her skirt a dare, a warning.

I stood in the half-light of the cloakroom for a long time, listening to the thud in my chest.

Permit.

Permutation.

Pernicious.

Sister Joan was feeding me spelling words from one of her many lists, preparing me for the Rocky Mountain Spelling Bee. We were sitting in the front den of the convent on a Saturday morning in

April. I'd never been inside before. There was a couch and two large, comfortable chairs. Gold drapes hung from the sun-filled windows. This was the part of the house where guests were received, and it felt very special to be there and rather strange that it was just the two of us sitting not far from where she, our principal, slept and took her meals. She wore oval glasses with tortoiseshell frames and, though stern, had a soft face, smooth cheeks with hints of blush. She was always impeccably put together. A small nun in her mid-thirties. She was beaming this morning. I'd done well in the arch-diocesan bee and I knew she was counting on me to place in the big one in May. That's why she was taking extra time with me. "Spelling will sharpen the good brain God gave you," she often said to me.

"*Pernicious?*" I repeated. "Definition, please."

"Wicked."

"Could you use it in a sentence, please."

She'd taught us spellers to ask all we could about a word, even if we felt sure we knew it. "Definition, derivation, use in a sentence—these are your guides, your tools. And asking gives you time to think," she always reminded us.

"Alcohol may have a pernicious effect on your health."

"A *wicked* effect?"

"Let's be more exact," she said, lifting the magnifying glass that dangled from a silver chain around her neck. She put the glass to her eye, then quickly bent her nose to her beloved Oxford diction-ary. She loved nothing more, it seemed, than dipping down like this, like a bird digging at the root of things. She flipped through the pages. "It's from the Latin, of course: *Pernicies*—destruction. The first definition is, 'Irreparable harm through evil.'"

She sat up and looked at me, letting the glass fall to her chest, where it tangled with her crucifix. I felt a little grin grow across my face and, comfortable and alone as we were in the nun's inner sanctum, I felt emboldened to ask a question unrelated to spelling.

"There really isn't such a thing as the devil, is there?"

She closed the dictionary and looked at me with grave blue eyes. I wiped the smirk off my face.

"Marty, make no mistake. The devil exists and he is here among us. And we must be vigilant. Vigilant in our prayers and our actions, because he's always looking for ways to tempt us. To corrupt us." She took up the list to continue our drilling, then let it fall back to her lap. "He was an angel, you know, at the right hand of God. Innocent and loving as a babe. There's no worse fall than the fall from such a height. He wants us there too, proud and fallen from grace. Make no mistake. The devil exists." She kept her eyes on me until I nodded. She suddenly seemed worried what, other than a speller, I might be. My tongue felt thick, the pit in my stomach deeper.

"*Pernicious* — P-E-R-N-I-C-I-O-U-S."

"Correct," she said.

I asked Sister Christine the same question the next day during my guitar lesson. Hoping she would be less solemn. Smiling, I asked, "C'mon, Sister, there's no such thing as Satan, is there?"

She went deadly serious on me. "Oh yes, he exists."

And I thought, *What does he look like?* And I thought, *My God, I've met him.*

I stood in the main john of our house, in front of the mirror, glaring at the red, raging zits on my chin. I reached up and pinched one that was coming to a head. I felt the pop, the pus. I glanced at my finger and saw blood. It was a lousy habit but I couldn't seem to stop it.

"You'll have scars for your whole life if you keep doing that," my sister Chris said. "Stop picking."

"I can't help it." I smeared some Clearasil on my face. Chris had lent me her Oxy 5. Nothing was working. Zits kept sprouting. "Why do I have all these goddamned pimples?"

I caught my sister's crooked smile in the toothpaste-splattered mirror. "It's just the evil in you coming out," she said.

14

THE SECOND SUMMER I was with him, Bob took his camp on the road. North, to Wyoming.

There's a Teton there with your name on it, he wrote in a letter. *You should come and see it. We'll raft the Green River.*

Where he got the idea, the big yellow school bus, or the girl friend, I don't know. We were just there, suddenly, that hot July between my seventh- and eighth-grade years, speeding up Interstate 25—pied piper Bob, thirteen campers, and Bob's nineteen-year-old cowgirl-friend, Karen.

The wind whipped across the rubber rafts roped to the top of the bus, creating an incessant banging overhead. Bob had his can of Coke propped on the dash. Each time he moved his hand from the wheel for a sip, he'd reach across the aisle to caress Karen's arm.

"If you're gonna keep speeding, you should switch lanes," I heard Karen say as she yanked at the brim of her cowboy hat. "I know how the fuzz around here thinks; my uncle was a cop."

I sat four seats back, behind Bob. I turned to the window, to the featureless flat, the endless tumbleweeds. This state was depressing as far as I could see, and so was I, I felt sure, with my face full of zits, my mouth stuffed with braces. My toes were hot and pinched in a pair of boots he'd handed me for the trip. They were cowboy-cool but way too small. I didn't tell him that when I tried them on. I gave a polite smile, said my thanks, figuring he must not notice that my feet, like the rest of me, were getting bigger. In the fifteen months I'd known him my bones had thickened, my hair grown long, my voice dropped.

I didn't know any of the other boys on the bus—a pair of brothers who lived on a farm in Loveland, some kids from Boulder who seemed to know each other from school, and a few others from out Nebraska way. Kip and Steve and the few other Bob-campers I'd met along the way were elsewhere this season. It seemed I was the only repeat camper from Bright Raven the summer before. How we'd all come to be here on a school bus in the middle of Wyoming was another mystery in the vague life of Bob. There'd been no fliers that I could remember, no real brochures, no parental permission slips. The whole adventure sprung from the seat of his pants.

Long after a lunch of peanut butter and jelly, well after dark, we were still driving toward Jackson, toward some ranch he'd lined up as our base camp. I could see that, despite all the Coca-Cola, he was sleepy at the wheel. Karen yelled out at one point when he nearly swiped an abandoned car parked along the shoulder of the road. Those who were dozing were startled awake.

"Let me drive," Karen said.

"No," he snapped. "You don't have a chauffeur's license."

A few miles later, Bob yanked the wheel and drove the bus right into the tumbleweeds, where he came to a halt next to a barbed-wire fence. He acted as though he knew exactly where we were, as if this was a campsite he'd reserved.

"Everybody grab your sleeping bags and get out."

We stood in the weeds and watched as he crawled atop the bus and untied the blue tarp that covered the rafts. Then we helped him lay it on the bumpy ground. We peed near the fence, then unfolded our bags and lined them up in two rows, tight as sardines, along the square of plastic. I glanced up at the shifting pattern of clouds and starlight.

"What if it rains?" I asked.

"Oh, for chrissakes, think positive," he said.

Bob and Karen took a walk after all us boys laid down. When

they returned, Karen went to sleep somewhere inside the bus—the floor? I wondered—and Bob squeezed his bag in next to mine. As we drifted to sleep, the only sound was the occasional, rocket-like whoosh of semitrucks approaching, then racing past, on the nearby interstate.

His hand awakened me. My eyes opened to sagebrush and tumbleweeds bejeweled with dew, our sleeping bags wet and shimmering with first light. It was cold and the sky clear. His fingers worked the zipper, wandered toward my belly. I had wondered if it might stop, now that he had a girlfriend, now that I was older, but I guessed not and answered his reach, scooted silently into his cocoon.

His warmth surprised me, surprises me still. The texture of skin, the way our bodies fit together. His lotion was stashed in his bag; he snapped open the lid and in no time was pumping between my thighs. The routine. I watched the sky, the last stars folding away into chalky blue. And then, as if called there, my gaze landed three sleeping bags away, square into the bright, brown pierce of Robin Hedrick's eyes.

At sixteen, he was the oldest camper on the trip. A somber, lanky guy from Illinois, he'd said very little to anyone outside of his dry comments regarding hicks and haystacks. Bob had told me how Robin was taking time away from the divorce, the trouble, at home. There was something about him, not just his age, which commanded respect. His silence, his cool, Chicago composure, and now he was wide-awake, looking at me, at my face jerking across the pile of clothes that was my pillow. The dawn had brightened enough so that I was sure he was seeing it clearly—that I was in Bob's bag, Bob's arms, that sex of some sort was going on. Perhaps it was because his face was so calm, but, instead of flinching, I kept looking at Robin as Bob pumped away.

Robin raised a brow: *Is it what I think?*

I rolled my eyes: *Yeah . . . weird . . . he's a pervert . . . Oh well . . . life's funny, isn't it?*

Robin blinked: *Yeah, funny.*

There were things, I realized, that I was dying to clarify. Key points I wanted to explain—out loud. I kept trying to send thoughts across the cold air, across the gently breathing boys: *It doesn't hurt, don't worry. He isn't inside me; he's just rubbing against me. No big deal.* This felt, still feels, like a very important distinction. Something I wanted Robin to know.

Robin, I feared, didn't understand, and I was plotting how I'd find him later, pull him aside and tell him to please keep it quiet and isn't Bob queer and don't worry, I'm cool, I'm not *this . . . that way . . .* and this was all going through my head when Bob came, and not quietly. I was sure Robin heard the groan because his eyes widened, blazed for a few seconds, as though he was witnessing a car accident, and then he looked away. Bob reached around to service me and I scrambled back into my bag, used my T-shirt to clean my thighs.

"What's wrong?" Bob whispered.

I buried my head in my sack, wondering what cool Robin might do. If maybe he'd find a shotgun, commit murder.

I dunked the greasy cookie sheet. How is it, I wondered, that Bob happened to choose Robin and me for kitchen duty? The pan clattered against the sink as remnants of oatmeal and raisins drifted down into the soapy water. I scrubbed Brillo across the burnt spots and searched for a question to fill the silence.

"Have you ever rafted?"

Robin nodded, then flicked his black hair up and away from his dark eyes. His bangs tumbled back down toward the bridge of his nose, swept across his cheek, like a curtain closing.

"I never have," I said. I watched his hands, his long, slim fingers turning the spaghetti pot, drying it with a blue dishtowel. Maybe he plays keyboards, has a rock band. "I've always wanted to river raft."

The fluorescent lights hummed like bees.

"I rafted the Grand once. In Utah. With my dad."

I was so grateful to hear him speak, to hear that his voice was untroubled.

"White water?" I asked.

"Yeah. It's cool."

We fell silent again. I ran the cookie sheet under the faucet.

"Ouch!"

"Hot?"

I nodded.

"Careful."

I turned up the cold. He took the pan from me and began drying it with his blue cloth. The skin of his arm was olive-colored, smooth and hairless. He wore funky leather sandals, gray corduroys, and a purple T-shirt. Standing this close, he was bigger than I'd realized. A head taller than me. He seemed older than sixteen, almost like he could be someone's dad.

I reached for a large skillet that had been soaking on the counter. As I dunked it, I thought again of the morning, of what Robin may or may not have seen or thought. Maybe what he remembered was very little. Maybe he'd blocked it out or didn't put it together or even really *see* it in the first place. Maybe he was sleep-watching and figured that what lay before him was a dream, of which he had only the vaguest memory. I often figured that. That what passed between Bob and me in the small hours was no more or less than a ghost story. Not real at all. Of no consequence. Someone else's life. Someone else's body. But then there was the way Robin had looked at me that morning, just before we'd gotten on the bus. The way his eyes pierced then darted when I caught his glance. I wanted to explain, to reassure him of . . . I didn't know what. I watched my blurry hands under the murky water, circling the skillet.

"The Grand and Colorado are the same river, aren't they? Sort of?" I asked.

"One becomes the other, actually. I think. Near the Utah border."

"Were you scared? Of the rapids, I mean?"

"No." He flicked his bangs again, then hooked them behind his ear so that they stayed clear of his face. He stood on tiptoe and slid the cookie sheet onto an overhead shelf. "Don't know if this pan goes here." He wiped his hands on his corduroys. "Doesn't much matter, I guess." He turned and leaned his bony hip against the counter and ran his hand slowly through his thick hair. I could feel his eyes. His face, full on, was warm, intelligent. "No, it isn't scary," he continued. "Running rapids is fun. You'll see."

I nodded, kept cleaning the clean skillet.

Then he asked it. "Does he do that a lot?"

I stared into the dishwater as if I might find there the word to go with the truth. What's *a lot?* I mouthed the opening of some answer but nothing came out. My shoulders moved slowly toward my ears, then dropped.

"Man, that's fucked up."

I put down the Brillo and lifted the heavy skillet to the faucet, rinsed it and passed it to him. He took it with both hands. He wore a silver ring with a turquoise stone . . . a girlfriend?

"For how long?"

I looked at the tiny patch of stubble on his chin, then right into the brown of his eyes. "What?"

"How long has he been doing it?"

"A while, but it doesn't . . ." I turned to the sink, reached through the warm water, and pulled the plug from the drain. "He doesn't . . . he doesn't hurt me."

Robin studied the skillet in his hands. "Really?"

"You know what I mean?"

He placed the skillet upside down on the counter in front of him, then turned to me. His eyes were kind and I loved him for that. That he hadn't screamed or snarled or snickered. He seemed incredibly calm. I stared at the place across his chest where it was written, in white letters, *The Grateful Dead.* I wanted to press my ear there and listen for his heart, to hear him tell me what I hoped was true—my secret was safe with him. The sink suddenly gurgled, sucking down the dirty water. We both stared toward the drain, at the swirling muck, until it was gone. Then we were called to bed.

It was to be a two-day camping trip. We rose before dawn to pack our bags and drive to the river.

A night of rain had given way to a morning washed clean and clear. Wyoming's sky was a bright and tender blue sailing over the tall pines that hugged the Green River.

"It's running high," Bob said, his voice containing his excitement as barely as the banks contained the swollen current.

He crouched to check the pressure and air caps on each raft and then walked around to make sure every boy had tied his life vest properly. He took charge of one boat, made Karen captain of the other, and divvied up oars and campers between the two. I was placed with her, a wooden paddle in my hands, front and starboard.

We lifted the rafts and moved them to the edge of the water.

"Listen up," Bob said. "We all need to work together. Keep your eyes peeled for rocks." He looked right at me, though he was addressing the group. "If you land in the drink, point your feet downriver." This made him laugh. He raised his fist high in the air, whooped loudly, and cried, "Let's go!"

Everyone cheered. We slid the rafts into the water and shoved off.

Not five minutes later there came the unmistakable roar of white water. A thrill rippled through the ranks and lodged itself as dread in the pit of my stomach. I looked down and pulled the straps of my life vest as tightly as they would go.

"Look sharp!" Bob yelled from his raft, thirty yards behind us. He let out another stupid *whoop*—his idea of an Indian battle cry—then screamed again, "Avoid the rocks!" His voice, full of delight, skipped across the clear, placid water and down toward the approaching rumble.

The sound of it was like hell's thunder. *We'll be juice,* I was convinced, *pulverized, then swallowed.* We picked up speed as the river narrowed, and within seconds we were in it, rising and falling in the wavy, foamy mix. Water splashed and soaked my legs, sprayed across my cheeks. The blessed land, the lucky rooted trees, were calmly passing us by.

Karen screamed orders. "Row, row! To the left, the left. Harder!" Lord Jesus, what kind of sport was this? I wondered. The Green, it seemed, had become a monster, a mortal enemy. The happy hollers from the boys around me ricocheted across the waves. Was I the only one hating this? We rose and dipped; shooting past ripped-up trees that had lodged against sharp, merciless rocks.

A huge, flat-faced boulder rose before us. "Hard left, hard left!" Karen cried. I rowed frantically, my arms burning, but the stubborn current had its way and we rammed straight into the rock. Half the raft slid right up onto the mossy face of granite so that I thought—it wasn't thought but sheer panic—we were going to die. I let out a shriek then cried, "We're gonna flip!" With that, my feet took me right out of the raft and up onto the boulder, where I promptly dropped my oar and clutched at whatever crags I could find. I crouched on the tiny summit like a trapped and trembling toad, whispering: *igneous, igneous, specks of mica.*

"Get back in!" Karen screamed as the raft slid immediately backward into the water, did a wild 360-degree turn, and continued its plunge downriver. I turned upriver where I heard a muffled version of Bob's orders. Through the mist of churned-up water I saw his mouth moving, his arm pointing frantically in my direction. They tried like mad to steer their raft toward me for a rescue but the river wouldn't have it. They didn't even come close to my perch. As they tumbled by, the boys, including Robin, had just enough time to lift their hands and offer me a mirthful, merciless *so long.*

"Stay put!" Bob screamed. "Just stay put."

I squatted on the tip of my midriver peak for more than an hour. An hour of solitude amid the roiling soup, an eternity to reflect upon my cowardice. Meanwhile, far downstream, they struggled to get the rafts ashore, hike through horribly thick brush, and get back on the water to perform the rescue.

"Hop down!" Bob yelled as his wobbly boat lurched toward me. I fell toward his outstretched arms and then straight into a puddle at the center of the raft. There I remained, soaked and silent, avoiding contact with anyone and everyone for the rest of the day.

That afternoon, we made camp along the eastern bank of the river. It was a beautiful spot, thick with pines. Through the small spaces between trees, I caught sight of jagged, snowcapped peaks. I wasn't sure, didn't care, if they were the Tetons and, if so, which was the one with my family name. Maybe I'd ask. Later.

As the light softened and the air cooled, I walked the trails that wound their way along the river. The quiet, the odor of pine, was calming. I searched for dry branches and kindling for the fire. I spotted Karen, unavoidable, heading my way down the path. She was dragging a long, dead branch. As I approached her I kept quiet. I knew she was pissed at me because Bob had been upset with her— as if she could have, should have, stopped me from jumping ship, losing an oar. I moved over to pass on the right but she shifted her dead log and blocked my way.

"That never should have happened," she said, lifting a hand, tucking a bit of her blond hair behind each ear. She glared past me down the path. "It never would have, not if you had any *balls*."

She might as well have jabbed her fist into my stomach. I had no wind; my eyes seemed to swell with heat. I pressed the kindling I'd been holding against my chest, stared down at a thousand crisscrossed pine needles.

"Cat got your tongue?"

I turned to watch her lumbering, slump-shouldered frame shrink away. *Say something!* the voice inside me urged. She was still within sight, the broad, blue spread of her Levi-covered ass sashaying down the trail. I dug for a word, a weapon that could be hurled like a stick or a stone, but nothing would rise to my throat.

—

Bob stepped over and placed his hand on the corner of my bunk near my head. He'd come from the adjacent cabin, where he and Karen were staying. He'd come to bid us all goodnight.

"You guys did a great job on and off the water these last two days," he said. "We covered good distance."

I turned my back to him and curled into the stiff sheets, which, like everything on this desolate ranch, smelled of must and mothballs. Unused and unswept for who knows how long, these cabins comprised another of Bob's shoestring arrangements, one of his twilight zones. Nothing but ghosts and bugs seemed to live here. But after two nights camping, it felt good to be in a bed, under a roof.

"Let's call it lights out in five minutes, OK, guys?"

Most of the boys were already drifting off. Robin was awake, though, across the room from me in a top bunk, and it was his face I watched, his gentle eyes, as Bob leaned over and whispered into my ear.

"You were great on that glacier today, kiddo." His breath, his compliment, was warm on the back of my neck. "You really slid down that mother; you're getting gutsy." He tapped the back of my neck with one finger. "Come visit me after lights out . . . OK?"

I held still.

"Marty."

I could hear how particularly, how much, he wished to see me and I turned my face to him. He tousled my hair and I felt the crazy muddle ignite inside me, the fire of rage and want burning me up.

Bob went for the light switch and, when I looked over, Robin tossed me a rueful grin. I tried to smile back but my face was frozen. The room went dark.

"Goodnight, guys," Bob said.

The door squeaked to a close. I buried my head in the pillow, pulled the rough blanket tight around me, and knew just what I'd do, the one weapon I could think to use. Silence. I closed my eyes, determined to sleep, to stay right where I was.

—

The next day—for the morning hike, for the meals, for the fishing—I stuck to my strategy. It felt right and good. In fact, I thought, I wanted this war of silence to last forever. For the rest of the trip in Wyoming, for the rest of my life. Borders closed, locked and guarded. Don't let him get near you, I thought. I'm thirteen now, for God's sake. Screw him, and screw his creepy girlfriend. And with every moment of my silence, with every maneuver to avoid him, a fury built within me. A mounting pressure that felt something like strength. Like *balls*.

That afternoon, I stood alone, tossing horseshoes near the empty, red-stained barn. Everyone else had gone to the lake for a swim, for the good fishing, but I was practicing solitude. It was sometime near five o'clock, still very hot. The mosquitoes hadn't yet risen off the nearby ponds. The air was dry and still. I was aiming a shoe when, with no warning at all, he appeared. I'd seen him go off swimming with the others, so I was startled. I pretended not to notice, but the white of his T-shirt, the weight of his stance, was vivid against the barn door. My heart began to bang for battle. I gripped tight to the shoe and tossed it. It landed well past the post, kicked up a puff of dirt.

"What's up with you?" His question drifted across the dusty barnyard, faded into the trees.

I shifted another horseshoe to my right hand, leaned forward, and swung it back and forth, enjoying the lethal heft of metal. I squinted, took a step, and let it fly. It arched high and way short, and landed with one flat thud. I saw out of the corner of my eye that he was holding his camera. The good one, the large lens. It had a fancy strap, a colorful, psychedelic weave that draped over his shoulder. He lifted the camera to his eye and pointed it my way.

"Don't."

He held it steady against his face.

"Don't!"

He hesitated, then let it drop and held it next to his hip. Long silence.

"Why didn't you come to see me last night?" I imagined my remaining horseshoe sticking out of his head, the way it would bleed, knock him cold. "Do you want to talk?"

It was a good toss—nearly a ringer, it smacked, ricocheted off the post, and skidded to a stop. I stuck my hands in my jean pockets and wondered which way to walk—the path to the lake or the one to the bunkhouse. Then I heard the *kriiick* of the shutter.

"I said *don't,* damnit." It was out of me like a shot, not the way I wanted. I sounded shrill and childish and I hated the way my will seemed to leak with the words. *Keep silent,* I thought, *best to say not one damn thing.* I stuck the heel of my boot into the dirt as if slamming on a brake.

"Oh, come on. A souvenir of Wyoming."

"Just don't."

I wanted to bolt, but not enough for my feet to obey. My heel dug deeper, carving a crater toward China.

"Let's talk. Let's go into the barn."

I shook my head. No way. No talking.

He hit the latch from beneath with the heel of his palm and the large door swung open. The cooler air from within, the faint smell of hay, brushed past my face. It seemed as though the barn had been waiting, holding its breath. He moved aside to let me pass.

"Watch your feet."

A board, easy to trip on, framed the bottom of the doorway. I stepped over it and into the dim light. The ground inside was less packed, soft in the soles of my boots. My eyes were drawn to the ceiling, which sloped steeply up beyond a high, wooden beam hanging like the transom of an old chapel. The sun spilled in from somewhere above the hayloft and cast its amber light in one rectangular chunk across the wooden wall to my right. The building was startlingly quiet, not an animal in sight, though the fodder and waste of them were mixed in the dirt, whiffs of their living in the air.

From behind me came the squeak of hinges. Bob was yanking

at the door. The back of his T-shirt was streaked with dirt and with yellow stains at the pit of each arm. His Levis were snug at his buttocks; I could see clearly the shape of his wallet, the white, rectangular fade of it stenciled on his left pocket. My feet moved backwards as if to find the spot to take a stand. The time had come, I thought, to find the right words to say what's wrong. To make an end.

The sight of light and trees from the barnyard narrowed to a sliver, then to nothing as the door slammed. The rattle of its closing sent an instant charge through me and my knees began to shake. I had to bend them to steady my stance. It was fear, it seemed, as much as desire that caused my dick to stiffen. Hunger and danger—fused. I folded a fist into each front pocket to hide the swelling. He grabbed the inside latch of the door and spun it until it snapped into its cradle. He set his camera on the ground with great care, the bright strap of it flopping in the dirt, then he stood with his back against the door. Dueling distance.

"What is it?" he asked. I studied the scratches and stains on the pointy toes of my boots. "Why didn't you come to see me last night?"

I glanced toward the locked door. Maybe Robin had added things up, was looking for us.

There were three fences, small pigpens, I guessed, or goat stalls, jutting from the wall to my right. I stepped over to the first one and sat against it, my hands still stuffed in my pockets. Bob moved into the room and stood near the large center beam.

He patted the wooden pillar. "This was built to last." He looked up toward the loft. "What's wrong?" I stared at a pair of reins and a bridle dangling from hooks on the wall behind him. "Why didn't you come?"

I let my chin fall to my chest. "I didn't want to."

"Why?"

"Because I didn't *want* to."

A fly dove recklessly at my face. I swatted it away.

"Why?"

"Because." My voice, barely a breath, was swallowed into the dirt. I searched for the fury that had grown and lodged itself like a tight ball in my chest, but it was gone, or melted, somehow, to nothing but sorrow. Useless for a fight.

"What is it?"

There was a rusty pail near my feet. I gave it a little kick and it fell with a clatter to its side. The bottom of it was caked with mud. "I have to end it," I said.

"What?"

"Everything." My throat clamped shut, my eyes filled up. Fucking tears, I fought them with all my might. I had a stand to take, there were things burning inside, things to say—about being older, the boots not fitting, Robin seeing us, Karen hating me—but, of all the words, only two fell out of my mouth. "I jumped."

He took a step toward me and I couldn't stop the flood of tears.

"That's OK," he whispered.

"No. No it isn't."

"The Green is a serious river ..." He moved another step toward me.

"Don't ... just don't." He stopped. "No one else would do what I did."

"Don't worry about anyone else. You're a great—"

"*She* even said it!" I looked at the dirt, wiping my face on the baggy sleeves of my large button-down shirt—a hand-me-down from Dad. "She said I have no balls." He was quiet for a time and with a new and sudden worry I whispered, "God ... don't tell her I told."

"Well, come on. We know that's just not true. Don't we?"

I looked up at him then, at the stupid grin on his face, at his pink hand slapping at the fly circling his brow. I stared right at him until his smile disappeared, until his hand came to rest.

"It's turning out all wrong," I said, my voice clamped in a growl.

"What is?"

"*I* am!"

He shook his head. "I don't think so."

"But look at me . . . at *us*. We are . . ."

"We're not *that*, I've told you! You're not *that*."

"How do you know?'

"*I know*. You'll see. You'll grow up and you'll meet a girl."

A girl . . . a girl . . . for an instant the image—long blond hair, breasts under a white sweater—flashed through my head and I grabbed onto it as to a lifeline. God how I wanted to believe him: me with a girl, me a normal boy kissing inside a barn, with Lisa or Tammy or Paula. It was three seconds of comfort to trust that he might see what I couldn't yet about my own body, about the way the world unfolds.

He stepped a little closer, his arms outstretched, his palms open. "We *love* each other. That's entirely different."

"Different from what?"

"From the way homosexuals are." A jolt of sickness at hearing the word aloud. A word not said but looked up in dictionaries of disease. "You and I are different." His head was tilted to the left, his face somber with facts of life. I looked at his glasses, held together at the nose by a hunk of gray tape, I looked at him and thought, *he must know*. He must have seen one, or some, of *them*. Seen what they are—these awful people without love. "We help each other, that's all," he said, reaching toward me, displaying the chalky calluses at the base of each finger. "We're two good people, helping each other. There's nothing bad in that. Homosexuals are people without love." He stepped closer and my knees began to shake again and my groin to pulse. He took off his glasses and hooked them into the V-neck of his undershirt. He bent down carefully as he got close to me and reached for the bucket near my feet. I took in the smell of horses and hay and of him, aware of how much I liked it all. The animal odors. The animal life. He took a step back, flipped the bucket bottom up, hitched his pants and sat on it like a rancher on a milking stool.

"Come here."

I didn't move. I remained, hands in pockets, leaning on my little fence, making believe I might stay put, stay blameless. He opened his arms wide and held them there, as motionless as the statue of a saint, and I knew I couldn't bear the being separate. "Marty, come here." His voice traveled down my throat like heat from a furnace and my legs moved toward the warmth, toward the body right in front of me.

"It's all right," he said, reaching for my belt.

As his hands worked my buckle, I thought I might melt for gratitude, for the relief of being touched. Thank God, at least *this* existed on earth. At least I'd found it. The consolation of flesh. He unsnapped my buttons one by one, then peeled away the cotton to get to me. He paid no attention to pleasuring himself. This time it was all for me, a gift, like sealing with a kiss the end of our quarrel. My pants fell to my ankles and I gazed at the burnt, bald crown of his head moving, at the wisps of brown hair spiraling clockwise. I gazed, utterly amazed at the way warm and wet could answer, for the moment, every aching worry, every troubling question. He took hold of my hips and I gripped his shoulders, closed my eyes. I knew I didn't really like him, that there was barely a trace of love here, and I knew what that made me and I tried not to care. And as I moved my hips back and forth I looked around the filthy, beautiful barn, and heard myself whispering, *Yes, oh yes.*

We left the barn and walked down to the lake to join the other boys and Karen. Some were fishing, some swimming. I sat down on a log, my body heavy with failing. I'd failed, again, to stop it. He asked if he could take my picture. Yeah, OK, what the hell. I still have it, me sitting on that log. In it I'm holding—I don't remember why—a rumpled piece of paper towel. My face is drawn, circles under my eyes, my hair a thick long mop, my lips parted in a faint effort at a smile, the clunky braces on my front teeth peeking through. My father's old shirt, white and baggy, barely tucked into my recently buttoned Levis.

Everyone else went up to dinner. I remained on that log, I remember, for a long time. I wanted to be alone. I wanted to listen to the birds, to watch the light change and soften over the lake. I remember observing how the changing breezes and the many bugs skating along the water caused little wakes of light, dappled patterns, to constantly shift. I watched the fish poke through the surface to eat what they could. The tall pines swayed, growing darker against the darkening sky. Movement, incessant song and movement, the world going on, and I remember thinking, so clearly, as I watched the gloaming, how I was not, could not be, a part of this. The natural world. I sat on that log at the side of the pond, wanting to ask the bugs, the birds, the beautiful trees: *How did this happen?* It was the first time, the first place, it occurred to me that I must leave here. Leave the world. *God made all that is,* I thought, *and it is beautiful, but I cannot be a part of it.* He could not have intended *this. This mistake.* I didn't think of it as suicide so much as the idea of ending being. That something, someone, so unnatural as I, could not remain among that which lives. This feeling, like sex, seemed to come from my body. A certain dreadful sense that the only solution to the error that has been made is to erase it. The feeling then moved from my body to a kind of rational argument: If something is bad, you must get rid of it. End it. Simple. *I am bad so I must go.* And I knew then that this was the only answer, the only choice. That I needed the strength to end what wasn't good. This one thing I had to have the balls to do.

The idea was born that day and would not leave me for years and years to come.

That night Bob came to my bunk after everyone was asleep. He jostled me and asked that I come to the room where he slept. Like a trained zombie, I pulled back the covers and followed him out.

I didn't exactly know if they slept in the same bed or what they were to each other but there she was. "Come on," he said, "crawl in."

She didn't seem to react at all. She lay on her side in the dim light, her back to us, maybe sleeping. I slid into his side of the double bed, then he got in and nudged me over so that I was in the middle. He didn't say anything, but the movement of his hands, the way he gently turned my body toward hers told me what was happening. I understood suddenly that this was his offering. My reward.

The air, the silence, is electric. What has Bob said to her? I wonder if they've discussed it, made a bargain about what to do with the kid. Did he tell her I was hurt by what she said? Did he ask her to make up, be nice? Bob reaches around with one hand and guides me toward Karen. I'm excited, my mind racing, thinking: *This is it, the thing that men do.* The natural thing. The thing I've been waiting for. I'm erect, a sign that I'm made the right way. It's surreal, the way she's not really there. A lump of flesh, or like a rock, really, with an opening into which Bob slides me—small plug into a cold socket. Has he made a compact with her? It wasn't two days ago that she insulted me, told me I wasn't a man. I slide into her thinking, oh my God; I'm *in* a woman. That part of a woman. It, she, feels rough, sandpapery. It does not feel warm or good and I understand in some way that this holds no pleasure for her but I don't care. All I'm thinking is how I'll be able to say from now on that *I've done it.* What boys do. It goes fast. I come, thrilled at my accomplishment. My sense of power is followed instantly by intense embarrassment. Awkwardness.

When it's over I crawl back over Bob to the edge of the bed.

"You see?" he whispers. Then he turns and makes love to his girlfriend.

An hour later I tiptoe back to the dorm and take my place among the sleeping campers. I look at Robin's shaggy, handsome head. The thought of waking him runs through my mind. Just for a second, so I could tell him what's happened. Not to worry, I can do it. No question. But I don't dare wake him, dare spill this new secret, and I crawl into my bunk. I stare above at the series of thick beams—

shaved logs—running the length of the room, and above them at the sloped, slatted ceiling. I wonder if the roof might fall in, crush me. I wonder why it is that I feel so terribly, terribly sad.

We are in Wyoming for three more days. The last night we're there, very late, he sneaks in to get me and takes me to bed with the both of them again. Once more he offers her to me or me to her. No words, just nudges and hand signals. She "accepts" or, rather, holds still and receives me. Coldly, as far as I can tell, but what do I know? It goes quickly, nonetheless, because I'm hungry to prove it for a second time. Prove that I'm capable. Then everything goes a step further. With more nudges and maneuvering Bob makes it known that he wants me behind him, to be inside him while he moves inside her. I oblige. It all strikes me as weirdly inventive, that such a configuration could exist. This is something, I think, he's been angling for all along. Attention from all sides, master-mind in the middle. How did he become this being, this thing—like a daddy longlegs weaving a big, sticky web? And how did we get here, tangled in it, like hungry prey, groping in the dark for food, for escape?

In the daylight nothing is said. Karen and I can scarcely look at each other.

15

SUMMER OVER AND back in the halls of Christ the King, my body vibrates. My bones are infused with a push that tells me I must fashion a dazzling public self. Be the best and busiest eighth grader ever. The push has always been there but now it's a kind of panic, an incessant, living prayer: *God, do not let shame fall upon my head.* For if it were to come, if the truth of things surfaced, I would die of it. And I had no doubt that shame could kill a body.

Even now I can see, nearly feel, my small body scurrying down the halls, running for classes and extracurricular meetings. It's a physical, an almost athletic feeling that I must jump higher, spell better, talk smoother, smile more broadly than anyone else. It's as if my life depends on this. On performing. It lives there in my knotted stomach, this imperative. Dazzle or you're doomed.

I run for class president and win. I know then that my picture will be placed—along with secretary and treasurer—at the very center of our graduating class photo. This is what I want, to be encased in the bright aura of achievement. Student Council. Boy Scouts. Great Books. Run. Run. The faster, the better. The quicker I move, the less any truth can be pinned down. By me or anyone else. The shinier my halo, the more I can blind them. If the arrows come (and there are awful moments when I feel sure they will, that trouble will surface), I'll have armor so golden, so thick, that nothing will stick. Not to the straight-A superspeller likes of me. Nothing will pierce. Not the good boy.

There are many moments I enjoy. I'm good at chatting with adults and I'm generally popular with my classmates. I love the attention I get from doing well, but I know that my quick body is a blight here in the holy halls of civilized life. My fellow citizens just don't know it yet. Every waking moment comes with the task of earning the right and making up for the wrong of being here. I knew I'd revoked my own membership, but every action I'd take would be a way of proving, of saying: *I still belong.*

It would be the odd moment cycling home or daydreaming in class that it might come to me. Like a whip-crack of dread. The thought of a news clipping, a rumor, a summons. The thought that somewhere there might be an authority investigating him. He'd be found out. And then, so would I.

Once in a while I'd get a letter from him, urging me to keep up my studies, to kick butt in the spelling bee, asking how I was and when I wanted to come visit and work on his new house. Sometimes he called.

"Marty, it's for you," my mom or one of my sisters would yell. I'd stand in the kitchen and speak briefly, quietly, on the phone with him—my counselor pal from camp, my mentor, my secret lover. I tried to resist the invitations, but the craving would rise up and I'd say, "Yes, OK," and arrange to spend another few days with him. I knew that somewhere in the course of the weekend there'd be the drug, the fix, the touch—that one thing that felt true beyond any Truth. He knew that part of me, the part that craved sex. Pleasure. He accepted it. Fostered it. He wanted what I wanted.

And also there was, during those long, winter weekends, the simple companionship. The holding of a hammer, the time spent together sawing wood, making things. He still had lessons he wanted to teach.

I remember coming home from one of these weekends to find that my minibike had been stolen. It was my prized possession. A shiny red, fifty-horsepower minibike. I was in shock. My dad could barely look at me; he felt so badly, his head hanging low. Turns out he'd taken it for a ride to visit his friend and have a bit of a nip. Innocently, he'd left it out front and someone nabbed it.

My motorized bike was months and months of paper route money. It cost way more than the guitar I bought. It was, at the time, the world to me. I could barely speak. Something so big, that I'd worked so hard for, gone. Vanished. I was numb with anger. I didn't know what to do.

I called Bob.

Gently, he calmed me. "God has reasons, plans larger than we could ever know. Look, Marty, you may never understand why. You've just got to figure that someone out there needed that bike more than you did."

It was one of the strangest notions I'd ever heard, but, even so, there was something undeniably wise in his words. A larger kind of thinking. And what he said sunk in, comforted me. The last thing he told me before hanging up was, "Marty, you've got to forgive your father. That's important. He meant no harm."

Eighth-grade weekends with Bob meant Karen too. She had an apartment in Boulder and sometimes we'd sleep there Friday nights before heading, just the two of us, up to the unfinished house where we'd work (and sleep) alone in sleeping bags. Or sometimes in the almost-finished bedroom with the fancy skylight, where you could lie on the futon and practice celestial navigation.

On those occasional nights in her apartment in Boulder, the three of us had sex. By now I was demanding that I get my moment with her, my chance to prove myself. Then Bob and she would do whatever it was they liked as I hovered on the edge of the action.

On one of those mornings, I remember Karen waking very early, with a start. She let out a sort of gasp, threw back the covers and dashed to the bathroom. There were large drops of blood all across the linoleum of her small studio, leading to the bathroom door. I felt a jolt of terror, thinking she'd cut herself or had a nosebleed or that she'd been hurt somehow. I noticed that there was blood in the bed too and in a panic I jostled Bob.

"Jesus," he said.

"What happened?"

"She's got her period."

"Oh," I said, sort of putting it together with the little I'd gleaned at home from my sister and mother about menstruation. Bob explained a bit more and calmed me down. Said it was something normal. Eventually Karen emerged, pale and upset, and with a wad of paper towels she cleaned the floor.

We spent that morning together packing up her studio apartment. She was moving across town, somewhere cheaper. In the midst of loading boxes into Bob's pickup truck, the two of them erupted.

"You live like a pig. You've left the place such a mess!" Bob yelled.

"Shut the fuck up."

"Everywhere you go, you leave a mess. Why didn't you clean up?"

"I'm working two damn jobs. What do you expect?"

Suddenly, Bob lashed out and smacked the passenger door of the pickup with his fist, leaving a dent. He bent over and cradled his hand against his chest. That could have been her face, I thought. I'd never seen this violent side of him, though I realized I always suspected it was there. That he did his best to keep it from me.

"Let's get out of here," he said, throwing a broom and then himself into the back of the pickup. I sat up front, wishing myself invisible.

"He's crazy," Karen kept repeating as we drove down the dirt road. "He's fucking crazy."

There was one time my parents confronted me about the mountain trips. I came home very late one Sunday. Karen and I had gotten lost riding some horses, transporting them from one ranch to another. We were to meet Bob but we'd gone down a wrong trail and it was well after dark when we finally found a highway and a phone. By then, Bob had called Rocky Mountain Rescue and had rangers out looking for us. It was a school night, my parents were concerned, and when I got home my mom made my dad say something. It was a short and vague sort of lecture, Dad sitting in the armchair in his pajamas, smoking a cigarette.

"Come in here and sit down."

"OK."

"You can't be going off like this and coming home so late. What about your studies? What's *going on?* What are you doing up there?"

"I'm helping out."

"Well, you can't just go off and come home so late," Dad said.

My mother nodded. I had the feeling that she wanted to know, to ask, more. But she didn't. Nobody pressed.

"I'm sorry," I said, seeing how honestly upset they were and how caring. And how powerless. Everything was too far along now for them to stop it, for them to have any grip on me. I looked at my dad across in the chair and Mom sitting on the couch. The seven feet between us was vast. I was barely aware of their preoccupation with making ends meet, with negotiating a crumbling marriage. And they hadn't a clue what I'd gotten myself into. There might have been an inkling beneath (I recall one occasion when they'd suddenly insisted on driving me to the ranch instead of Bob picking me up. "We want to have a look," they'd said.), but the conscious thought would never have been allowed to blossom. That a tall and charming man, a guy associated with St. Malo, a fellow I'd said was once a seminarian, was a pedophile. Unthinkable.

"Well, don't be home so late," Dad said, stamping out his cigarette.

"OK."

We all went straight to bed. That was the last of it. The closest we'd ever come to a showdown.

—

Sometimes I felt scared and I liked it. All the concealment was a kind of strange power. An entire and buzzing inner life. A four-teen-year-old on a three-speed Raleigh, getting it every which way. I was getting away with murder, with pleasure, with crimes, and I was pulling As, I was pulling focus for all the right reasons. I got second place in the televised Rocky Mountain Spelling Bee (a joy-ous occasion, a prize TV!). I was spokesman for the class, top of the Catholic heap. I was oh so nice. Naughty and nice. My face was the frantic mask of a chipper boy. I was expert shape-shifter. Secrecy, my engine. A machine so loud it makes it nearly impossible to lis-ten for what's in your soul, to hear what's authentic.

I was aware in some way that the jumble inside of me was cor-rosive. I didn't know then how my psyche was urgently fragment-ing, stuffing the appropriate story into the appropriate corner of the brain to summon at the appropriate moment to deliver the appro-priate impression—depending on the place, the person, the time. It is amazing how efficiently the mind can erase from the heart the details, the truth of the narrative.

Sometimes I think, I dream, of going back there for a moment, back there to the boy on his bike, the boy I'm remembering now, and asking him how he did it, held it together. How, what, he re-ally felt. I want to ask him exactly what words he would use to de-scribe the muddle of it all and if I'm even close to telling it like it was.

What he withstood, what he soaked up like a sponge, I'm wring-ing out now, and I know it's him, it's the boy, who's summoning me to tell. He's the one who insists, believes, that all the fractured pieces can be spread on a white page, examined, and woven back together with words.

16

I CAME HOME one afternoon and found a formal-looking letter addressed to me sitting on the kitchen table. I opened it and was confused by a tangle of unfamiliar names. Then I saw Robert and Karen and understood that this was an invitation, that they were to be married. The thought of it, the news of it, was shocking. Especially because I'd been busy boxing up thoughts of them and shipping it all away. I'd managed to be out of touch with them for nearly four months. The last contact was a call I'd made thanking them for the gift they'd sent me at Christmastime. A beautiful hardback copy of James Fennimore Cooper's *The Last of the Mohicans,* inscribed: *Merry Christmas, Happy Birthday, and Happy New Year, Love, Bob and Karen.* The very sight of the inscription shamed me. I'd taken a pen and scribbled until their names were unreadable and hid the book at the back of my sock drawer.

I threw the invitation away and went downstairs to do my homework.

Several days later Kip (charming, bacon-frying, also-sleeping-with-Bob Kip) called. He said his mom was going to drive to Bob's wedding. Did I want to go? "Yes," I said without much thought. Suddenly it seemed the right thing to do, and I realized I wanted to wish them well, that I wanted, in fact, to witness the normalcy. Their wedding would tell me that what we'd done and who we were was over, that everyone, including me, was moving on into the respectable.

A few Saturdays later, I put on a suit and a tie and spent the afternoon in a tiny church in the mountains, watching Bob and Karen walk down the aisle. In my memory it was a priest who presided, though I don't recall a Mass, so it might have been a mountain minister or justice of the peace. I remember feeling awkward sitting there with Kip in the last pew on the left—two of Bob's musketeers bearing witness. For some bizarre reason, Kip's mom remained outside in the car. She wasn't welcome. Bob had had some sort of quarrel with her, but she was so devoted to Bob, was so under his spell in some way, that she brought her fourteen-year-old son to the ceremony anyway.

Their figures, Bob in fancy black, Karen in white, standing with their backs to us at the altar, were surreal. There was that strange disconnect from the hidden things we'd done, who we were, and the ordinariness of a public ceremony. I recall that Karen was pregnant, already swollen with the reason for marriage. I never even spoke to them that day, save for a quick nod and a whispered *congratulations* as they moved past. I sat quietly in the back and smiled as they walked up the aisle and out to the pickup parked in front of the church. It all happened so quickly, with so few people there. No drinks, no food, no toasts. I knew the occasion was meant to be full of hope and happiness but the whole thing struck me as pathetic. Unreal. Somebody opened and held the door; someone else tossed a bit of rice. I saw that Bob was grinning as he took Karen's hand and they ducked into the truck. Then they were gone. A honeymoon? Just going home? I never asked.

We drove back to the city. Kip's Mom asked, "Was it nice?"

We nodded, and then sat in silence all the way home. The one good thing, I kept thinking, was that now I could say to my parents or anyone who happened to ask: *Oh, yeah, Bob? Him? I don't see him anymore. Well, he got married, he's having a kid. Just a regular guy.* The whole strange event gave me a certain relief that he wouldn't be found out. Relief that he was through with little boys and so trouble was less likely to come to his door, less likely to come to mine.

I got home and took off my suit and sat on my bed. I'll never touch him again, I thought, or allow him to touch me. He is wed, going to be a father. And I'm going to grow up now. High school soon and then I'll get into the best college I can. Stanford, maybe. And when I get married, it'll be to a good woman, and we'll have lots of kids, and I'll do my best to be honest and good. To be a citizen. A lawyer. A senator, one day.

I knew this now. I sat on my bed and felt the sharp stab of my convictions. And of my lonesomeness. I hated that I felt lonesome, but I did. The one person who knew my body, my secrets, had just been married. Wedded to a woman I didn't like.

17

THE BUSY-BOY BRAVADO, the manic performance that carried me through my last months at Christ the King Elementary, crumbled upon my arrival at Regis High. This was the place, I felt, the moment, to become a man. This was the big league now, no grade-school games, no singing nuns, no girls allowed, and in the face of it, I was utterly overwhelmed. Here was a brotherhood of boys taught by a fellowship of priests. Here was the revered Jesuit institution where my Dad, uncles, and all of my male cousins were educated, and the second I laid eyes on it I was stricken with shyness.

Constructed in the 1880s, Regis High School was a monolithic pile of giant rose-colored stone, a four-story monument to Catholic maleness. It was the most oppressive edifice I had ever seen. Carved in granite over the large doors of the main entrance was the phrase RELIGIONI ET BONIS ARTIBUS. And above that, faded rays were chiseled around the letters *IHS,* the Greek monogram for Jesus, known in English as the symbol for *I Have Suffered.* Each time I saw the carvings on the face of that mammoth building, every time I hiked up the wide steps past Father Fitz, barking at everyone to hurry to class, every fear I harbored about who I was and what I might be on my way to becoming was galvanized. I felt I was marching into a men's-only holy club to which I could never win membership. A place where my face would flicker the wrong and sinful desire, where I'd move in a certain manner and all would be revealed. Because, somehow, this community of men would know. They'd know where I'd been, what I was.

Everything about the place, the dank halls, the priests living on the fourth floor above our classrooms, the rusty pipes and cracked tiled floors, the very odor of its history, heightened my dread. My deepest longing was to measure up. And my bottomless terror, that I'd already failed. As I moved from class to all-male class, particulars kept creeping from the pit of my stomach, up the back of my throat. There was the indisputable fact that he'd stolen my first orgasm. It felt, in some mythic, fourteen-year-old way, that that single act of thievery had doomed me, made me incapable of real manhood. He'd yanked it from me at just the wrong moment and now it was fated, encoded, that every drop of my Catholic seed and the rush of pleasure that came with it, was linked forever with him. I couldn't shake the feeling, so strong in the dim rooms of this old school, that my deeds stuck to me like a bad smell. A stain.

How many students, how many priests in this institution held secrets? Countless of them, surely. But I felt that mine was the only, the worst possible, one. And the weight of it began to crush me.

For the first few months, by sheer force of will, I kept my studies up. But as the weeks went on, I couldn't concentrate through the haze of depression. I hadn't the armor to withstand the humiliation that seemed the main method, the core of the Regis curriculum. There was terrifying Mr. Getz, who smacked the science tables where we sat with a yardstick whenever we didn't answer quickly or correctly. There was the ancient priest who taught Latin and Algebra, his cassock smeared with chalk from impossible calculations, with the dust of dead verbs. He gave pop quizzes, where disgrace awaited if you hadn't memorized the lesson as well as the page number that the lesson was on. The message was clear and everywhere—get through all this, then you'll be one of us. A strong, smart citizen. A good Catholic man. Dads all over town spoke of their time at Regis with the awe and affection of soldiers having served together through war. They would speak of the great

Jesuit tradition of intellectual curiosity and rigor. Of this brilliant Society of Jesus dedicated to discipline and education and the pope. A society that included great leaders like the paleontologist and writer Pierre Teilhard de Chardin, and the passionate activist Father Daniel Berrigan. A society I was born into, in which I was meant, and wished, to take a proud part.

In the course of those dreadful freshman days, no hour was worse than gym. The place where body and masculinity are most nakedly revealed. At Regis, phys ed was lorded over by a beady-eyed man with no hair and less humor. Mr. McPhee. He forced us to participate in each week's alternating activity in a furious nine-month tour through every sport known to man, from boxing to wrestling to basketball and rope climbing. No matter how ill equipped we were, no matter how terrified, he screamed at us (me) through every miserable activity. He was insanely strict about two things: jockstraps and showers. Each session began with his checking the one and ended with his observing the other.

His vocation, whatever it was (actual Jesuit or lay teacher, I can't recall) was buried beneath his mound of sweaty sweat clothes. Always in his hand was a clipboard, and around his neck a silver whistle, which he blew often and loudly. The first whistle was our signal to line up along the black (not the red!) line in alphabetical order, arms clasped behind our backs. He would walk along the row of boys, his tennis shoes squeaking, his baldpate reflecting fluorescent light. At random, he would pause in front of three or four different boys, reach under their regulation red shorts and quickly, deftly (years of practice) hook his stubby index finger under the elastic of the required jock. *Snap!* He did all this without ever taking his eyes off the face of the boy he was checking. We were all ordered to stare ahead at attention. If the jock wasn't there (which happened only rarely), if you were wearing mere underpants, he simply marked it on his board without a word and everyone knew you were two demerits closer to the six that brought you JUG.

JUG: Judgment under God—a kind of punishment handed out

at Catholic school, usually in the form of detention, suspension, and, occasionally at this Jesuit high school, forced participation in a boxing match with the dean of discipline in a vacant lot behind the field house. This instilled in most students a sense of mortal terror, which of course was the point. I never actually knew anyone who'd boxed with Father Fitz, the dean. The rumor was enough.

At the end of class, McPhee would blow the whistle again and stand at the end of the shower stall, where each boy was required to get fully naked and fully wet before being checked off his list. No shower, two demerits. He stood there, his eyes moving slowly from boy to clipboard and back to boy. The tepid water, the tense atmosphere, the beady eyes of Mr. McPhee, kept things quick and furtive. His presence did offer one bit of solace—it crushed my abiding fear of getting an erection at the worst possible moment.

The single class that came as a relief was Brother Tom's Freshman Theology. He was a compact, athletic man with very small but very bright blue eyes. He had a tiny mustache, which he constantly rubbed with the side of his index finger as if it were a bit of dirt he was trying to brush away. The first several weeks of school, Brother Tom was subdued and nearly as strict as all the other teachers. But after winter break, the moment we left the Old Testament behind and began with the New, he was like another man. A light, an actual twinkle, began to burn in his blue eyes. We were witnessing a man smitten. And, suddenly, an easier grader.

"Do you see what a radical this guy was? What a lover of life?" he asked, clutching the crucifix, caressing the Corpus as he spoke, needing, it seemed clear, to hang on to the very man of whom he talked. His voice rose in pitch, and his body, onto the balls of his feet, as he spoke.

"Did Jesus fall in love?" he cried out one day.

We boys generally thought so and cited Mary Magdalene.

"So, you think he liked women?"

"He must have...*after a certain age*," said handsome Kevin McKenzie, with his perfect Groucho Marx inflection.

"Did Jesus have a penis?" Brother Tom asked, tapping Christ's feet tenderly.

The room went dead silent.

"Well?" he asked again.

Silence, genitals retracting all over the room.

He spoke slowly, softly, rising up on tiptoe.

"We need to accept, to love *all* of Jesus, his body, his manhood. Look, what I'm saying here is that it's important we not be afraid to ponder the question of humanity and divinity. Are we bodies with a spirit or *spiritual beings* with bodies? And can we not see our bodies, the desires that course through us, as sacred? I think there's something we can uncover when we meditate on Jesus as God become man, God as flesh." He held up the cross. "Here is God as flesh. He gave His only begotten son. Who are we? Can we accept the sanctity of our bodies, our own desires, even our imperfections?"

"Are you saying we're like Jesus?" Kevin asked.

"Are you of God?"

"I guess . . ."

"Well, I purport that you certainly are. You are, Mr. McKenzie."

"But I'm not the Son of God."

"Not *the* Son, but *a* son. With all our imperfections, with this wonderful physical body of ours"—he touched his chest, his stomach—"I think we must recognize the ways in which we are divine." He brought the Corpus to the side of his face, to his cheek, in a delicate and shocking gesture. "Look at the ways in which this radical, wonderful teacher, was *human*. Like us. Bring him close to you."

If I was beginning to experience the Church as a dark and oppressive wall of silence, an impenetrable cultural monolith (which I did, I do), then here was a chink of light in the wall. A man who dared to talk of the body, of desire. I loved the way he was trying, it seemed, to work out his own thoughts and ideas in front of us. Things, I imagined, he was in conflict, in doubt, about. He trusted us with that, wanted us to think and query. His questions touched

off in me the ache of my own unanswerables, a veiled remembrance
of all the unspeakable things colliding deep in my own heart. A
few times, I actually went home after school and started a note to
him. *Brother Tom, could we talk . . . ?*

But my, *the,* wall of silence stood too solid and terrible between
us. How could I find the words that might leap over, go through,
that cultural wall? I couldn't. Even if I did find words, I knew
they'd never have risen to my throat. The things in me were too
terrible, I thought, too buried, for language.

If I'd ever found the voice, the courage, what might I have described to my freshman theology teacher? Could I have told him
about the man who entered my life? How I hated him? *And listen,
Brother, it's not just that. It's also that I think I love men. Boys. I dream
of them. I think maybe that's the way I was made. That's my imperfection.
Now do you still think me divine? I'm torn down the middle. I want to be
of you, I think, but I cannot. I went back, you see, again and again. Up
to the mountains, inside a barn, inside a sleeping bag. And it was wonderful and terrible and I am ruined. And I will do nothing in this life but
shame my father, my family. Shame this holy school of men. I must get out
of this skin, out of this wretched life.*

18

WHEN IT ARRIVED, at an unexpected moment, I experienced the news as both shocking and inevitable.

They wanted him in jail.

I heard it at a drive-in movie with John, my sister's seventeen-year-old boyfriend. It was nearly winter; I'd made it through three months of the Jesuits. It was a rerun, a film with Peter Fonda and we'd come because we'd heard about a scene with a nude girl on a motorcycle. John (who'd attended and loved St. Malo) was at the wheel and as we stared up through his dirty windshield and munched our popcorn he said, ever so casually,

"You remember that guy from Malo? Bob?"

I kept my eyes on the giant screen. "What? Who?"

"Bob? He did some weird shit. Stole some stuff. He's going to go to jail."

My bowels squirmed. "Wow, really?"

"He messed around with boys."

"Gross," I managed to say.

"He's in deep shit."

Silence. Peter Fonda, thirty feet tall.

"He ever do anything to you?" John asked.

"No. No." My heart had taken off, was racing.

"Listen, Father G. wanted me to ask. If anything . . . like that . . . ever happened to you, you could talk to him and well . . . they'll take care of it. Of him." I focused on keeping my face blank as my being went into spasm. I shrugged my shoulders, shook my head. It was all so twisted. Why was John asking me this? Why was he asking on behalf of an archdiocesan priest? What did John know, what did Father G. know? Who were *they*? Why do they think I'd know something? Mercifully, John let it drop, didn't bring it up again.

I was sleepless that night. And the next.

I had always sensed that trouble awaited Bob, that the Law would come down on him. And the very thought of it, of him being dragged into a public mess, a court of law, caused my lungs to contract in terror. *Catholic Schoolboy Molested by Camp Counselor.* That headline would be the end of my life. I'd drown along with him. After hearing the news from John, I awaited in dread a legal-looking letter, a summons, a terrible phone call forcing me to go somewhere and spill the shameful beans. But I heard nothing.

It had been nearly a year since I'd seen Bob standing in his dark suit at the altar. Every day, every month that went by without hearing anything from him made me feel the relief of being further and further away from the dirty picture. I'd vowed after that sad wedding to never, ever, have anything to do with him again. It was a solemn, self-preserving promise.

But after that night at the movies with John, an odd and powerful idea began to take hold of me: *I must see him, face to face.* The sense that, no matter the danger, I had to confront him before he vanished into jail, would not leave me alone. It became an obsession. This thing grew within me, this beastly, crazy hope that the way to absolution, the path to release, was to look him in the eye and denounce everything that had ever passed between us.

My braces were off, my voice had dropped, and my suit size had changed. I could speak to him now with some authority, couldn't I? I could tell him a thing or two and wipe the slate clean. Then it'd be all over. I'd go on with my real life, I'd have a shot at being a good person. This would be my chance at becoming a man, a father, a citizen.

One Friday night, some weeks later, my obsession forced me to make a move. I slipped the car keys from their hook in the hall.

Dad was gone, Mom was asleep on the couch in front of the TV, exhausted from work. I took Daisy, her yellow VW Bug, without permission, without a license. I was fifteen, too young to drive legally, but I'd learned well from him just how to do it. How to sneak, how to use a clutch. I started the engine and headed west. If I found him, I thought, *then* I could forget him. Forget the whole damn thing.

I shifted to fourth, released the clutch, and held steady at sixty miles an hour. Daisy strained to keep up with the mammoth Blazers and Chevy pickups climbing past us along the Denver–Boulder freeway. I kept patting the dash. I wanted to thank Daisy the car for its effort, her loyal company. Daisy was the only one in the world who knew where I was, which way I was headed.

Mom's Chanel knockoff was embedded in the plastic of the bucket seat. Every time I moved my legs a wave of perfume wafted up like a girly-ghost, following, watching me break the law, make a fool of myself. Again. I opened the window a crack and sucked in the night air.

You're doing this because you're weak, a voice said. *No, Mart, because you're strong,* said another.

The ashtray was open, stuffed with lipstick and toothpicks and floss. The instruments of Mom's passion—dental hygiene. I imagined her cleaning her mouth, painting her lips as she sped down Speer Boulevard each morning to her new job. A woman possessed to save what teeth she had left, to be on time for the job that would buy her what she wanted most—a divorce.

I rolled the window down so the cold wind tore across my face; the half-formed fragments of what I might say when, if, I found him, whipped through my brain.

Long time no see . . . have you finished the house?
How many other boys did you . . . ?
I got my braces off.
Goodbye . . .

The rush of air screeched through the vents and the frayed rubber lining of Daisy's door. It sounded as if the world was screaming: *What the fuck are you doing?* I didn't know what I'd say to him. I'd stolen the car. This was a mess. Here I was again, my body flying off somewhere I didn't mean for it to go. That alone place where you make it up as you go along, where desperate need becomes the mother of sinful invention. Panic rose from my stomach and clawed at the back of my throat. It didn't want me to breathe.

I leaned forward and took great gulps of air. I recognized this— the adrenaline. The anticipation, so much like the sex, like the stuff that happened with him and me out in the secret zone, out at the edge of the world where not a soul knew where we were. It was the insane thrill of a hidden life, of sneaking off and cheating on the world to which I'd vowed, again and again, to belong. If I were normal I'd be on my way to the Friday night Regis–Mullen basketball game. I'd be cheering with the others, raising my fist, wanting the Jesuits to cream the Christian Brothers.

Instead I was stealing away, like I had so many times during the affair. *Affair?* Christ . . . is that the right word? The criminal affair. The love affair. Is it even possible for a kid to have an affair? It implies choice in the matter. *Yeah, well, that's me. I chose, didn't I? Again and again.*

I hugged close to the solid white line that ran along the shoulder of the right lane. Smooth and easy, holding to the speed limit. Everything by the book. Headlights kept rushing up from behind and blazing into the rearview mirror, lighting me up. They'd press close, then scoot into the left lane to pass. I kept thinking that the next pair of lights would go red, start blinking, pull me over and ask questions. Sometimes, as they zoomed by, I could make out the shape of a face, a phantom head floating by, someone with a license, the right, a good place to go.

I shifted to third so Daisy could climb the long hill outside of Boulder. The pitch of her engine rose as I put the pedal to the floor. A van roared past, its headlights blinding. I caught sight of my face in the mirror, the red, raging zits covering my chin. I reached up and pinched at one.

I crested the hill and the lights of Boulder came into view. In the distance, the windows of the two tallest buildings, the university dorms, were ablaze with a busy student body. I rubbed my chin again, wiped the blood on my jeans. I didn't want him to see me like this, livid chin, poison coming out. From here, I figured, it was less than an hour to his place. I thought of pulling into the overlook, turning around at the next exit, but I didn't. My foot stayed on the gas.

The traffic in Boulder wasn't bad. I drove slowly, not sure but trusting that I'd recall which way to go. I'd nearly reached the north end of town when, as soon as I saw it, I remembered it was after the Dairy Queen, a good mile after the last light on Twenty-eighth Street, that I should turn and climb west into the canyon.

Before long, the walls of rock grew higher and the road was deserted. The moon was out and gibbous, and I caught glimpses below of the bright white water where the creek grew narrow enough to make rapids. The VW fought its way around the sharp curves, the headlights casting eerie shadows along the cliffs. I honked the horn as I drove through a tight overhang. Bob had always done that at this very spot, but the bleep of Daisy was nothing to the blast I remembered from the truck. Another mile or so and I spotted the yellow sign urging you to climb to higher ground in case of heavy rain. With it came the memory of the night Bob shot the deer. An age ago, it seemed.

The canyon walls widened and gave way to the clearing where houses began to appear. I passed the shop with the neat, suburban-looking lawn and the sign that said: *Cider, Beef Jerky, Antiques Here!* My heart sped up. The idea that he could be close—if he was home, if he wasn't already arrested—frightened me.

I spotted his VW in the gravel driveway—an older, paler model of Daisy. The truck was nowhere in sight. Other than a light in the kitchen window, the house looked dark. I couldn't bring myself to stop the car. I drove on, climbing up the canyon toward Nederland, realizing I was looking everywhere for cops. What if he was being watched? What if some authority saw me? I might be questioned, dragged into it.

I pulled over, yanked the wheel, turned around, and within moments was parked in his drive. My body had taken over. My head was full of thunder but I could hear my feet crunch through the gravel and up to the doorstep. I looked on as my fist rose and knocked.

And he was there. Standing tall and quiet, silhouetted in the soft light of the kitchen. He didn't have his glasses on. His eyes looked puffy and tired. And like a performer who'd been a wreck in the wings but knew just what to do upon entrance, my voice rolled out low and steady.

"Hello, Bob."

He remained still, seemingly placid, and stared at me. For an awful moment I wondered if he'd actually forgotten. If I really was one among too many and he was rifling through the boy files in his brain.

"Long time," I said.

"Yeah," he agreed. And that one word, that single sound of his voice crawled across every synapse of my nervous system—head to toe—as if my body recalled in an instant everything that had ever passed between us. "Come in."

I followed him through the kitchen and into the dim light of the living room. There was the faint smell of fresh paint. He'd done a great deal of work in the months since I'd been there. Wires were hanging from an unfinished fixture on the ceiling and a wood door off its hinges was leaning against one wall. Otherwise, the house appeared finished.

"Place looks great," I said. "Nice carpet."

"Thanks."

He was wondering why I'd come, of course, wondering, perhaps, if I was one of the enemy. I could see it in his pathetic manner and I could feel the stupid smile I'd stuck on my face to reassure him. Why did I need to reassure *him?* Why did I care? He gestured for me to sit with him on the lip of a step that encircled the stone fireplace in the middle of the room, stones I'd helped carry and cement into place. He had on his usual Levis and white T-shirt. He folded his hands and let them droop between his knees. His eyes were lowered, looking, it appeared, toward his scuffed penny loafers, the dimes still there—tails right shoe, heads left.

"What is it?" he asked.

"Last time I sat here it was all plywood and sawdust," I said, digging the car keys into my palm. I could barely hear the gurgle of the creek behind the house, beyond the sliding glass doors that led out to the deck. Other than that it was perfectly quiet. The air was thick, somehow, with grief, with troubles. A place under siege. "I wanted to see you, I . . ."

I heard the cry of a baby. Bob raised his face toward the stairs that led up to the bedroom. The room where I'd slept and wakened with him many times. The bed with the skylight overhead.

"Karen, look who's here," he said.

She came down the steps slowly as though she was in pain. Perhaps from childbirth, perhaps from everything. She still had her long blond hair. It was tied in a ponytail. She'd gained a good deal of weight. She had a pink blanket in her arms, a tiny child inside.

She barely acknowledged me as I nodded, her freckled face stone cold, her jaw set, it seemed, for a fight. God only knew what crap she'd been through or was in the middle of and I'm sure she thought I was bringing more. She wanted to erase me, I'm sure, as much as I wanted to erase her. Those months that our lives overlapped were fraught with unspoken jealousies, confusion, and that awful, cold sex. We'd made a twisted triumvirate—a thirteen-year-old boy, a nineteen-year-old cowgirl, and Bob in the middle, spinning his web. I'd thought of her as so grown up then, an adult. Seeing her again—me nearing sixteen, her barely twenty-one—she seemed as helpless and young as the crying babe in her arms.

"I've got to get her a bottle," was all she said as she walked past us and out into the kitchen. I heard the fridge open, a pan going on the stove.

"So, what's up?" he asked.

I stared at the fireplace, at the mound of gray ash, searching for a line. He kept silent. Time passed.

"I wanted to see you . . ."

The little girl's crying had become loud. I could hear Karen cooing, humming high notes. It didn't seem to help.

"How are you doing with the Jesuits?" Bob asked.

"Oh, not too bad. Not great."

"You'll always do great."

"I wish we'd never met. I wish I'd never met you."

The baby's crying stopped. I imagined the bottle stuck in her little mouth.

"I'm sorry you feel that way," he said, tuning his baritone toward patience.

"I'm ashamed of every single thing that ever happened between us. I'm ashamed. That's what I wanted to say."

"OK."

"I'm not *that way*."

We sat in silence for a minute or two more, both of us staring into the black space, into the fire that wasn't there. And then, as if upon orders from above, we both stood. I put my head down, my hands into my front pockets, and without a word, he led the way out of the living room and straight to the kitchen door. I glimpsed the child perched on the counter, sucking at the bottle Karen held. Clueless blob of pink. Karen never looked my way. I never learned the child's name, only that it was a she. Bob stuck out his hand. I looked at it. God—the size of it, the chalky blisters. We shook. His grasp was firm and kind and in an instant I heard my feet on the gravel. The car door slammed and the engine was running and I worked the clutch as he had taught me, smooth and swift out onto the canyon road. I pointed Daisy downhill and tumbled past the antique shop and the silent homes, slid past the walls of rock that had been carved by this creek for a million patient years. I moved east, leaving him behind, and I waited.

I waited for a sense to rise within that I'd done it. Just the right thing. I'd said it and now it was over. For good. I'd never see him again. I was clean and forever different. I'd said my piece and I could go on and be a man now. I waited until the cliffs of the canyon fell away and the lights of the city came into view. I waited for tears of relief or a wave of peace. I'd earned it. I'd come all this way. I waited as I drove through Boulder back to Denver, as I coasted silently into the driveway and placed the keys back on their hook. I waited but nothing came, not one thing. Numb. Not tears nor peace. No sense that I was better for having faced it down, figured it out, or received absolution. Not then and not by the time I woke the next morning and smeared Clearasil on my livid chin. Not by the time, some months later, I heard word he was to be sent to the state prison.

19

I started a collection of orange and yellow capsules. Shiny little pills. I'd begun stealing them around Christmas, one or two at a time, from bottles in the medicine cabinet in our main john. One color had to do, I think, with my sister's acne and the other, I believe, my mother's sleep. I wasn't terribly scientific in choosing my poison. I figured enough of anything swallowed with a tall glass of milk would do the trick.

I placed them in a sandwich baggie that I kept hidden at the back of my sock drawer, next to *The Last of the Mohicans.* As it grew, my secret stash looked like a collection of sweets, a bunch of little jelly beans I might have given up for Lent and was squirreling away until I could gobble them all on Easter morning. But I wasn't waiting for the Resurrection. I was waiting for the courage.

As I gathered the capsules, I tried to gather my will. If there's one damn thing I could be brave about, manly about, let it be this. That I can take the fucking pills. That I can take the step that will get me out. Out of this body. Out of this place.

Mornings before school as I reached for socks and a pair of Hanes, I'd glance into the way back of the drawer near the book, next to the stupid spare jock (the one I needed as backup for McPhee) and check on the pills. The candy-colored sight of them was a comfort. Secret exit, private plan.

Soon, I'd think, eyeing the little baggie. *Soon.*

20

ONE FRIDAY AFTERNOON after I got off the bus from Regis I came around the corner of our street and was surprised to see Daisy in the driveway. Mom must have got off work early, I figured. I opened the front door and headed to the kitchen for a snack. Mom was alone at the kitchen table, filing her nails. She didn't look up when I walked in. Her chin was on her chest; her eyes focused on her fingers. What I could read of her face said stony. Something was up. Mom could go from sunshine to frost in an instant, especially since she'd gone back to work. It was a matter of gauging and adjusting.

"You're home early," I said.

"The judge had a meeting."

Her consonants were clipped.

"T.G.I.F.," I said.

The sound of her nail file filled the air, a rhythmic *cha-cha-cha*.

Her focus was fierce, her filing almost savage, like something you might catch on *Wild Kingdom*. "Grooming Habits of Suburban Mammals." For a moment I watched the curls of her frosted hair jiggle with the motion of her task.

I opened the fridge and grabbed Wonderbread and ketchup to make a blood sandwich, then took a seat two away from Mom. I noticed her scuffed high heels on the floor near the chair where her feet were delicately crossed. There were holes worn in her hose at each reddened heel. Her pink polishes and bottles of cuticle strengthener were lined up in front of her, along the edge of the Formica table, like a battalion of toy soldiers.

A vague smell of the sea swam through our landlocked air. I glanced at the stove, where a cookie sheet was lined with thawing fish sticks. I squirted some ketchup on my bread and tried for conversation.

"Mrs. Lachada was out in her yard. Almost every time she sees me she calls out a spelling word. Today it was *rhododendron*. I wonder if she has any idea whether I'm spelling them correctly."

Scrape, scrape. *Cha-cha-cha.*

The house was quiet. I knew my older sister was working at the pizza place, and I figured my two younger siblings were out playing. I took a few more bites of bread, stole quick glances toward Mom. Something was definitely on her mind. I wondered what. Maybe she was just exhausted. My eyes landed on her blouse. It was pale green and had ruffles up the middle, ending at a tight collar around her throat. It looked like a secular version of what a nun or a priest might wear, something Roman that's meant to cancel everything from the neck down, now and forever amen.

She'd pieced together these work outfits from hand-me-downs she'd received from a close friend. Her *feminist friend,* my dad had once said. *Gloria Steinem.* He whispered *feminist* as if it were the curse of the modern world. As if, I gathered, it was the cause of divorce.

The news of my parents' separation came as a surprise to us kids. They weren't fighters, not that we knew of, anyway. I don't remember ever hearing my dad raise his voice but for one time, when a car sped down the street near where we kids were walking and he howled with anger. There had been a recent afternoon, before Dad moved out, before they sprang the news on us, when I'd overheard part of a conversation and got an inkling that all was not well. I'd come in from riding my bike and was on my way to the bathroom when I heard my mother say, "But I just don't know how to live . . ."

The sound was awful, stopped me cold. There was a terrible silence. "It's just something I have to do," she whispered.

Then my father said, not unkindly, "That's just nonsense."

They noticed me then, and abruptly stopped their conversation. I nodded and walked to the john. It was just a few weeks later that they gathered us in the den. Mom was very put together, sitting up straight. "It's the way it has to be for now," she said to us. "I don't know how else to put it." Dad sat alone in the big chair, not saying a word. His hand, now and again, passing over his anguished face.

"Oh, damn," Mom muttered.

"What?" I asked.

"Broke one."

We caught eyes for an instant. Icy blue. "Some sandwich?" I asked.

"No thanks."

Cha-cha-cha.

There was a broach jiggling on her chest, stuck there like some badge. It was a gold turtle with its head barely peeking out of the shell. It looked as if it had crawled to her right breast where it could rest for a time before moving on or until it found the courage to roar—like Helen Reddy. I couldn't say exactly why but the lonely turtle depressed me. I guess I thought of it as Mom—a determined creature, barely hanging on, sticking her neck out after eighteen years of marriage. There were very few relatives in either branch of the family who were warm to her at present. Not now, not after she dared to come out of her shell, break the rules. Some, like my paternal grandmother, made it pretty clear she'd never speak to her again.

Mom looked up at me a moment. "How's school?"

I shrugged. She knew I wasn't happy at Regis.

She nodded and tried, it seemed, but failed to flash a smile. The crow's-feet around her eyes (which had been known to light up a dazzling smile) looked cracked under the cake of her makeup, old

tributaries fanning out from a dry lake. Her red lipstick was lus-
terless too, after a long day, a long week at city hall playing clerk
to a judge. Forty-three had landed hard on Mom. She'd defied the
tribe and the arrows were flying from every direction.

As I chewed my last bites, I fingered the mail on the table in
front of me. It was piled next to dad's old ashtray. The one with
the Moran family coat of arms shellacked to the bottom. *Lucent in
Tenebris,* "To shine in darkness." There were the usual bills—
Mountain Bell and Public Service, and the colorful coupons for sav-
ings at King Soopers. Next to the pile nearer to Mom was the new
copy of *Time.* A familiar sight with its red borders and shiny paper.
It was Dad's favorite magazine. "Their journalism is solid, the way
it should be: tight, bright, light, and right," he'd always said. In
black ink in the upper corner it said: 75¢ and the mailing label was
glued there with Dad's name on it. That is, my name with a *Sr.* attached, almost like my own derivation, I used to think, from the
Irish. I liked seeing Dad's name in typeface. It reminded me of
his bylines in the *News.* Made me think of Dad the journalist who,
despite the tense atmosphere and the harsh critics, was writing rea-
soned and objective articles about the explosive situation concern-
ing the recent court-ordered busing. It was strange seeing his name
with our address, which was no longer his address. "Look after the
lawn, will ya? Soak the burnt spots." Those were his final words to
me on the day we stuck his suit-rack and some shirts into the trunk
of the Chevy and he left for his one-room bachelor pad. A little studio with no yard. No mowing or clipping or watering. Or children.
None of the things that seemed to sustain him.

I ran my fingers across Dad's name, thinking how I'd make a
stack of his mail again and bring it to him on Sunday. My fingers came to rest on the grave face of the serviceman who'd made
the cover of *Time.* His chest was full of medals—a Vietnam hero of
some sort, I guessed. He had a black mustache and the strangest
look, I thought, as if he'd had the wind knocked out of him. His
eyes peered directly out from the photo, straight at you—a pained

but stoic soldier. His nametag said: Sergeant Matlovich. He had a blue cap on, exactly like the one I wore my first year in Scouts. He looked worried, somehow. Then I saw the unbelievable words written there below his somber face.

"I Am a Homosexual."

Right on our kitchen table, in front of Mom, in front of me, that ten-letter, five-syllable, Greek word.

Cha-cha-cha.

She must have seen it, too, when she got home. That's it. She must have.

Was she looking at me looking at it?

"I Am a Homosexual." The Gay Drive for Acceptance.

I had actually picked it up. I was holding the magazine.

I flung it back down on the table and covered the sergeant's face and that word with the phone bill, then went to the sink to rinse my dish, wash my hands. I held on to the edge of the sink for a moment, then turned on the hot water. My face burned. What a horrible lapse. How could they put such a thing on the cover, knowing that it would arrive on kitchen tables all across America? The walls and the floor seemed to vibrate, move inward. There was too much pressure, the kitchen way too small for a mother and a son and that magazine. I stuck my bloody plate under the faucet. The reddened water smelled sweet as it swirled around the drain. Why, I wondered, did I feel so humiliated? Implicated? *It's a magazine; it's not you.*

I'm not that way, I'd told him. I'd gone all the way up there and told him. I'd put it away, vowed: *Never again.* And there'd be girls in my head from now on.

As I scrubbed the dish clean, a crazy notion came into my head, sent waves of shame through my chest: *There are pictures, lists, inside that magazine and mine is there among them, next to Bob's. Soldier Bob.* It was absurd, it was impossible, but it felt like *Time* was a bomb ticking on the table and if it went off everything would blow into the open. All I'd done with him. All I am.

I rinsed out a glass and drank some water.

Out the window I caught sight of my little brother in his wide-ribbed corduroys and plaid shirt. He was with my little sister, who was still in her CK uniform. They zoomed past the front yard on their bikes. My head felt as if it was shrinking. Shrinking like the room, the walls closing in. I picked up the cloth to dry my dish.

An orange sun was sinking toward the Rockies. It blazed through the shutters, throwing vertical shafts of shadow and light across the turquoise-colored walls. Dusk would descend soon but it was still broad daylight in California and Hawaii and on the other side of the globe. They'd be receiving *Time* in those places too. Reading all about it. People everywhere would be talking about the sergeant and the fags. What made Matlovich *do* such a thing? I caught a ghostly reflection of my face in the window. I could see the whites of my eyes, the pimples on my chin lit up by the sun.

I rinsed the last bit of soap down the drain, turned off the water, and draped the dishtowel over the faucet. I went to pick up my pack and get to my room. That's when the scraping stopped.

"I can tell you one thing." So, it was her voice she'd been sharpening all this time. I turned and watched as she unscrewed the lid of her pink polish. "I think I'd rather find out one of my children was dead than homosexual."

The words—*dead, homosexual*—hung in the air like unpinned grenades. And it was the second one, coming all the way from the Greek to the front of *Time* and out my mother's tired, red lips, that crashed across our kitchen floor—a five-syllable blast, a crisp, clinical strike.

I stood absolutely still in the silent aftermath. My brain could not produce a response as I watched Mom dip the tiny brush into the bottle. The acrid chemicals wafted through the air as if it was Revlon who'd manufactured the bomb, won the battle.

Sick to my stomach, I moved to the stairs, past Mom's bowed head. She was busy with the delicate painting of her digits. I glanced from her jiggling, frosted hair to the sergeant's obscured face and felt revulsion. Hatred. For him. I hated what he was and that he'd done this in my kitchen; he'd done it in front of the whole world. He'd told.

I went to the basement, down to my room, and shut the door.

21

IT WAS A particularly sunny day in March and Brother Tom was deep into the beatitudes. He loved them. He said they were, in fact, great "attitudes of being." He held his well-worn Bible in his right hand and reached out over our heads with his left. "It's always in Christ's own words that we find the gems, the real guidance. The Prophet." He pointed now to the page. "Listen:

> *How blest are the poor in spirit: the reign of God is theirs,*
> *Blest too are the sorrowing; they shall be consoled,*
> *Blessed are the meek, for they shall inherit the earth."*

We paused there for a good while for a lengthy discussion on the meek. "It's our job, our calling, to be aware, to come to the aid of those less fortunate." He paced in front of us, caressing the text —Gospel according to Matthew. "And it's you, you young guys, who have to be the radicals now. Radical and brave enough to see through the lies of modern society and hang on to these Christian ideals. The real human ideals. The old farts get caught up and tired and forget sometimes what's true and—"

He was stopped by a knock. A small white note in the hand of a student on office duty was carried into the classroom. The boy passed the piece of paper to Brother Tom. This caused a stir. It happened rarely and usually meant death (as when John O'Neill's grandpa died and a note came asking for him to go home) or, more often, punishment. A summons from Father Fitz.

Brother Tom, I could see it, was trying to be casual as he looked up and over to me. He nodded and, oddly, used my Christian name. My heart did a flip-flop. I got up, my feet on automatic. *What did they have on me?* I'd been late to school twice but that was due to snow, a stuck bus. Fitz had caught me once with my shirttail out, reprimanded me, but I had no demerits so far as I knew. No points stacking up toward JUG.

"Marty, head to the dean's office." He held out the paper. "I'm sure it's nothing."

The room was silent as I took the note. I didn't meet his or anyone's eyes. I walked toward the door.

"Mr. Moran, tell Father Fitzpatrick we want you back quick, cause we're into the good stuff, Matthew: Chapter Five. Tell him: 'Blest are they who show mercy, mercy shall be theirs.'"

"I can't say that."

"I know. Just trying to get a grin out of you. Haven't seen your teeth for weeks."

He rubbed his little mustache and smiled.

I walked down the empty hall past the battered lockers, the portrait of Saint Ignatius Loyola, the solemn photos of matriculated men. His office was the last door on the left, next to the west entrance. I approached and waited just outside the door. I could hear his labored breathing. He was seated at his desk, his big nose bent toward an open manila folder. Sitting on each of his black shoulders was a sprinkling of dandruff. He always had it, as though daily he'd walked here through his own private snowstorm. I glanced at the small chalkboard stuck on the wall above his head. J. U. G. was written in chalk at the top with five or six names scribbled below. Mine was not among them. Not yet, anyway. Dangling from a nail in the upper-right corner of the board, like fat, swollen hands, was a pair of brown boxing gloves.

"Shut the door, take a seat," he said without looking up.

The door creaked like everything in these haunted halls, then clicked to a close. I sank into the middle of three straight-backed wooden chairs. I'd not sat in here before. Not much to look at. His old desk and a file cabinet. A couple of reference books were propped near his phone. On the binding of the largest was inscribed *Libreria Editrice Vaticana*. He remained quiet; flipping through what I guessed must be my life. My heart hammered to think what he might know. That what was written in there could be the truth. He sucked in breath, blew it out. I smelled the alcohol. Even we freshmen had heard talk of his problem. He was the first person I'd ever known to whom the world referred, in a gentle and pitying way, as alcoholic.

"Mr. Moran?" His head was still buried in my folder.

"Yes, Father." I studied the blood vessels, like delicate veins of a leaf, crisscrossing his Jimmy Durante nose and spilling out across his sagging cheeks. He lifted his head, folded his hands, and focused his bloodshot eyes on me.

"In the space of one term, you've gone from near the top of your class to very near the bottom. Did you know that?"

"No, Father."

"Well, you have." He pushed his glasses to the top of his nose. I tried to spy what was on the page in front of him, but all I could make out was a column of scribbles and the usual embossed *A.M.D.G.* (*Ad Majorem Dei Gloriam*—to the greater glory of God) at the bottom of the stationery. "What's going on with you?"

"Nothing, Father." I glanced up at the portrait of Paul VI.

"Look," he said, taking off his glasses, "going from sixth in your class to one-fifty-sixth is not nothing. You are known as a disciplined student." His eyes were rheumy. They blinked at me. "Do you see why I've called you here?"

"I think so, Father. You want me to do better."

"Yes, that's true." He spread his elbows along the desk and leaned forward. "And I want to know what's weighing on you." I had thought this seat was for punishment only. I was totally thrown in the face of concern. "Are things all right at home?"

I shrugged.

"I know about your parents' separation, Marty. I'm sorry."

His use—first time ever—of my Christian name, his "sorry," caused my throat to close. I saw that he meant to be kind, and I craved the kindness, but I was terrified to let anything leak out. A leak might lead to a flood and I could feel, looking right at him, how every door of me was slammed shut. He was reaching out, and I sat there, numb. A blank.

He took out a white handkerchief and blew his nose. Then he stood and, with great, wheezing effort, tucked my life away into the bottom drawer between McLaughlin and Moroni.

"Have you thought about joining a team?" he asked as he closed the drawer. "Soccer or swimming? Something physical, outdoors, something to do with other boys. What do you think?"

I stared at the floor, at the soiled cracks between the ancient tiles. I had not one clue how to speak from my hiding place, how to get out from under my own JUG. "Maybe soccer," I whispered.

He sat back down.

"Good. You think about it. Good for you to get out and do something physical with the other boys. You'd better get back to class."

"Yes, Father." I stood and walked to the door.

"Marty?" His baggy face was all goodness. "If you'd like to talk . . . I'm here."

"OK."

"Get those grades up."

"Yes, Father."

I walked back into the empty hall full of male eyes, with the firm knowledge that I was falling, like my grades, to the bottom of the barrel. I couldn't keep it up, the act, the will. I thought of heading out the door, walking west toward the hills, but, instead, stepped into the boys' room, into one of the stalls. I locked the door and sat on the toilet.

I hung my head between my knees and wrapped my arms around my ribs as if to hold them all together. I felt like a little kid who'd

fallen on the playground, banged my head, doing OK ... until the
adult reaches out and offers sympathy. It's then that the tears come,
that the sorrow and unfairness of harm washes through you. The
want of pity. I hated, but couldn't stop, the tears leaking. And hated
that I didn't understand my sorrow, couldn't pull it apart, look at
it. All I knew was that there was this immense ache at the center
of me. I didn't really know how much I was trying to bury. How
much I was working to hide the attractions I felt, to hide the places
I'd been and the hunger left in the wake of what happened. I don't
think I knew how much I missed him. I'd banished him. They'd
banished him. He'd been my friend, for Christ's sake. My fucked-
up love. He knew my secret. He knew my body. This not divine
body that would never hold a good Catholic man. A citizen, a husband, a father. Despicable.

I looked up at the rusty pipes and down at the filthy floor, whispering over and over: *You've got to get out of here. You've got to get out
of here.*

On the bus ride home I held my list of irregular French verbs. *Va-
loir: je vaux, tu vaux, il vaut* ... I couldn't concentrate. I glanced up
to see the streets thicken with people and construction as we approached downtown Denver. Suits and ties, secretaries and shop-
pers everywhere. I watched one man in a pinstripe suit with shiny
cowboy boots rifle through his briefcase as, on the same corner, a
group of Native Americans (Ute? Arapaho? Cheyenne?) huddled
together on a pile of parkas in the shade of an old building. They
passed around a paper bag. I'd see them there most every day as the
bus stopped at the patch of red lights on the West End of town.
They looked so lost, next to all the Plexiglas and steel. Visible but
hidden beside the busy march of foot traffic, the honking horns. It
was as if they were camped there in defiance while crazy, anxious
white men built a city higher and higher around them.

The bus came to a halt at a congested corner not far from Six-
teenth Street. I leaned my head against the window and watched

a bricklayer at work. He stood alone at the corner, constructing, brick by red brick, a wall, which now stood about hip height to him. He was fast. He'd place a brick, swipe his trowel along the wet cement, line it up, smooth it out, pick up another one, and repeat. His arms were thick and sunburned. Globs of cement landed near his feet and on his yellow boots. His blue jeans were worn to white, covered with dust. He had a brown beard and, above it, ruddy cheeks and forehead wet with sweat.

As I watched him, a wave of anguish moved through me, a force that seemed to scoop away whatever will I had left. Why in the world was he making a wall? Doesn't he know it will come to nothing? Why all this futile activity? Everywhere I looked was movement. Movement infused with some purpose, some essential ingredient gone missing in me.

Look at it, I thought, gazing up the busy street. This life is nothing but a lie. Couldn't we all just agree to stop, for God's sake? Lie down and stop? *Remember you are dust,* the priest says, *and to dust you shall return.* There's the truth. I looked back toward the bricklayer. His lips were puckered. Actually puckered, and I could see that he was whistling. Whistling while he shoved another brick into place, while all the world, including me, moved past. He has a wife, I supposed. And kids. Is it for them that he's whistling? Working? What possible reason? I couldn't know and didn't want to. All I knew was that would never be me. I'd never make it that far.

22

I GOT OFF the bus and walked toward home. I could hear the song from our corner.

Will I ever find the boy in my mind, the one who is my ideal?

The voice was spilling out onto the street. Mom was home early, had one of her favorite records going.

Will I recognize the light in his eyes, that no other eyes reveal?

She sat in the big chair in the living room, a bag of Hershey's Kisses in her lap, head thrown back, high heels kicked off. She'd made it through another day at the office. I dropped my knapsack and landed on the couch. She sat up and took me in. She was surprised, I knew, to see me stop so close. I'd been avoiding her. We hadn't talked much since I'd kicked a hole in the wall at the end of the hallway two weeks before, just after I'd called her a bitch.

Or will I pass him by and never even know...

"How are you?" she asked, picking up her chocolates. I could hear it in her voice, the tone, like I was a box of explosives labeled: *Fragile, handle with care.* It wasn't just the hole in the wall. I'd been behaving horribly. Really mean to my younger siblings and outright hostile to my older sister. Recently Mom had dragged all of us in for a few sessions of family counseling to discuss the divorce, the tension in the house. She was trying, God knows.

"That song...again," I said.

"I love it." She popped another chocolate in her mouth.

"Langford?"

She nodded and plucked another from the bag. With her pol-

ished nails she tugged at the little white ribbon—*kisses kisses kisses*
—then peeled back the foil.

"Do you want one?" she asked.

"No, thanks. Is she still alive?"

"Who?"

"Frances Langford."

"I think so."

"She sounds so sad."

"I love her voice."

"I think I need to go to public school."

"Really?"

"Yes."

"Well, with all the busing, the problems, I don't think that's an
option. Have you mentioned this to your father?"

"Doesn't matter."

"Well, let's give it some time, some thought."

I stood, went downstairs to my room, and shut the door.

There were enough of them now. I counted twenty-something
pills, piled up and waiting. I stared.

*Wait till summer. It's not so far away. Go to the mountains and do it
there, just disappear.*

No, chickenshit. Get it over with. Do it now!

I sat on my bed and struggled to devise a plan. The first thing
that occurred to me was that I was scheduled to give a reading at
the All-City Youth Mass a week from Sunday at 7:00 PM. Ten days
away. I'd promised, was honored, to do it. (I'd become very involved
with the Catholic Youth Organization, one of my extracurricular
attempts to shine; to find Jesus.) Wouldn't that be fittingly dramatic, I thought. Stand before them, the way you like to do, articulate and capable and nice. Greet all your CYO friends. Then go
home and die. That's the bargain. Ten days, no matter what. I put
the pills back in their hiding spot.

The next evening, I altered the bargain slightly. It seemed to me
that I should at least make a final effort to tell someone what I was

planning. Maybe that would change things. At least give it a try, I thought. There was a girl whom I adored. She played guitar at Mass, had the kindest demeanor, the most beautiful soprano voice. For some reason, she was the friend I thought of. *Nancy,* I could hear myself whispering to her, *I think I have to kill myself.* I saw her that weekend in the community room, doughnuts and juice after church. I sat with her and it was *hellos* and *how are yous?* I tried to tell her with my eyes. Didn't work.

The following week, I remember, I took long walks at night around the neighborhood. Just moving in a depressive trance. A couple of times I stole the car (still had no license) and drove aimlessly around town, lugging with me this ache to connect, this unbearable sorrow. I remember driving the VW in circles under the ghostly street lamps in the parking lot of the bowling-swimming center—Celebrity Lanes—stopping the car in the back by the trash containers to scream at the world, to masturbate. To find reprieve. But nothing seemed to work, to give relief. I was parked there once, done jerking off, my head in my hands, when a Glendale policeman drove up. "What are you doing here? Are you driving?"

"No . . . no. I'm just waiting for my dad."

He looked at me a long while.

"Why are you sitting in the driver's seat?

I shrugged.

He finally drove off. I waited a long time before I started the car and made my way home, heart pounding.

When that Sunday arrived, I repeated what I thought was my final bargain: *I'll go to Mass, I'll do the first reading, I'll see everyone, and then I'll come home. I'll wait for my sister to get in from her job at Angie's Pizza Parlor. I'll try to speak to her. If she stops and talks, I'll take it as a sign. I'll tell her what I'm planning.*

I waited at the kitchen table after Mass.

It was well past eleven when Chris flew in the front door, smelling of grease and pizza dough.

"Hey," I said. I stood and moved toward her, toward the hall, which led to the bedrooms and bathroom.

"Hey," she said, dropping her backpack and keys on the bench. Her face was stern, her long blond hair a mess. She went straight to the bathroom and shut the door. That was it. A two-second encounter. She was my last chance, my sign from God to go ahead with my plan, and she didn't even know it. I wanted her to ask me what I was doing up so late, sitting at the table. I wanted her to read my mind, but how could she? She had a job, she had a life, she was coping as best she could. So much fell to her as Mom went to work and Dad moved out—laundry, cooking, babysitting. She was already scheming her way out, saving every dime possible so she could find a place of her own. I didn't realize any of that then. All I felt as I watched her disappear into the john was that nothing would ever change. That I'd never be able to speak to anyone, really, about anything. Ever. It was too late. I'd never be able to correct what was wrong with me. There was no priest or parent or sister who could possibly hear this story, this shit. I had no choice now; I had to be brave enough to follow through.

It was nearing midnight. I decided to take one more walk. I moved past all the dark houses on our end of Glencoe, then around to Flamingo Street. I walked by George's old house; I hadn't seen him in months and months. He'd moved. The one time I did see him we'd smoked a joint and stared at the sky, talked of nothing. Never of Bob.

I walked up the street and sat on someone's grass. Across the street, in the vacant field near Cherry Creek, I could see the Four Mile House. George and I used to ride our bikes right by it. It was named for its location in relation to the center of downtown Denver. It was where, in the old days, carriages from St. Louis and other parts east stopped to freshen up horses and clothes before making an entrance into town. Now it was abandoned, the white paint peeling from its three fancy stories of slatted wood, tumbleweeds piled in the huge yard. It stood there like a giant Victorian ghost in the moonlight. I stared and wondered how many people had passed this way, by stagecoach. Through time.

I got up and moved under the hum of street lamps, past the quiet houses. I was in a stupor. I remember finding myself back on my own street and just throwing myself down onto the Newcomb's front lawn. I rolled back and forth, squeezing my rib cage as if to keep my body from flying apart. There was the smell of grass. There were my arms around my chest. I was rolling like a guy who'd been punched in the stomach in a barroom brawl. *Stop it. Stop it.* I remember telling myself: *You're out of control, losing your grip.* I kept my arms tight around myself as though staving off an explosion. I will be a bomb, I thought, of bone and blood, scattered, splattered against the street and the walls, a message written in red: *Remains of an unspeakable boy.*

I heard a horrendous noise, like a dog, an animal howling or dying and it scared me, made me leap to my feet. I looked around. Everything was quiet and I realized the sounds had come from me and I was afraid that someone had seen or heard. I hurried down the block, back to my house.

I opened the fridge, poured a tall glass of milk (milk!), and went to the basement, to the privacy of my bedroom. (My little brother had long since moved to his own room upstairs.) I sat on the bed and swallowed the pills. It was easier to do than I thought it would be. Once I'd decided, I didn't hesitate. Pouring the milk. Carrying the glass down the stairs without spilling. Taking the pills out of the baggie. Swallowing down the orange and yellow pile, two or three at a time.

I took off all my clothes and put on my red checkered robe and sat on the edge of my bed. And waited. I wrote part of a note saying goodbye, saying how I just couldn't bring myself to speak to anyone, that I was sorry, that I'd tried to be a good Christian. That I wished I loved myself. I didn't finish it. I just wanted the sleep, the rest, to come.

I woke with my head at the foot of the bed. My robe was flung open. I tried to close it, didn't want to be seen naked. But my arms didn't work, they were asleep. I scooted around and put my feet, my toes, onto the floor, the orange carpet. The color made me think of the pills and I was hit with the dread of remembering what I'd done. *Oh, shit. I'm going to die.*

I stumbled toward my desk. I didn't know why I was headed there, something to do with the telephone? An idea of calling for help? I reached toward the phone but, instead, swiped at my clock radio. It crashed onto the floor. It had those large numbers that flip and when the clock landed upside down they tumbled backward, scrambling the time. The numbers were stuck, unable to turn, and the clock wheezed and clicked as the digits tried to flip forward. I remember (the memories so sharp despite the medicated blur) feeling such regret that I might have broken it. I liked that clock. It had fake paper stuck to it that looked like wood. Matched my paneling. It had a radio tuned to a cool talk/jazz station. Big numbers, loud alarm. I broke it, damn. A flash of panic, of terrible sadness, shot through me. *I've done it.* I was staring at the upside-down digits, at the crumpled clock, and that's the last thing I remember before my face fell toward the bright orange carpet.

The next picture stuck in my head is of Mom trying to wake me, panicked: *What have you done?* she was asking. *Are you on drugs?* She was pushing up the sleeve of my robe, examining the veins on my arms. I understood at once that she was looking for needle marks, looking for signs that she was living with an addict. Feeling hurt and disappointed, I thought, *Ah jeez, lady, you're barking up the wrong tree.* I kept trying to close my robe, cover myself. I didn't want her to see me this way, my new patch of pubic hair.

I recall then that somehow I'd gotten upstairs. Time was warped —minutes were hours and hours seconds—but I was curled up in the big chair in the living room, vaguely aware that I'd gotten there on my own. My words were thick and slurred as I announced I wasn't going to school, that I felt very sick.

My mother was standing in the hall, angry, frantic. Getting ready for work. She made some calls. Doctor? Hospital? All was confusion, my sisters and brother gone off to school already. She grabbed her raincoat from the hall closet. I watched all this blurred flurry from the chair. Then, suddenly, my father was there. She must have called for him. She pulled her car keys from her bag. Then she went out the door. I understood that my dad was going to be here, stay home from work. I talked some nonsense to him about a bad flu. I got up, stumbled to the bathroom, and threw up.

I never went to a hospital, never had my stomach pumped. I don't know how they figured it wasn't serious enough to call 911. Maybe since I could sort of talk, because I began throwing up. I don't know. But, as much as that day was a haze, as foggy and thick as the hours were after I took the pills, I remember so clearly Dad standing in the hallway keeping an eye as I came and went, in and out of the john, to get sick. He stood motionless, clueless, the poor guy, hunched near the bathroom, next to the six-inch hole I'd kicked in the hallway wall. He had a cigarette. Swept his hand across his face, over his thinning hair.

"You OK, tiger?"

It was the only, the sweetest, thing he could think to ask this strange boy who'd done such a strange and violent thing. Next time I'd make a more serious attempt. Next time, in fact, I tried to put a .22 rifle to my head, the one Dad left behind when he moved out. Thank God I shot the thing through the paneling of my bedroom wall and the bullet went through the banister of the basement steps and ended up somewhere in the storeroom. But that would be later. Months later. For now there was only this: the two of us alone in a home that was no longer his and a father's ragged voice gently inquiring—

"You OK, tiger?"

I wiped my mouth with the back of my hand and nodded toward the man with the cigarette at the end of the hall. The man unable to approach, unable to ask his son what happened. And I was relieved he didn't, because I wouldn't have known where in the world to begin.

Book II

WAKING

I

HENRY AND I are living now across the street from a New York City public elementary school. We moved in this past winter, in the early days of the new millennium. Nineteen ninety-eight and ninety-nine had been boom years for us, good steady work, good steady life. I turned forty and, after nearly fifteen years together, we'd arrived at the courage and the down payment to become homeowners.

"Steps from the Cloisters," the *Times* real estate section had said. "A Cabrini Blvd. Junior 4." *Junior 4.* Somehow that sounded cozy and affordable (somehow, I remarked to Henry, it sounded gay) and just the thing for us. As it turned out, there was an ideal space for Henry's baby grand piano and a small guestroom off the kitchen. We made an offer on the spot.

During the week, students gather on the playground just opposite us before classes begin. Their chatter builds and rises to bounce against the surrounding apartment buildings. The kid noise mingles with the birdsong that drifts along our tree-lined boulevard. The symphony of it sneaks in bits and pieces through our window, across our bed . . . reveille.

Then a whistle blows. Away go the hula hoops and jump ropes. Away go the basketballs and screaming children. The obedient little bodies line up and disappear inside the old building, and everything (even the birds, it seems) goes silent. It's eight o'clock.

Sometime later, after coffee, a whistle blows again (it almost al-

ways takes me by surprise) and out the children spill like water released from a dam. Colored parkas, pleated skirts, and navy blue
pants splash across the tarmac. Watching them take to the slide and
swing from the jungle gym, screaming with terror and delight,
awakens in me a kind of joy. They land and jump and run to do it
all again. It's a dance wild enough, I think, to wake the dead.

I remembered someone telling me that a famous saint was en-
tombed inside the church that stands a few steps up our street.
Shortly after we'd moved in and finished unpacking boxes, I went
to investigate.

There was a buxom nun with a sturdy blue skirt and black veil
standing on the steps as I approached the side entrance of the
chapel. "I grew up in Denver, Colorado," I told her. "I lived not far
from the Mother Cabrini Shrine. I always thought she was buried
up there in the foothills."

"No, dear," she said. "They have the mountain, we have Mother."
She pointed toward the altar inside the church. Sure enough, there
was the holy corpse, encased in glass, laid out front and center, for
all to see. I was ready for a good bit of Catholic gore, like in Italy.
The head of Catherine of Siena, for example, which is as creepy and
desiccated as any monster out of Edgar Allan Poe. What I found,
though, was a small body covered with gray robes. Her hands were
folded delicately over her breast, rosary beads entwined in the fingers. Besides her hands, her face was the only visible flesh, and it
all looked decidedly waxy, very Madame Tussaud's. I stepped down
the hall into the Cabrini Gift Shop, where there are countless books
telling and retelling the story of Mother's struggles, of her great
work with poor immigrants and lost orphans. I asked the young
woman at the cash register, "So that's really and truly Saint Frances
Xavier Cabrini in there?"

"*Si, si,*" she said, continuing to nod as she counted and stacked
small blue pamphlets entitled: *How to Pray the Rosary.* I picked one
up, my head suddenly filled with the image of my grandmother

and great aunt Marion (both long dead now) sitting on the green couch in the den, fingering their black beads, saying their daily rosary. The pamphlet explained that Mondays and Thursdays are reserved for meditation on the Joyful Mysteries, Tuesdays and Fridays the Sorrowful Mysteries, Wednesdays and Saturdays the Glorious Mysteries, with Sundays being reserved for any and all mysteries depending on the season. Only fifty cents a pamphlet. I dug for two quarters.

"The thing is," I said to the girl in the blue flannel skirt, who, I guessed, attended school next door at Cabrini High, "Mother's head looks fake, somehow. You know . . . like wax."

This made her stop what she was doing. She turned her young, dark eyes toward me and then, with one swift motion of the hand, she made a clean chop across her throat and said: "Mother here, head Rome." With that she took my fifty cents and I pocketed the pamphlet.

"Why is her head in Rome?" I asked Henry, who, having been raised that way, is wise to many things Catholic.

"Oh, they do that as part of the beatification process. I think. They watch how the head decomposes, or something, to be sure she's the real deal."

"You're kidding."

"No. It's part of counting up the required saintly miracles."

"So saints not only live differently than we do, they rot differently too?"

Henry shrugged. "God only knows."

I'm watching the kids again. I figure noon recess must be nearly over. There's a boy out there alone at the edge of the playground, one hand hooked around the chain-link fence. I've noticed him often this past spring. He almost always has a book, and when he's not reading it, he holds it by the front cover so that it flops open, pages dangling, as he observes the passing traffic. Sometimes his lips move as if he's recounting a story or memorizing the lines of a play. A little Huck? I wonder. A little Hamlet? I wish I could hear him. I wonder what the story is. A sanitation truck catches his interest. He follows it with his eyes until it takes a right off our little boulevard and disappears. At times he glances up toward my window and I wonder if he can see the middle-aged man at his desk trying to string together a few decent sentences. The boy's hair is a brown mop, bangs cut straight across the brow. He's adorable—a little miracle frozen there at the fence. I'm twenty yards, thirty years away from him, but I swear I was there—same playground, different city—five minutes ago, hanging at the edge, looking at the world going on.

There's the whistle. Loud. I wonder if the saint down the street hears it. I wonder if she sees all the bodies lining up, all the living getting back to business.

Once, not long ago, my mother looked at me with such tears in her eyes that I felt my heart crack open. We'd just gotten out of the car and were standing in the drive of her brand-new New Mexico home. Her two acres of hard-won peace and retirement. She was holding some groceries. Her fingernails, I noticed, were short and unadorned except for the soil of her land, the evidence of her effort to make green things grow on her bit of beloved desert. The snow-mantled Sangre de Cristos rose jagged and blue in the distance, framing her beautiful face. She'd been talking of her Boston childhood. How horribly lonely she'd been, how frightened when she walked home from school, not knowing whether her mother would be fine or knocked by drink to the kitchen floor. "God, I'm sixty-five years old and still speaking of this," she said, tears filling up and spilling out her blue eyes. "Still longing for a mother, I guess. Trying to figure it all out. Forgive me—I just need to know that, before I go to the grave, someone has heard my story."

I reached over and took her hand. I told her that I was glad to listen. That I believed I knew exactly what she meant.

2

MOM PICKED ME up at Regis on Wednesday afternoon, the week after I'd taken the orange and yellow pills. She was in a panic about what I'd done and wanted me to get help. She insisted I see a psychiatrist. The doctor was warm and plump. Somebody's grandmother, easy to talk to, easy to charm. I told her how my parents' divorce had set me off, sent me into a terrible depression. But that I was fine now. In fact, I was planning on running for president of the Catholic Youth Organization. I had lots of plans, I felt much better. Even as I spoke, I believed my chipper song. I was good at it. There was truth in it—the pulling up of the bootstraps. Somewhere down below, though, down there in the pit of my stomach, I was aware of a burial going on, the kind of forgetting you do in order to go forward. I was determined to smother the facts of what happened and to entomb the worry of turning out wrong.

There was one specific idea I chose to share with the psychiatrist. Public high school. I said I thought I'd do better there. I said it, knowing that it would get back to Mom. The notion of attending the local school had begun at some point to shine in my head as a kind of beacon. My older sister, Chris, had recently made the switch to public and I think that inspired me. Gave me courage. And there was that steady inner voice (that mysterious companion) that had grown up within me since the moments and days I'd so suddenly come of age. And I heard it telling me, like a crossing guard standing on the corner, pointing up the street: *Walk this way, this will save your life.*

To hike five blocks east, along with the neighborhood kids, seemed such a simple course of action. And I wanted simple. I wanted to get out from under, start anew. I wanted to distance myself from the weighty world that had delivered a slew of saints and one troubled man to my doorstep. In the vaguest way, I understood that attending public school would contribute to the forgetting I longed for.

My parents took the request seriously. They were glad, it seemed, to have a concrete suggestion from their sullen son, this overachieving kid who'd made such a strange and bungled mess of things.

I walked that September morning to George Washington Public High School and it was as if, in an instant—by dint of one decision—the earth went from black and white to color. There stood a shiny, secular building, a four-story structure without a cross, without a bell tower, built by the grace of public taxes. A big new school with not a Roman collar in sight. The size, the sheer multiplicity of its beings, loosened something within my chest. *The world is vast,* this place seemed to suggest, *there are limitless possibilities.* And, at least initially, I enjoyed the anonymity. And I realized that I harbored a hope that among all these beings, I might find someone *like me.* Whatever that was. I didn't know. Someone unholy, perhaps, but good. Good in a secular sort of way.

In those first weeks, I would stand against the wall of the giant lobby and observe the life-forms as if I'd landed on the surface of Mars. A busy planet not five minutes from my own house. After all those months with Jesuit boys, the colored skirts and ponytails left me dazzled. There were young men wearing yarmulkes who toted basketballs. There were high-tops and high heels, saris and Afros and radios, dreadlocks and sweethearts and six-foot black men who called each other nigger. There were boys with beards and hair longer than Cher's. Elephant pants and bell-bottoms embroidered with peace signs. Here was a catholic world.

The bulletin board near the office listed clubs beyond my imagining. With the Jesuits there'd been Sodality, of course, and choir and sports. Here there was Greenpeace and Caduceus, Drama and Golf. There was the Black Students' Alliance and Amnesty International and even a collective for Transcendental Meditation. The rules and warnings regarding absenteeism and weapons, crimes and expulsions, were so different from Regis' demerits and JUG for not completing an assignment or for having your shirttail out.

There were countless wings and stairwells with little arrows and numbers stenciled discreetly up on the walls to help you find your way. Even after I got my bearings, I had this habit of looking up for direction, as if looking for something I'd missed. The starkness, the lack of adornment, was startling. No bloody martyrs, no drama nailed to the walls. The one splash of artful color in the hallway was a portrait of our most famous politician, George himself, father of our country. I stopped once in front of the glass-enclosed case that held shelf upon shelf of gold and silver figurines. Metal-muscled athletes, compact little heroes dribbling or kicking or passing. Not a bloodied arrow or a plucked eyeball in sight. These were the tough men and women with their eye on the goal, going for the gold. And standing there looking at the taut little statues, the public crowd rushing by, I had to admit that some part of me yearned for the broken bodies and melancholy eyes of the men and women who gazed heavenward. That army of souls whose deeds, whose fervent wishes, had so little to do with this world and nearly everything to do with the next.

I just don't know how to live, I remembered my mother saying. I fretted that this was true for me too. That I was damaged goods, not fit for this existence. The idea that, soon, I'd have to *get out* would not leave me. And that when the moment came, I'd have to come up with the courage to do the job right. I kept my head down, trying to hide the dark, ungovernable feelings shooting up from within as well as all the crushes that I knew were flashing across my face. The brilliant boy in front of me in history, the quiet guy next seat over in AP English, the handsome tennis coach. *God, stop with the guys!* I told myself continually. *Stop.* As I put my nose to the books and worked to get As and keep up appearances, I thought incessantly of suicide.

It was near the end of that sophomore year, on a bleak night when no one else was home, that I pulled Dad's .22 rifle from its rack. It wasn't any one thing, beyond sheer terror and loneliness, that incited me to take the gun down that night. It was an abiding desire to give up the act. The exhaustion of hiding the truth. But I didn't follow through. At the last second I put the slug in the wall and not in my head. I found my way to the next day, and the following. I continued my trudge through the school year. I remained a steady and quiet kid, getting good grades, getting the lay of the land.

I look back at the months and years after the pills, after the dark night with the rifle and the new days at public school, and I see now that certain elements began to rise and converge. Life-saving elements.

Luck is a matter of character, a teacher once told me when I dared to say how lucky I felt I'd been. I don't know if that's true. What I do know is that my life began to lift again, to change. What do you call it when human events and, most remarkably, human beings start showing up to bless your life and you're able to open your eyes enough to see it? Blind luck? Good fortune? Fate? Here's what I do know. A kind of light emerged and something within me was smart enough to move toward it.

I trace the first glimmers to a moment at the kitchen table on a Friday evening early in my junior year, just after tuna noodle casserole. The four of us Moran kids were finishing up dinner. The TV was blaring at the end of the table where Dad used to sit. The younger kids were arguing about what channel should be next when they came upon a special presentation of *Willy Wonka and the Chocolate Factory.*

The characters were singing their cheery Oompa Loompa melody, a tune easy to follow and, as I put my dishes into the sink, my throat opened and I sang along. The sensation in my chest, the sound coming out of me, made me giddy. I turned circles in front of the fridge, mimicking the choreography on the screen. My older sister's face was buried in an algebra book, her features hidden behind her long, blond hair. Suddenly, she lifted her head, enough so I could see the glint of blue through the tangle of hair. "Jesus Christ," she said, "you've got a loud voice." My little brother and sister seemed amused, grins growing across their faces as I continued to bellow and dance. I'd never, in any way, thought of myself as a singer. I'd joined in the hymns at church, of course, and sung a bit with Sister Christine during guitar lessons, but that was it. Now my siblings were applauding as I took a little bow. It was this odd, spontaneous moment in which (as happened when reading at Aunt Marion's Mass), some ham in me dared to swell up and pop out. Standing there on the linoleum floor, putting the milk back in the fridge, I laughed. So did my siblings. It was a sudden burst of delight on an otherwise dreary school evening. I went to my room humming, pondering the strange statement from my distant sister. "You've got a loud voice." And I wasn't mistaken. She'd been smiling when she said it.

Two weeks later I was walking through the lobby at school when I noticed a bright orange poster. On it was drawn a large cartoon figure of a hefty man kicking up his heels. He was wearing a toga, or something Roman-like, and was running, apparently being chased by a scantily clad, large-breasted blonde. His sandals were skimming along large red letters that said: *A Funny Thing Happened on the Way to the Forum.* Below, in the right-hand corner, was printed the following information:

Auditions, October 14, 15, 2:30–5:30, Auditorium. Sign up, Room 228.

Without much thought, I moved through the crush of students up the stairs and across the hall to the drama room. My head had the slightest conversation with my feet. *What are you doing?* My body's reply: *This is the way it is.*

I signed my name on the clipboard hanging near the door.

The following week, I sat clutching sheet music for *Camelot* against my knees, my legs jerking up and down. *The whole thing's absurd,* I kept thinking. *I'll never go through with it.* There was a row of folding chairs lined up in the hall just outside the entrance to the auditorium. They were all occupied with students like me, holding music, humming softly, appendages jerking. *This is crazy,* I kept thinking. *How could anyone do this?*

"Next."

He was pointing at me. This guy with copper-colored hair (*Is that dyed!?* I wondered) was telling me I was *next.* I stood and, avoiding the eyes of the others folded in their folding chairs, I walked past the boy with flaming hair, through the door, and onto the stage of the enormous auditorium.

"Music, please." It was a deep, disembodied voice bubbling up from somewhere. "Down here," it said. I walked forward and saw a guy seated in the orchestra pit behind an upright piano. A white guy with the biggest Afro I'd ever seen—a globe of curly black hair topped with a tiny purple yarmulke held in place, I noticed, with a bobby pin. "Music?" he asked again.

I bent down to hand him my song. He stood to take it. His yellow T-shirt cried, *Godspell!*

"Tempo?"

"Fast," I whispered.

"OK." He gestured for me to move back toward center stage.

I shuffled back and forth, stuck my hands in my pockets, took them out. I bent my knees to keep them from shaking.

"Dive in, baby lamb!" came a female voice from amid the dark sea of seats. I squinted and saw, several rows back, the outline of a hairdo and the glimmer of glasses. I stared.

"Darlin', did you hear me?"

"Yes."

"What are you singin'?"

"'Camelot.'"

"Lovely."

"Go ahead, Allan," she yelled. The music began and, miraculously, so did I.

A law was made a distant moon ago here . . .

I got three lines in, blanked, and stopped singing. *Oh well, that's the end of that,* I thought.

"Oh! You're a tenor!" she cried. I saw the head of hair stand. She moved briskly down the aisle toward the stage. She seemed excited. She was small. Well dressed. She had a lovely scarf and a huge grin. "Did you bring any other music?"

"No."

"That's OK. Have you got nice legs?"

"What?"

"John?"

The boy with the fiery hair was at my side.

"This is John, my assistant."

He nodded at me. "Fabulous voice," he whispered. "Ms. Priest likes you."

"Darlin', would you mind throwing on a pair of gym shorts and letting me have a gander at your legs?"

I shrugged and mumbled something, assenting but embarrassed.

She said, "It's part of the story, honey. One of the characters has lovely gams, wears a toga. I'm sure yours are great. I just need a quick look."

John handed me a pair of gym shorts and pointed. "Last door, up right."

"What? Where?"

"Wing three, off up right." He pointed again.

I followed the general direction of his finger. I found the door to a small room and returned with bare legs and stocking feet.

"Turn once around, darlin', would you?"

I spun, they gazed. It was oddly intoxicating. Attention. Eyes coming at you, lingering on you. The ham in me was definitely pleased. The drama lady (that's how I thought of her then) came to the edge of the stage. "Sing something else for me. Anything you know."

"Without music?"

"Yeah, a cappella."

I saw the boy at the piano stand and lean in.

"Um, I really don't know much...except church stuff or ..."

"*Something,* honey, you know *something*. Whatever comes into your mind."

"OK."

The floor of the stage was slatted, varnished and beautiful. I stared down at the swirling grains of wood, clutched the hems of the gym shorts, and sang the first song that came to my head.

Will I ever find the boy in my mind, the one who is my ideal? Maybe he's a dream and yet...

"What show's that from?" the piano player asked when I'd finished.

"That's not from a show," John said. "That's from life."

It was a cross between sports and choir, church and an unending party. Putting on a show had to be the fastest way on earth to meet people. There was Phil, a small, adorable guy who played the comic lead. He taught me all the important terms in one afternoon. What *wings* are and what *up* and *down* mean, which turns out to be something quite different, of course, when you're on a stage as opposed to off. He showed me a shorthand for recording movements, called "blocking." For years to come I'd use the symbols Phil taught me, and think of him every time I scribbled in my script: *x d r* for "cross down right." There was Kent, the man who played *all* the leads (even though he was my age he seemed like a grown man) and had the biggest voice and personality I'd ever seen in a high school student. I was convinced he'd been belting high notes and tapping out time steps since the womb. He took great pains to teach me the basic elements of stage makeup. I watched him paint his eyes—liner, mascara. My God, suddenly this place, this permission, to wear lipstick and rouge. Lots of it. All in the line of duty. All part of getting the story told. I wasn't that keen on eyeliner but I took it as a sure sign that I'd landed somewhere different, where the usual rules didn't apply. I was aware, as I watched this dynamic thespian, of a wonderful feeling of delight and liberation. "You don't want those spotlights washing you out," he told me in his resonant baritone. "Your face, your eyes, are the windows to your soul—the *character's* soul." As he continued to apply his cosmetics, carefully chosen to enhance the rich black of his beautiful black skin, he spoke of the nuts and bolts of trodding the boards. He dabbed a bright red dot on the inside corner of each of his eyes. "This," he proclaimed, "is a comedy dot. This helps your eyes look farther apart and more distinct. Good for laughs. There are comedy dots, red, and tragedy dots, white. That's what you've got, comedies and tragedies. We're in a comedy." He turned to me. "Open wide." He dabbed at the inside corner of each of my eyes. "So here's *red!*"

"What if something is comic and tragic?" I asked.

"That rarely happens."

My first dance partner ever was sexy, sultry Cynthia, who yelped on opening night when, during our big number, I fell going through her legs and took her skirt with me to the floor. She forgave, invited me over for Sabbath dinner, and taught me the Hebrew for *Ruler of the Universe.* I met and worked with Pearly, a crackerjack jazz pianist. We stayed up nights in his basement, where he rolled joints and taught me Cole Porter tunes. I became smitten with Jan, a keen-tongued comedienne who shocked us all by deciding to sing a verse of her song from the lap of a distraught man in the third row. I marveled as she twirled her fingers through the man's thinning gray hair, belting out lyrics with the worldliness of Marlene Dietrich. She was sixteen going on forty. We all were, it seemed—

a collection of odd kids feeling quite adult in this histrionic sphere and, though we couldn't have fully realized it then, a group of students who had the fortune to be at a fine school at an extraordinarily creative time. As it turned out, many in this group would go on to make lives in and around the arts.

When I first stepped before an audience, a bundle of nerves wrapped in a toga, I could scarcely believe it was my own body. Right on cue a voice resounded *(whose throat is that?)* and the limbs attached to the trunk I called Martin instantly inhabited a character named Hero and his bumbling love for the girl next door. I felt myself rise up and lean into the presence, the touch of all those human eyes and ears. It was a lightness of being, a momentary pardon for all the secrets and sins. They were smiling out there. They weren't seeing bad or damaged, so it seemed. They saw, I think, a kid with rouge all over his cheeks, red dots in the corners of his eyes, and a mouth open wide, belting high notes as if his life depended on it. And what I saw written across the field of faces was rapture. A collective delight. How astonishing it was to stumble upon such genuine life while at the business of pretending.

And there was something familiar about it all. Something *church*. The huge auditorium, though it didn't have the flying buttresses and jutting steeples of a basilica, had the grandeur of a space built for mortal communion and prayer. Though I was dressed for a silly musical, I couldn't help feeling a bit the altar boy in front of the congregation. Different costume, different stage, but a ritual nonetheless. In the coming years, I would come to think of theater (when it's good) as a place of epiphany. Not the transformation of the Body of Christ, but of every body present. Humans fused by a jolt of laughter, by the thread of a story. And from this very first experience of *Forum* I felt, even in all the irreverence, in all the courtesans chasing Pseudolus, in all the raunchy jokes, that there was something sacred. A celebration of what's human and what's here. I stood there, an essentially ex-Catholic, uncovering a new faith. And when the curtain call arrived I bent my head, my body, into the praise, and felt no quarrel with living, and the voice in my head said: *This is joy. Remember this. This exists.*

When the ovations stopped and the lights went out, I was back confronting the infernal wishes to die, the hollow sense of unbelonging. But I knew that something had changed. Not only had I connected with classmates in a genuine way, not only had I discovered something really fun that I was good at, but some force had made its way in and, without my even knowing it, was rearranging molecules. The playful collaboration, the applause, was an embrace I'd been longing for. Like Hero, I was giddy with love, but mine was for the stage, and rather than knock me off my feet it seemed to set me right back on them.

There was, in my class, the absolute coolest group of guys. Ken-Mike-Dave-Jeff-Barry. Everyone agreed, in that unspoken high school way, they were cool. All the more, I think, because they had no sense of themselves as being popular. They were just good at things. They played a wicked game of basketball and got straight As. All smart, all straight, all handsome, and, by chance, all Jewish. I revered them.

They were close, they'd known each other since kindergarten. I was new and could barely hold a basketball, but I got good marks and this helped, at least, in holding a conversation. Sometimes I would conquer the crush and find the courage to turn around in class and say something to one of them about an isosceles triangle or the fall of Rome or *Death in Venice*. Mike played the trumpet and turned up in the pit for *Forum*. In the lull of rehearsals, in the atmosphere of theater, it was easier to talk. I don't know how the subject presented itself or when, but the idea of going camping, of maybe climbing Longs Peak, came up.

"Yeah, man. We should do that," Mike said in his straightforward way.

It wasn't until later the next year that we actually camped and climbed to the summit of Longs. But, meanwhile, other plans got

made. I joined Mike and the gang to drive to Winter Park and ski.
One trip turned into several. Then it was smacking tennis balls
with Ken or Barry or getting high and hanging out all together to
watch *Saturday Night Live*. It was going to Ken's to study for a physiology test. Then Jeff got us into TM and we'd gather to transcendental meditate in his parents' pitch-black sauna. Then there was,
"Dave's got an extra ticket to the Nuggets game" and, "You can't
miss Ken's birthday dinner." By the time junior year was over, I'd
somehow become something I never dreamed (especially when I
was drowning among the Jesuits) I could ever become. One of the
guys.

On one trip, Dave drove. The night was clear. I don't know why,
but we never seemed to bother with tents. We found a ledge above
a creek across the highway from the trail, threw down a tarp, lined
up our bags. Mike and I searched for kindling; Jeff sat on a big rock
and meditated. We ate simply around the fire. We had boots and
water at the ready for the next day's climb. We hit the sack. Ken
wrestled Jeff until Jeff could barely breathe for laughing. At ten
thousand feet we were flying high, staring at the stars, talking a
mile a minute.

"I didn't get it at all."

"I think he was saying his idea of hell was other people."

"But what's the existentialist thing?"

"Meaningless universe."

"Fuck that."

"I never got through it."

"How'd you pass the test?"

"Is that girl from Manual still calling you?"

"Once in a while"

"Hey, northern lights."

"Not till August."

"It's glowing over there."

"You're stoned."

Next day we stood strong at fourteen thousand feet. Mountain conquered. The wind knock-you-down wild. Our home state lay glorious at our feet. All directions clear as far as you could see. "This is the best," Jeff said. And it was. We sat on our parkas and ate peanut butter sandwiches and I had but the dimmest thud of remembrance in my chest, the merest thought, of how many times I'd crisscrossed these peaks with Bob. Of how I struggled against the sense that I'd somehow sullied all of this, could not belong in these parts. That noise was drowned out by the sheer pride I felt in being among my new friends. Climbing with these guys was like regaining the high ground. Rediscovering home. Finding trust and strength in my own male body. I couldn't have explained it then, can barely now, but I knew that being near their self-confidence and their kindness, at simply being among them in this uncomplicated way in the middle of our mountains, in the middle of our high school lives, was healing beyond measure.

I was confused and frightened of much that was in me, including the love I felt for them, but I never had to hide who I was. Not what was essential. And a day would arrive when they'd come to know Henry. Come to know my story. And I would come to know their children. A day would arrive when Mike would tell me, *Man, you're one of the bravest people I know.* And I would look at him and the others and remember there was a time I thought bravery for me impossible. Living, unthinkable. That I wasn't man enough for it. How would I ever begin to tell them that so much of the courage that grew in me came from what I saw reflected in their eyes.

Lucky.

Not long after that first musical was over, the irrepressible drama lady, Nancy, cornered me in the hall one day and asked if I was planning on taking part in the next project. The spring production of *Oliver!* "You have a shot at a good part." I walked away calculating that if I were to get into the show, then I'd have to postpone killing myself for several weeks. If I started, I couldn't possibly miss rehearsals. Let everyone down. I'd have to wait until summer.

I got into *Oliver!* and, when it was over, the summer came and I had to postpone my plans again because I was cast in the all-city production of *West Side Story*.

. And so it went, death deferred because I could hold a melody. Because I got the part, got to sing. Suicide on hold for rehearsal, for a hike with friends. I began to figure that, maybe, if I could quell the demons until the next ovation, the next peak, then I'd never take more pills or use the .22 rifle again. After all, the first principle you learn in this line of work is: *The show must go on.*

3

ONE EVENING AFTER a performance of *Forum,* I was at my dressing table mirror in the cafeteria—the area that, by night, magically transformed into backstage. I sat scraping pancake from my face when a redheaded woman in a long pink gown and fur coat entered the room. I watched as she threw open her arms, smiled broadly, and hugged a few students she knew. "Congratulations, sweetheart!" I heard her say. She looked as though she'd arrived not at the lunchroom of a high school, but at the opening night of the Metropolitan Opera. Maroon-colored jewels dangled from her ears, sparkled over the fluffy collar of her coat. Her grin, which she bestowed generously on all who cared to take notice, was blue-eyed and blinding. I turned back to my mirror, figuring she must be someone's glamorous mom or a kooky official from the school board. A few minutes later I heard her say my name, and I turned to see her moving in my direction, her hands extended as if to embrace.

"You are simply terrific," she said. "I'm Winnifred Magoun."

"Thanks," I said, picking up a Kleenex to wipe the cold cream from my hands.

"Have you ever studied voice?"

"Oh . . . no."

"You should. You have an *instrument.*"

The word struck me as odd. Did she mean my throat was like a cello?

"I'm just doing this for fun," I said.

"Of course you are. Doesn't mean you can't study. I'm a voice teacher. Why don't you take some lessons with me?"

"It's great of you to ask but I really couldn't. Schedule and, you know . . . money and all."

"Of course. Well, thank you for a wonderful performance." She leaned into me. "You should just see the *color* of your aura." I stared at her. I'd heard of such things, but only vaguely from flower children who'd appeared on the news. She laughed, reading my face, my thoughts, I felt sure, and whispered, "I'm not kidding—a shimmering blue-green light spreading right out to the last row. *Gorgeous.* Congratulations on a great performance. Goodnight."

"Thanks, goodnight," I said as she turned away.

She waved to a few more kids she seemed to know and then glided out of the cafeteria, leaving in her wake the distinct aroma of an exotic perfume.

"Who was that?" I asked Barb, one of the girls I'd seen speaking with her.

"Winnie. She's an opera singer—Brico Symphony."

"She's a little eccentric."

Barb shrugged. "Yeah, she is."

"She said I should study voice with her."

"Well, that's cool. She's got all the best students."

"Really?" I felt flattered but, knowing that ultimately this whole theater thing was a lark and knowing that, if I lived, I was planning to be a lawyer, I forgot all about her.

Several months later, on the closing night of *Oliver!* she was standing at the cafeteria exit as I left to go to the cast party. She had on a different gown, just as bright, just as glamorous.

"Hello again," she said.

"Hi, Mrs. Magoun."

"Call me Winnie. I have something to tell you." She laughed. "First of all, you were wonderful tonight. And second of all, I don't care about schedule conflicts or money or any of that. I am *supposed to be* your teacher. You call me. I'm in the book."

We shook on it, my one hand enfolded by both of hers, and she bid me goodnight.

I stood in the mist of her exotic perfume, wondering what in the world she meant by *supposed to be.*

I was instructed to enter her front door without ringing, take a seat on the blue couch in the living room, and wait to be summoned. I arrived a bit early and did as I was told. Among the books on her shelves, wherever there was a bit of space, little plaster and porcelain figurines of elves and knickered gnomes balanced on teeny tree trunks and dangled from bells. There were little white fairies and winged angels. I sat eyeing the knickknacks thinking, *Oh dear.*

The loud vibrato of a tenor wafted through the room. His voice emanated from somewhere deep in the house. I recognized the word *Amore* floating on a series of very high notes. Italian...*love.* I listened as love competed with the drone of a lawnmower somewhere down the block. I kept thinking of getting up and leaving. I felt vaguely embarrassed to be there, to be taking her, and singing, seriously. Soon, the cheery, chunky tenor walked through the living room and gave a wave as he moved briskly out the front door. I heard her call my name. I nodded at all the little tchotchkes, stepped around the corner past a hallway and into a large den.

Her flaming red hair—beauty-parlored to perfection—and laser-blue eyes beamed at me from behind the keys of a black baby grand. "Welcome to the studio," she said. I glanced around at the walls. There were several photos of students, I figured, past and present, smiling in eight by ten or costumed and singing in various theatrical productions. There was a large mirror positioned behind the piano so you could watch yourself sing. Next to it was a chart of vowels and a colorful poster on the physiology of the throat.

"Come on in, stand there."

She pointed to a music stand. A box of Kleenex sat on the end of the piano next to some vocal books—Vaccai, Marchesi. There was a stack of sheet music weighted with a rock on which was etched: *On some other plane it already happened, and it was perfect.* She took a sip of coffee, her pink lipstick marking the rim of the cup. She set the cup back down somewhere near the base keys. "That will be your bible," she said, pointing to the book on the music stand: *Twenty-four Italian Songs and Arias.* "We'll start with 'Oh Love of My Heart,' page 35. Do you read music?"

"No."

"No matter. Put your hand on your breast."

"OK."

"Everything starts with the breath. Everything. Do you feel your heart?"

"Yes."

"Rhythm, meter, is born with the beat of our hearts. Inhale through the nose, out through the mouth. Another." She smiled. Her eyes looked as though they might burst blue all over the room. "Good to breathe, yes? Good to just stand and be, isn't it?"

I nodded.

"Everything is vibration, dear. Light, sound. Your chords vibrate and the waves of energy coming from you affect, rearrange, the energy of the universe. That's what I saw you doing in that theater— changing the energy. You have such *full-being.* Such *joy.*"

I dropped my head and laughed.

"You think I'm jesting?"

"Well . . . I'm not . . . I don't know."

"Well, I do. Sing an 'Ah' for me on this arpeggio."

I sang up and down the scale, making as big a sound as I could.

"Now, easy jaw. Give me an E on each note of this chord." Her fingers moved across the keys, her eyes fixed upon my face. "Relax your forehead, darling. Good. Again." She stopped playing. "You have a beautiful sound, you know. And the world is in need of beauty." She leaned back, her swivel chair squeaking loudly. She fiddled with the top button of her fluffy white blouse. "You think I'm crazy, don't you?"

"Yes."

This delighted her no end. We both laughed.

The half hour passed quickly. She stood and crossed around the piano. Her sensible black shoes and polyester pants suddenly made me see her as the housewife, the mother of four sons, that she was. She put out her hand. "Come again next Thursday at four o'clock. Does that work for you?" I nodded, taking in the scent of her.

I stepped out with my vocal book, with my instructions to learn "Caro Mio Ben." She'd given me a cassette on which she'd recorded the Italian pronunciation and the melody. A young woman was sitting on the couch near the knickknacks, waiting her turn. I drove off thinking how unfortunate that this woman Winnie didn't live in the *real* world, how I'd return next week and thank her and explain that this just wasn't for me. I turned onto Colorado Boulevard aware, suddenly, that the lovely smell of her was preserved in the folds of my shirt. I drove north, humming the whole way home.

The following week I arrived and sat on the blue couch. This time there was a soprano in there and it wasn't Italian but French. Something about a white moon, about tranquillity. Glancing up at all the little elves and fairies, I prepared to tell her how I just didn't have the time for these lessons.

The soprano departed, I entered, and when I saw Winnie sitting behind the piano grinning at me, what I'd planned to say vanished. I was aware of a swell in my chest, wondering if it might be related to the word she so often repeated—*joy*.

"You've been raised Catholic, haven't you?" she asked after we'd sung a few scales.

"Yes."

"Me, too." She got up from the piano and took a huge paperback book off one of the shelves. "We Catholics—lapsed or not—are steeped in the mystical. Don't you think? We're primed."

"Primed for what?"

She sat back down and studied the big green book in her hand as if deciding which chapter she meant to look at. Then she stood and held the book across the piano. "Here," she said, "I got this for you. Keep it. Read it. I have a feeling you'll find it fascinating."

The Nature of Personal Reality, it said. *A Seth Book.*

"Who's Seth?" I asked.

Winnie laughed. "Oh, darling . . . well, I'll just tell you. Seth's an *entity* from beyond this physical plane. A wonderful woman named Jane Roberts channels him."

"Channels?"

"Yes." She was smiling at me. "I wish you could see the look on your face. Listen, I'm not sure why I'm giving this to you. It's just that I'm *supposed to.*"

"Supposed to?"

"I can't really explain it. An intuition, an instinct. In any case, it's good to read new things, isn't it? Get another perspective."

I nodded, flipping through the big book. "Thanks."

"You read some and let me know what you think. Like most things, some of it may speak to you and some not. We'll talk about it."

"Does it have to do with singing?"

"Yes . . . in that it has to do with everything . . . with how you perceive this life. Your life. You are a very old soul, you know."

"Seventeen."

"I'm talking about other dimensions. Your body may cease to be, Marty, but you will not. You've had and will have many lives."

"Are you talking about reincarnation?"

"Yes." She sat back down and took a sip of coffee. I felt a certain thrill and fear at discussing what struck me as vaguely blasphemous, crazy. In my head I saw cows in a field in India. I saw dark-skinned Hindus with turbans. I saw a wacky suburban voice teacher. But, at the same moment, I realized everything she was saying struck a chord in me. Every word—and the way she spoke them—seemed to loosen a knot within, to land in my gut with the comfort of truth. "Read a sentence or two," she said.

I glanced through the first few pages.

The great creativity of consciousness is your heritage . . . each living being possesses it. . . . What exists physically exists first in thought. . . . The spirit becomes flesh . . . each individual's soul, then, is intimately connected with what we will call the world's soul, or the soul of the earth.

I looked up.

"Food for thought," she said. "Look, put it aside for now. Just check it out if and when you want. How's 'Caro Mio Ben' coming?"

We worked on the song awhile and then, just before our time was up, she stood and said, "Marty, there's no place within you that isn't creative. You are a part of *all that is*. You can accomplish whatever you set your mind to." She came around the piano and embraced me. I let my head rest against her shoulder. "You know," she said, "all I'm doing is reminding you of things you already know."

So it went for months. Music and metaphysics. My lessons grew from a half hour to an hour. "We need more time," she'd said, "to talk." Walking into her studio, sometimes, I felt as though I was stepping through some invisible door into an alternate, neighboring reality. A wild new terrain with a redheaded guide. A guide who suggested: *Look at it another way. Listen to your intuition. It's guided you beautifully so far, hasn't it?*

We'd be in the midst of working on a song, me belting . . . *Maria, Maria, say it loud and there's music playing* . . . she'd lift her fingers from the keys and start speaking, our eyes locked, her crows'-feet radiating from bright pools of blue. "We are completely free of space and time, Marty . . . breathe. Breathe. You're holding onto those notes as if for dear life. Notes are not for holding. They are to be lived and let go of. A note lives even as it dies . . . like us."

Much of what she spoke of baffled me. I disagreed; I didn't know what to think. But our conversations stimulated and comforted me in a profound way. Her presence, her ideas, the music, brought to me miraculous moments of serenity. I experienced a palpable sense that my body was a vehicle of spirit (as Brother Tom had once suggested), a porous collection of molecules, not a limited sentence of doom, a weighty problem. Sometimes, in the midst of our discussions, it was as if the room cracked open and I saw everything (including my own being) in some eternal, larger way. I couldn't have put it into words but it was the rush, the delight of perceiving separateness as an illusion. A shimmering sensation of *all* being *one*. (A few years later, when I dropped acid on a glorious evening in California and the world revealed itself as one continuous tapestry of love, I thought of Winnie and her lessons.) Our talks made me feel—if even for a moment—that my fate wasn't sealed by the trouble I'd been in. That despite who I was (perhaps even because of it!) I had a real chance at being good.

Often, I'd leave her house as if on a cloud, flying from our discussions about dimensionality or past lives. And very often, the farther I got from her home, from her lessons, the volume of other voices would grow and crowd in to tell me that she was nuts and that these ideas were nothing more than a cheap way to escape the hard truth of living on a troubled planet.

I did share with her, at times, how much I struggled with depression. I wasn't specific, I didn't know how to speak of the fear that I harbored regarding my sexuality, what I saw as the darkness of my desires, of "what I'd done." That locked in me was a belief that I was an aberration. That I wrestled with the desire to kill myself. I remember asking her,

"What if who I am . . . authentically, is bad? Wrong?"

"Not possible."

"How do you know?"

"I know."

"But you don't really *know* me."

"I know that you have love. That you honor life. Of course you struggle. I see that. We all do. I'm terribly sad at times. There's a hell of a lot of pain to be experienced on this dimension. But, I remind you, there's infinite joy too. And there is much you are meant to do, to give, in this life. And I know that you are preparing for it, for what you are to give. That's why we're here, after all—*to serve.* To serve others. What I am doing for you, you will, in some way, do for someone else, for others, one day." She spoke so matter-of-factly. I looked at her, at her flaming red hair and bright eyes, and dared to believe her. "Our brains are not capable of grasping all the dimensions we are working on, living on, at once," she said. "It's our intuition that guides us."

"Faith?" I asked.

She nodded. "Yes . . . a *knowing*."

I think hers was the most vivid faith I had ever encountered. Strong, like Aunt Marion's, full of joy like Sister Christine's, but connected to a secular world, a singing world. She offered a glimpse of God, a vision of light, in daily doings, in art. A light that I sensed could outshine the dark, that could begin to mute the shaming voices of a Catholic upbringing.

Winnie attended all her students' performances. She had a little purse into which she'd snap away the evening's program. She'd bring them home and put them on the piano so that her students could witness the achievements of their colleagues. She took all that we offered, onstage and off, very seriously.

As my senior year was nearing an end, I received news that I'd been accepted to Stanford University. I told Winnie of my plans to head for Palo Alto.

"What will you study there?"

"Pre-law, I think. I plan to be a lawyer. Like my grandfather."

"Well, I'm sure you'll do well in whatever you choose. But some-one should tell you, darling, there's no doubt that, if you want, you could enjoy a career in the theater. It can be a wonderful life, you know."

"But that's not a *real* life. A real living. It's crazy."

"Not crazy, it's important work. It's a way to channel the divine, Marty. Music, theater, can be a passport to the infinite. Healing for you and for others. It's a way to reach people."

"It's so competitive, though. It would be impossible."

"Most of the great, challenging things in life seem unattainable. But if you set your mind to it...." She stopped herself and picked up a volume of arias, set it on the piano. "Whatever you choose, your life will be beautiful. I just know it. All I'm saying is that, if you want, I believe you could be a professional."

Professional.

The word moved through me as something sacred. It rang in my head like a distant, impossible dream.

4

IT'S 1982 AND I'm living in a big loft with three friends. The corner of Broome and West Broadway, SoHo, New York City. Raw space, raw talent, four crazy kids, cheap rent. There's Kim—actor/puppeteer. Amy—actress/chanteuse. And my old friend from high school days, Jodi, who's attending film school. We call each other "Broommates," and all of us are pounding the pavement, waiting tables, serving drinks, singing show tunes, whatever it takes to make ends meet. On the sixth floor lives a cranky young woman who (though none of us know it yet) will soon be introduced to America as the "Material Girl" and whisked away in a limo by Sean Penn. On the first floor is a store featuring a fat man who guards shelves of live chickens and rabbits. He butchers them there, or you can take them home and do it yourself. We figure that that's what the many Italian families in this Italian neighborhood must do. He sits next to our stoop in a folding chair. When friends come over, they scream toward our third-floor window and we throw down a stuffed sock with the key attached. Chicken feathers scatter everywhere. We four are consumed with the push, the drive, to unlock the secret, discover the combination, that will bring success. I buy *Backstage,* the actor's rag, and go to any audition I can find—up back stairwells, into the basement of churches, to sing an uptune or deliver a dramatic monologue that might land me a job. I wait tables, sell typewriter ribbons over the phone, sew buttons on the eyes of Woody the Woodpecker for the Macy's Pa-

rade, model naked for an art class, hand out fliers in Times Square
for an aerobics studio, wait tables. And more tables. Ballet becomes
my religion. Ten dollars a class with Maggie Black, a small and
mighty New Englander. The finest dance teacher ever in the whole
world. She strengthens my spine, lengthens my muscles. "Wide
back, long neck, Marty. Straighten your standing leg. Good!" She
talks about *line* and *simplicity* as Plato discussed the Forms of the
Good and the True. Her discipline and grace remind me of the
nuns back at school. She's as rigorous and positive as the electrified
city that surrounds us. The ninety minutes of her crackling voice
over the live piano, the physical repetition, the routine, is a godsend. Her daily class pulls me through the ache of being unemployed, misemployed...nowhere. The daily angst of doubt and
fear. Doubt that I've got what it takes, fear that I've made all the
wrong decisions.

In the space of three years, I'd matriculated at Stanford, come
out as gay, quit Stanford, entered an acting conservatory in San
Francisco, and moved to Manhattan. Now, instead of taking classes
in public policy and economics, I was scraping together rent and
cash enough to study pirouettes and pliés. To learn to belt high
notes and croon Broadway ballads. Instead of studying Tocqueville,
I was memorizing Cole Porter. Eating pizza for dinner, bran muffins
for lunch. It occurred to me regularly that I might be insane. But
I was also replete with the resolve to give this artist's life a go, to
see if I could make it. And even in the darkest moments, I knew
there was no going back. At least, not to Stanford.

I'd really thought that life would become lucid the moment I entered the great university. I thought that everything I'd secretly
struggled with in high school would melt away as I embarked on
this grown-up life in a brand-new state. I'd see to it. I had, in fact,
forced myself to visit a Denver psychiatrist just before leaving for
college. Sitting there in his office amid the Tinkertoys and teddy
bears of his trade, I'd made myself express the affliction I feared was

growing in me, the problem I wanted to conquer—*Homosexuality.*
He sat in his khaki pants, unbuttoned cardigan, and red bow tie,
he sat there like Mr. Rogers in his cute psychoanalytic neighborhood, and gently explained how the brain is like a switchboard. He
reminded me that I was, indeed, the "operator" and, as a disciplined
young man, it was my task to get the girl messages through. To
make the right bulbs light up.

I'd left there all circuits smoking, thinking him an idiot, but the
word *discipline* rang in my head and I sat down and reaffirmed, again
and again, the paradigm that had grown in my mind. The strict
plan that I would take with me to university: poli-sci, pre-law, lawyer, Catholic husband, father, senator, and, finally, happiness. I'd be
good. And rich. I'd make my mother proud. I'd will it so.

But forces stronger than will were at work. Between classes, my
feet kept taking me away from studies and off to auditions. First
it was the all-school musical *Gaieties!* followed soon after by the
dorm's Shakespeare production. I landed a lead in *Gaieties!* and then
played Feste in *Twelfth Night.* I fled campus as often as I could and
went to the theater in San Francisco. I sat in the balcony of the
Geary Theater, thrilled beyond measure to see men and women
playing Shaw and Chekhov and Stoppard. Playing for a living!
Weekends I visited my high school pal, Ken, who was at Berkeley.
These bayside cities were liberating and exotic, especially in com-
parison to lily-white Palo Alto. Ken and I went to People's Park,
saw women there dancing topless, smoking joints. One night I ven-
tured on my own to the Castro district in San Francisco. I saw guys
(so many of them!) spilling out of doors and onto the front stoops
of gay bars. Tank tops and mustaches moving to an earthshaking
beat. I observed from across the street, repelled and fascinated by
what seemed an impossible, sinful mirage. There were gay coffee
shops and galleries and bookstores. One Sunday when I went to my
first opera, *La Gioconda,* I saw a guy on the steps of city hall wearing a button that said, I AM A COCKSUCKER, and holding a sign:
WE ARE EVERYWHERE. In utter panic I ran around the corner. *Not*

here, not here, not me! my switchboard was shrieking. How sad their gay ghetto, I thought, how embarrassing their lives. Even that lanky politician, the goofy guy on TV, Harvey Milk. Even he, whose courage somehow thrilled me, embarrassed me.

On the 27th of that November, Harvey Milk was murdered, along with Mayor Moscone. I sat vigil in my dorm room, a storm of sadness and indignation and confusion raging through me. I don't recall saying one word to anyone ever about the tragedy. About all the feelings surrounding the terrible event unfolding not thirty miles from campus. Sadly, I did not want to reveal even the slightest connection to those people in the streets. Those fags who'd lost their brave leader and were daring to rise up in outrage.

I meant to buckle down into my freshman track, but I was continually drawn to the city, to these arty, sexy, urban places, even as every fiber of me was fighting it. I walked that idyllic campus, moving between mad bouts of despair and ecstatic bursts of defiance. Despair that I was still battling these "dark" forces within and yet a stubborn sense that my desires had to somehow be good. They were mine and they were real and maybe they were pointing the way toward a life, toward an authentic self that had little to do with this technocratic school. That had not one thing to do with "lawyer" or "marriage" or "church."

In the space of one evening late that first semester, a single event broke the floodgates and cleared the path.

It was a cool autumn night a few weeks after I'd finished playing Feste. An elder classman recognized me at the library and stopped me to say hello and to compliment me on my performances. I recognized him. He was a star athlete. His name was Dan and he was dazzling. He was extremely popular and clever. He was sometimes involved in creating the halftime antics at the football games, which had made the Stanford Marching Band so famous. He asked me over to his off-campus digs for drinks. Sure, I said. Later that night, sitting on the edge of his queen-size bed, we got stoned. We talked quietly of our aspirations. Though he was studying medicine, he wanted to be a musician, guitar, and I confessed that I couldn't stop thinking about being an actor. That I felt a passion for the stage and was beginning to think I didn't belong at Stanford. That I should look for other schools.

He touched my knee and seven thousand volts shot through me, switchboard blown. "You should," he said. "You could be a *professional*. You're absolutely dynamite."

The light in his brown eyes, the Hawaiian dope, his fingers brushing my dungarees, I was a goner. His room was tiny. We were knee to knee. I was aware, through the warm hum of THC, that I wanted one thing in the world more than any other. To kiss him. I wanted to hold him and be held. It was clear as clear as anything I'd ever known. Solid and real and vibrant and fabulous. His hand moved up my leg—the sky on the Fourth of July—and written in lights across the universe, across the inside of my buttoned-up head and the gooseflesh of my arms, there it was: *Hello, you want this. Here it is.*

It felt as shocking as it did inevitable.

Awkwardly, shyly, the star athlete and I managed to get horizontal. The warmth of this boy near my own age, near my own body, was some kind of beautiful, breathing truth. It was like holding (after all those high school years of denial, after all the awkward dating of girls) my future. God, here he was in my arms, this smart and funny and talented guy and I liked him. I really liked him.

It was wildly erotic and frustratingly chaste. I wanted more but couldn't even bring myself to say a word, much less kiss him. Lying right there next to me, he'd suddenly gone away. Disappeared. I could feel it. He was more afraid, it seemed, than even I. We'd taken off our shirts but still wore pants and I was holding on for dear life and wondering just what (everything, I hoped) would happen next. If there might be love here, if we'd sleep together and make scrambled eggs in the morning, if maybe he felt the same, when, with a jolt, he jumped up.

"It's late, you'd better go."

"Sure," I said, my face burning as I buttoned my shirt. We shook hands. I thanked him for the dope and the chat and went out into the dawn, knowing somehow (and I was right) that this would be the last time I'd ever hang out with him.

As I wandered through prettified Palo Alto, my belly burned with a pang I'd not experienced before. A powerful push, a vivid ache, at the base of my pubic bone. And it occurred to me exactly what it was. I wanted to have made love with him and the hurt was that it hadn't happened. The simple fact of it cracked open inside of me, cracked me across the head, and I paused there on Palm Drive and said it out loud. *Get over yourself, for chrissake. You're gay! Deal with it.* And when I reached campus I sat on the cement wall near the post office in a kind of trance. The sun was just rising and it seemed the earth had shifted on its axis. The position and quality of light, the rhythmic hiss of the morning sprinklers, the slow sway of the eucalyptus trees, all of it was strange and vivid and alive and new with what I'd finally admitted. I hadn't slept, I may still have been stoned, but everything was lucid. I sat there neither happy nor sad but utterly determined to harness the force of what I felt. To make adult sense of it. I stared at the maze of post office boxes, at the empty plaza, and a clear and tender thought came up to surprise me. Came up from the deep and fell out of my mouth: *He didn't make you this way, you know. Bob didn't do it. This is who you are.*

My plane landed at Stapleton International for Christmas break, and though my stomach was in knots, I plunged right in. My sister, Chris, was first. She took me to McDonald's and I told her my news. She listened and said, ever so calmly, that she thought I might be an actor and was always sure I was gay. "What?" I asked, incredulous. "Marty," she said as she ate another greasy fry, "you never walked, you always bounced."

Mom, I knew, would be trickiest.

It was early evening, a few nights after Christmas. I sat at my desk, down in my old bedroom, next to the cheery yellow bunk bed, over the blinding orange carpet. I was on my swivel stool, just like one of those seats you can spin on at the counter of a coffee shop. Mom came in and sat at the foot of my bed, across from the desk. We were both silent. I'd already shared with her my disappointment with Stanford, my intention to find another school with a theater program. This had caused mild protest, heightened anxiety. *What about your scholarship? Why not finish out college? A degree is so important these days.* And then there was just the basic divorced family-holiday stress—whose house to go to when, to cover all bases, keep everyone happy. Tension was high, everyone exhausted.

"Any thoughts on what you might want to do for your birthday?" Mom asked, pulling pieces of invisible lint off the folded laundry in her lap. "If you want to invite a few friends, I'll make some dinner."

"Thanks, Mom. That sounds good." I felt weak, sick in the stomach. I swiveled away toward my desk, pretended to write something. "I'll think of who to call . . . maybe Jan and Cynthia and Mike and Kelly, if they're around and—" I knew, suddenly, that it was the moment. I turned to face her. Her hands were resting on the T-shirts and underwear in her lap, my Fruit of the Loom. "I have something I need to tell you," I said.

Instantly, her eyes hardened. Grave, panicked. She'd been stoic when I'd discussed the acting thing. Now I watched her chest rise as if readying for a fight, then slump again. Why did I know she knew exactly what was in the air? Ever since I stepped off the plane, the strain between us had been palpable. I had the words planned, they were simple, but I needed a way in, a beginning, and it eluded me.

"Ummm . . . ummm . . . Mom . . ."

It came like a death rattle out of a parched throat. "You're going to tell me that you're homosexual, aren't you?"

Oh my God, they were right, mothers do always know.

I managed a timid nod, only vaguely aware of the sharp disappointment I felt at being robbed of the chance to say it for myself.

I watched the blood, the life go right out of her. She was whispering, shaking her head: "I knew it. I knew it." Her hands went to
her face and then, as if running toward an emergency, she gripped
the laundry and fled the room.

I was home for one more terrible week. We said not a word to
each other. For the first three days her face was swollen with grief.
I understood—felt the ache of guilt—that she felt guilty. She was
flogging herself with Freud, I knew it. "Aggressive Mother, Passive
Father." I'd heard her talk about it before, in general, in relation
to other people, but now I was her own clinical classic, a monster
she'd created.

Two evenings before I was to return to Stanford, Mom was at the
sink rinsing the dinner dishes. She was wearing her long red night-
gown, not unlike something the bishop wears to High Mass. She
had on her yellow rubber gloves, the ones she wore to protect her
hands and nails as she cleaned the kitchen. I was sitting at the table
when, suddenly, there was the terrible sound of cutlery crashing
into the sink. I turned to find her bloodshot eyes right on me, her
latexed arms held aloft as if she were a surgeon waiting to be handed
her scalpel. Water and bits of tuna dripped from her elbows. She
raised her wrists higher, as if in supplication to the brutal gods of
fate, and spat out three words which she and I would recall many
years later over cocktails, through stitches of laughter. She looked
at her nineteen-year-old son and with all the anguish of an empress
losing her grip, breathing her last, cried out:

"Et tu, Brute?"

I just stared, we both did, two drama queens at a standstill, playing the end of a bad scene. After the appropriate beats of silence,
she went back to the dishes and I exited to my room. Next morning, I was on a plane back to California, not to return to Denver for
another two years.

I waited a few more months before dropping the bomb on Dad
when he and his new wife came for a visit to Palo Alto. (He'd re-

married during my senior year of high school, a woman he'd met in his apartment complex.) I was terrified to speak, and struggled with the notion that, with him, perhaps everything was best left unsaid. But I also felt a determination to get it over with; I knew that he was likely (if he hadn't already) to get the scoop from someone else, and I wanted him to hear it from me.

It was a warm night. He and I went outside and leaned against a parked car. Eucalyptus in the air, stars in the sky. "Dad, I want to tell you . . . I think there may just be a distinct possibility that I'm essentially . . . sort of . . . a homosexual."

He looked down, I remember, and swirled his cocktail, stared at the cubes circling there like little frozen fish. He looked up then at the chunk of heaven hanging above my fancy college campus and said: "Well . . . there are things about me you don't like."

For some stretch of magical minutes I actually felt overjoyed. *That wasn't such an awful response,* I thought, gazing, as he did, skyward. *This is going to be OK. Neither of us have dropped dead.* He seemed calm and I read this as acceptance, even closeness. It was certainly better than the disaster I'd experienced with Mom.

We walked around the block. The cool California air was soothing. Peace reigned. We shook hands, said a solemn goodnight, and I headed back to my dorm ecstatic, mission accomplished.

The next afternoon I was to meet Dad and his wife in San Francisco's Chinatown. I took the train in after classes. The entire ride there and then walking the steep and narrow streets, I felt deliriously happy. I was looking forward to seeing him, being together in the light of this new understanding. I caught sight of them waiting on the sidewalk outside the restaurant and I broke into a run and threw my arms around my father. He clutched. His body was like a stone. With his arms glued to his sides, he muttered something about his cigarette: "Careful . . . watch it." He tossed it from his fingers, looked down the street. His eyes, shot through with blood, would not meet mine. He couldn't disguise his disgust, his disappointment. What emanated from him was utterly animal, involuntary. I'd read the books. I understood immediately that he needed time, space. That what I'd said had sunk in overnight and was poisoning him. I felt for him even as it devastated me. All the more because I could see he couldn't help it. He had no way, no vocabulary, for coping with the son in front of him. It suddenly occurred to me that what had passed between us the night before had been eased by alcohol. It wasn't yet five, he hadn't had a cocktail. *Go easy,* I told myself. We stood there in the bustling street, frozen and despondent. It was as if, I remember thinking, Everest had risen up between us and someone had commanded him to strap on his boots and climb up to meet me. And everything in his face, in his slumped frame, said, *I just can't. This I cannot do.*

"I think the restaurant's this way," his wife muttered, flicking her Virginia Slim into the gutter.

At our miserable Chinese dinner he and his wife got miserably drunk. At one point she blurted: "I don't understand how you could do such a thing to your little brother and sister—they *looked up* to you, you know."

When, some time later, I finally reached my sister Chris on the phone, I burst into tears telling her what had transpired. She tried to calm me, told me to give Dad time. "You know, he thinks that Malo guy did it to you. Made you gay."

"Christ . . . how much does he know?"

Somewhere along the way I'd shared a bit of the story with Chris and, as will happen (as she now informed me), she'd talked to Dad about it.

"What did you tell him?" I demanded.

"Just a little. Marty, after a point it's not that hard to put it together. The rumors about Bob were around. It was in the paper when he got arrested. I guess Dad had suspicions. I don't know. Put stuff together."

"He never said anything."

"Of course not."

"Bob had nothing to do with this! This is a separate thing. This is part of who I am. It has nothing to do with what happened then. This is who I am, I'm telling you. I finally know that to be true! It's part of me . . . no one *made* me this way."

"I know, I know, be patient. Just give them time."

"There isn't enough time in this life."

That summer, I got a job at Disneyland as an "All-American College Singer and Dancer." Five shows a day in the frighteningly fascist Land of Tomorrow. My first professional paycheck. The following year, I left Palo Alto to attend theater school and, upon graduating, found my way to New York.

It was the winter of '82. Short on cash, long on hope, I believed that, no matter how crazy or hard it seemed, there was no going back. And one rainy Wednesday after the matinee crowds had spilled from the Broadway theaters, I served a bowl of soup to our regular customer, the actress Kathy Bates, at Joe Allen's Restaurant, and she looked up at me and said, "You know, Marty, you're going to make it. It will take the head of a bullet and the heart of a child, but be patient. All of this, the whole shebang, it takes sacrifice. It takes a mountain of patience."

She smiled, and I thanked her, and that night, instead of taking the subway when I got off work, I walked all the way downtown through Chelsea and the Village. All the way down to the Broome Street loft. I walked knowing this was it. I was head over heels for Manhattan.

5

MEN.

It is there above the door, carved in white marble, in bold classical script. Like a commandment. So I enter.

I'm the older one. At twenty-two my body is finished finding its height. He couldn't be more than fifteen—the young man at the urinal—sixteen, perhaps, with his long, skinny frame and steel-rimmed glasses. In raggedy cutoffs and leather sandals, he looks the lost waif. I glance about for a parent, but he seems to belong to no one.

He's at the very back, past the damp, concrete room where you can wash the sand from your feet or sit on a wooden bench and change in and out of your trunks. He stands still under his curly brown hair, staring straight ahead at the sloppily painted brick. A slice of sunlight falls across his cheek. I take a position two away and open the fly of my baggy swimsuit. I study the walls, gray with countless coats of paint and etched everywhere with graffiti: *The Tigers Suck, Yor Motha farts to.* The disembodied laughter of children echoes through the room.

I play serious at the business of peeing as I feel him look up at me. Over to me. He's giving off something I know. An admission, an admixture of desire and fear that clings to him even as it radiates toward me. I know then that, in a certain way, we are the same. I feel sure his heart is pounding like mine, his knees shaking. He's got the madness; that unrest that sends you searching off-limits where your mother or friends could not in their wildest imaginings think you'd be—pulsing with want in front of a public toilet, your bike, your car, perched near for quick escape. You should be at school or work or meeting a friend, *should* be more careful, but you're not. You're here alone at the edge of your world . . . hunting.

I think I know this about the green-eyed boy: he's longing. I glance over. He looks me square in the face, God bless him. His eyes are bright, pleading. His brow furrowed with the look of a tenth grader awaiting his report card. A delicate gold chain with the Star of David glimmers at the V-neck of his white T-shirt. His glasses, slightly damaged—bent—are barely clinging to the bridge of his elegant nose. Everything about him seems fragile. He's been knocked down, I imagine. Teased. Perhaps for the soft look in his eyes or the tenor of his voice. He's been slapped, I think, so that his glasses tumbled to the tarmac where the other guys shoot hoops. My heart breaks for him and I say with my steady gaze— *I understand. I hated recess, too. I would never slap you down.*

I'm looking at the green-eyed boy, at the smattering of picked-at pimples on his whiskerless chin. At his hair, cut in the perfect, silly shape of a bowl. I watch his gaze drop toward my hands as I shake away the last drips of pee. Then his eyes rise to my face; proposition electrifies the air.

I nod toward the three stalls to our left. He's anticipated this. Instantly, he scurries, chooses the last one and leaves the door ajar. Heart hammering, I follow him toward the metal closet where piss and ammonia sour the air. I step in and close the latch, the click of it like confessionals I've entered before—closing a door, drawing a curtain to expose secrets, ask forgiveness. But here there's no somber velvet, no red light that snaps on when you kneel to begin, *Bless me father, for I have sinned,* and my back is pressed against the stall. *My God, what am I doing?* He faces me and with not a trace of hesitation he reaches for my swimsuit. His fingers tremble as he pulls at the drawstrings and slides my trunks down. He takes me then, gently, into his hands.

I'm stunned by his quickness, his will, his intent to touch what he wants. His eyes feast with the madness of a starved child who's found the answer to his craving. As if this zone of flesh, this piece of me, is his subsistence and he's blind to any other appetite. His smooth face speaks of worship too. There is something holy in his touch and I understand. I allow. I'm drunk with being wanted. *My God, where,* I wonder, *from whom did he learn such things? So soon?*

Thirty seconds, a minute, perhaps, has elapsed. I swivel and sit on the toilet. I draw him toward me, fumble at the buttons of his cutoffs. Who is this boy? What is his name? I pull down his shorts. Where is his school? What language does he speak? He places a hand on my head. I feel it tremble. Is his family large, his father alive? I take him to me. I'm terrified. I can't believe I'm doing it. And a thought rises from just beyond the veil of consciousness, from somewhere deep in my body, that this is somehow familiar. This is very like what he did with me when I was small and he sat on the bucket in the barn. Just as he did when the door was closed and all the other campers were at the lake. I flash on it, how I looked down at the sunburned crown of Bob's head, like the red eye of a storm, moving back and forth, wisps of his brown hair spiraling clockwise. How I closed my eyes, so grateful for the relief, for the five seconds of . . . *Oh, God.* . . .

"Ohhh," the boy sighs. I'm startled, pierced by this first hint of his voice—high pitched. I glance up to see his eyes clenched, as if he's hurting. His glasses have slipped; they're ready to fall from the tip of his nose. His hands rest with a timid grip on my shoulders. He throws back his head. I can't see his face now. Just this new-sprung triangle of hair, the smooth arch of his torso, the glimmer of his necklace. He's breathing shallow and fast and then, and then, my God! A sound. A click. A step. An intruder.

We both jump and instantly hike up our shorts. I'm seized with terror, with utter disbelief at my transgression. Still sitting, I retract my legs, stick my feet in the air, and balance like a clumsy frog on the edge of the toilet. They mustn't see four feet, I'm thinking. Mustn't count four legs. And at this moment, holding on to the toilet-paper dispenser, legs in the air, heart racing, I know who *they* are, all lined up just outside the stall: Sister Christine, my parents, a phalanx of police, all of them with handcuffs, JUG, humiliation, at the ready. They're out for vice and I'm it. Moral questions zing through the fetid air. I confess. I'm lost. How did it come to this, to toilets, to me in a men's room with a boy? This cannot happen. Give me jail. Excommunication. Shit.

The young man stands still. He's much calmer than I. Perhaps because the word *minor!* isn't shrieking around his brain. From my precarious perch I launch into a round of charades: *Button up,* I point. *Tuck in. You. You go. Me... I'll follow.* My arms flap instructions. I finish with a single finger to my lips: *Shhhhhh.*

He surprises me again with his sureness, self-possession. He even manages to toss me a crooked grin as he snaps the last button of his fly. Then he gently unlatches the squeaking metal door and slips away. I hear the brisk patter of his sandals across the concrete as I rise to close the latch. Beads of sweat fall from my brow, splatter across the floor. I stand perfectly still. I listen intently for any sounds of trouble beyond the pounding of my criminal heart.

Nothing. No one.

I walk, then, out into the glare of sun, into the blaze of noon. The boardwalk is busy with bodies. I watch a shirtless, potbellied dad pass by, pushing a stroller. I send my gaze far down the beach to the tall, rickety roller coaster rising up, hazy in the distance, like a lost and ancient city. The one called Coney Island. I look around for the green-eyed boy and spot him. He's draped over the fence along the concrete path that leads from the men's room back toward the Atlantic. His arms dangle over the top railing, his fingers stretch toward the sand as if searching for heat—a lonely, loose-limbed boy on a summer afternoon. I walk toward him. I want to say something kind. I want to tell him to *please take care, be well.* I'm not a foot, a word, away from stopping when he turns his head and looks right at me.

I pretend not to see.

I step across the scorching sand, regretting my silence, regretting everything. I make my way back to the folks I'm visiting, old Colorado friends who are helping me find my way in the big new city. I kneel down and resume the building of castles with their youngest son.

"Hi, Christopher," I say.

He smiles, so glad to see me—Uncle Nice. He takes my hand and with sweetest trust, leads me right to the edge of the patient water.

6

I GIVE UP Sunday afternoons now and again. A family duty, a welcome break from Manhattan. I take the train. Metro North. About an hour up the Hudson River to Maryknoll. Often, the train seems to be filled with women and children on their way to visit the men inside Sing Sing—Ossining's other major institution. At the station you hear the gypsy cabs organizing: "Prison here, Maryknoll this way." On my first trip, when the taxi approached the hill where the Mother House and the priest's residence are situated, I was astonished at the sight. The Maryknoll compound rises like a vision of Asia on a Westchester hill. It's much grander and bigger than I'd imagined. The main building (the one for the men) is palatial, and with its enormous red-sloped roof and oriental architecture looks as if it's been transported directly from Imperial China. The cabby asked, "You want the guys or the gals?"

"The Cloister, please."

"That's up here on the right."

Sister Rachel, the portress, greets me at the chapel door and leads me down a long hall smelling of snuffed candles. We pass crucifixes and statuary sculpted of wood and bone, works from the Maryknoll missions throughout Africa and Asia. Sister Rachel deposits me in a small, simply furnished parlor. A table is set for lunch. Marion will arrive through a door that leads to the interior of the cloister. On the ceiling I can see the rust marks left from the grate, the mesh of metal that in days past completely separated visitors from the contemplatives.

"Sister Theo will be right with you."

She arrives now in a wheelchair. Her face is calm, beams the warmth of a woman happily wedded to her way of life. We speak in the same quiet way we did when I was twelve. She listens. She is always curious about my progress, my thoughts. I tell her about the loft in SoHo, my three ambitious Broommates, my various crazy jobs. She's concerned, I sense, but careful not to ask too much about my personal life. "You've got to keep your heart and mind clear in that city. Do you get to Mass?" I hate to lie but I nod vaguely. She doesn't press, doesn't ask which parish.

She tells me more about how their day is structured around contemplation, communal meetings. She tells me that the entire community offers constant prayers that I might be able to quit the restaurant business for work as an actor. I'm grateful. I'm surprised to realize how much I want, how easily I believe, that their prayers have real power. We eat tofu or soy cakes and salad and sip decaf coffee.

After lunch and midday prayers the other sisters carry folding chairs into the parlor and we make a circle to discuss current events. They have dwindled to thirteen, mostly old. It is an exhausted vocation in some ways but these women are all vigor. I feel awkward with them at first, boy caught in the ladies room, but after a few visits, I get used to it. Enjoy it. I'm the special Sunday visitor, the guy center stage.

"Tell us, Marty, what do you do all day? How do you look for work in the theater?" asks Sister Grace.

"When I'm not working in the restaurant, I go to as many auditions as I can find."

"What do you do at auditions?"

"Whatever they want . . . usually I sing or read from a script."

"Is Times Square as busy as ever?"

"What does it mean to you to be an artist?"

"What do you think of Cardinal O'Connor?"

The questions keep coming. They really want to know. I try to be frank. They inspire frankness. Comes a moment Marion throws a smile my way. "Marty, won't you sing us a song?"

I do. I have an uptune and a ballad prepared.

Who will buy this wonderful morning, such a sky you never did see!

I throw in a pirouette, once, a back handspring. The sisters all gasp and laugh like crazy. Things loosen up and Marion recites a poem by Longfellow, beautifully and by heart. The sisters tell me what's really going on in Guatemala, the Sudan, El Salvador. They've lived there, they know the people of the mountains and the deserts. Speak their languages, pray for them and for Mr. Reagan whose policies, they say, have caused countless deaths. "Imagine, Marty," says Sister Theresa, a serious woman with an unwimpled pixie-gray hairdo. "Maryknoll made the CIA list of organizations most hostile to the Reagan administration."

"Our phones have been tapped," adds Sister Madelaine.

"We're not sure of that," says Theresa.

"Yes we are," says Madelaine. They all nod. "Imagine, that in this world, teaching someone to read is rendered subversive. When someone is starving you don't ask what faction they belong to."

Sometimes I return to the same question . . . what's it like here? How can you live this life?

Marion answers most pointedly. "I desire to go all the way for God. Life is only for love, Marty, and sacrifice is the language of love."

"And sacrifice isn't necessarily deprivation, or suffering," Sister Grace adds. "It's an offering. It is a way of *drawing close* to what we respect and love." I am amazed at the deep hum of comfort I feel in their presence. These are messages I want to hear. This is kinship that echoes my boyhood.

I glance, again, at a beautiful drawing on the wall of a young John the Baptist. A long-haired man with a handsome and melan-

choly face. I experience a familiar twinge of warmth, of want, each
time I look up at him.

Sister Theresa says, "In a world that has lost the sense of God,
our lives serve as witness, as a reminder, of the supernatural." The
circled sisters nod.

"Who drew that?" I finally ask one day, pointing to the gorgeous
man on the wall.

"Your Great Uncle Augustus Tack. He was a famous artist, a
painter like your sister, Chris." Marion tells me to be sure to visit
the Paulist Church at the corner of Sixtieth Street and Ninth Avenue. "Across from Fordham, where your Great Uncle Ted served
as a Jesuit. There is a mural there painted by your Uncle Gus. A
superb composition that includes some beautiful text."

(One afternoon, I heeded her advice and visited the church—and
still often do. Deep into the nave, on the left side, is a painting of
the funeral procession of Saint Theresa, the Little Flower. There is
a quiet place to kneel and, in the dim light, study the colorful work.
The text Marion spoke of is stenciled in gold on the wall next to
the fresco. It says, in part, *Love will consume us only in the measure of
our self surrender.* Somehow I feel sure that this is the very thing Marion hoped I would read.)

The sisters always stuff my backpack with homemade bread and
cookies. When I hug Marion goodbye she says, "It's so good of you
to give up your time to come visit. It means so much to me. And
the other sisters."

"I'm glad to come," I tell her.

She whispers into my ear, "Keep writing. Let me know how you
are and what you're thinking. I'll do the same." On my way out the
door, she slips me a five (her allowance for a month). "For that aw-
fully expensive train, dear."

She wheels herself into her sanctum and I exit, into the world,
onto the noisy train, into the roaring city.

Sacrifice is the language of love. I keep hearing the phrase as I gaze
at the Palisades during my melancholy ride along the Hudson. I

hear it as something true and beautiful, as something to live up to. Then I hear it as something stern and old and oppressively Catholic. When I get home after that first Ossining visit, I go to the dictionary.

Sacrifice.

Sacrificium: Sacer–sacred; *facere*–to make, to do.

Sacrifice. To make sacred.

7

THE NUNS' PRAYERS? Perseverance? I begin to find work. Real work. A summer at Williamstown Theater Festival, a stint in Maine doing Shakespeare, a short-lived Broadway revival of *Oliver!,* an Equity card, a quick tour of the musical *Doonesbury,* during which I get to hang out in various bars with the brilliant Garry Trudeau. Life is a blast, it's suddenly full of signs that I just might actually make it. Make a life in the theater. I'm being paid, making good friends. I even book a television commercial (a "Japanese buyout," they tell me) for Nescafé, in which I play a dancing coffee bean. I leap as high as I can in the bulky costume, sweat like crazy; deposit the check. Here it is, the professional life Winnie spoke of.

I fall for a formidable colleague named Alexa. A supersmart girl with a large and embracing Philadelphia family. I want it to work. Our relationship makes me think again about the possibility of being a husband, perhaps a father—*Sacrifice is the language of love.* But it's so much confusion and subterfuge. I can't stop, don't want to stop, looking for men. It ends painfully and as we part I vow I will be alone for the rest of my life. Just give me work. Work.

It's the beginning of my third year in New York, January of 1985, and I land my first off-Broadway play. It's an experimental music-theater piece. An opera based on a Gertrude Stein novel, to be directed by a young woman named Anne Bogart. "She's a big deal, very avant-guard," a friend-in-the-know tells me. "Look, her picture's in the *Village Voice* this week. She's doing some wild production of a Wedekind play at NYU." Though I find the Stein script bizarre and completely inscrutable, I'm thrilled to be one of the eight performers cast. To be working in New York with this up and coming woman director whose photo is in the *Voice*.

There's an actor in the piece. He's got cool leather boots—some kind of funky Asian design. Sleek black jeans. Bald head with long hair on the sides, which billows wildly out over his ears as though he's standing in some great and constant storm. I keep watching him. "He's from *Juilliard*," the other actors tell me. I learn that he's performed at the Guthrie, Arena Stage, and with Richard Foreman's Ontological-Hysteric Theater. He's a *real* actor. His presence, his originality in rehearsals, is astonishing. He's ceaselessly inventive, everything he does physically, an elegant surprise. His ideas, his sudden bursts of genuine emotion, are inspired and startle me. Seem to startle everyone. He's like the furnace in the room, the one you go to to warm your hands, your mind. Who is this man? Thirty, bald, beautiful.

Henry.

The rehearsal room is electric, happy. Everyone is doing strong work. We believe—Anne inspires it somehow—that we are creating the most beautiful and important piece of theater in the history of the universe. *The hymn of repetition . . . Life is the hymn of repetition.* We belt out the Steinian verses, repeat the exacting choreography we've invented together. I sing and move with the budding sense that I am an artist among artists. I am bursting with the happiness of work.

It's the end of the second week of rehearsal. We are in the midst of a physical improvisation in which we are moving rapidly around the rehearsal space on a gridlike pattern. Suddenly Anne screams, "Do something this second that you're totally terrified to do!" And instantly, I'm tackled. I'm taken straight (and somehow gently) to the floor by this man called Henry. We are nose to nose, my back pressed to the slats of oak, his eyes burning into mine. Laser-beam scary. I have the most distinct feeling that, until now, no one in this world has ever really looked at me. It's as though his being enters in, circles my heart, my liver, lassos all vital organs and declares: *Here I am. You've found your match.* The moment is over as fast as it began and we're on to the next exercise. When the stage manager calls a break some minutes later, I go out into the hallway of the huge, dusty rehearsal loft and find a private corner in which to cry. I'm utterly baffled. I very seldom weep and don't know why these tears come, except that something about the encounter with him has shaken me. Shaken something loose. Ten minutes later we're back in rehearsal and move on with the staging of Stein.

The third week, he begins to walk with me from rehearsal to the subway. We discuss the play, our Catholic, middle American families. When we get to the stop on Houston Street, he pulls a rose from his knapsack. "Here," he says. The following afternoon, it's a box of chocolates. Not much said, a furtive smile. Out of rehearsal, he's a quiet guy. A few days later, February 23, 1985, he stays by my side all the way to the loft, where he meets the three Broommates, where he wakes the following morning, still at my side.

8

MEN.

It is there above the door, carved in white marble, in bold classical script. Like a commandment. So I enter.

I'm the young one. At twenty-seven my body is finished finding its height. He's probably forty-five, the lone guy at the urinal, fifty, perhaps, with his tall, heavy frame and beret. He seems to belong to no one. He stands still, staring straight ahead at the sloppily painted brick. A slice of sunlight falls across his shoulder. I take a position two away and open my fly. I study the walls, dull beige with countless coats of paint. Sounds of revelers from the nearby park echo through the room. I should be working, singing, writing. *Should be* doing something, anything, else.

I play serious at the business of peeing as I feel him look up at me. Over to me. He's giving off something I know. An admission, an admixture of desire and fear that clings to him even as it radiates toward me. I know then that, in a certain way, we are the same. I feel sure his heart is pounding like mine, his knees shaking. He's got the madness; that unrest that sends you out searching off-limits where your mother or teachers or, dear God, *your lover,* would not in their wildest imaginings think you'd be—pulsing with want in front of a public toilet.

I thought sure this would end. That the grip of it would cease. Why is it happening again? Why am I allowing it? It's like a trance, familiar the way it creeps in, creeps out from behind the angst. A hankering. A hunger that says only *this* food will do. Only this will soothe the sharp edge of anxiety. All my nerves screaming like spoiled brats hooked on it long ago. *Get some,* the synapses shriek, *get it now.*

It's crazy, standing there full-bellied and famished, fly open, holding myself out because that's the ritual, the prayer before a meal with a stranger. I stand there exhausted from the wish to be two places at once: Here and not here. The chaos feels ancient and I'm scraping up reasons as I stroke myself:

I was born oversexed, marked with a family gene; it's in the blood, an overactive libido. I should look into this, get help. But, for now, I just have to see, please, this one thing swollen with proof that I'm here. Allow me this one quick glimpse of another man.

It's OK. Chill out. Just taking care of an animal need here. That's all. That's it. It is my earthly right as a guy to feel the pulse, the pleasure, the aliveness of body. This is what men have done since God knows when, since we were cavemen, for chrissakes. Don't let the enemy, the old Catholic guilt, crush what the body desires, deserves. It's cool, you're not hurting anyone. Stay put.

But why are you looking for aliveness inside a toilet? It's deadness, isn't it?

No, it's just a few minutes of fun with the damned. A few moments to enjoy, then on my way.

Go home and enjoy. Get out of this shit hole.

This is what I'm choosing.

If you think you're choosing you're crazy. This is desperate behavior. This surely is one thing you should be able to control, to sacrifice, to give up for love, for Lent. Stop hunting up excuses for being a rogue.

And I watch the man. I glance up at his skeleton smile (*are my eyes that vacant?*) I watch him play with himself. At least I'm being "safe," I think. I'm not doing anything dangerous in the midst of this horrible epidemic. At least I have *that* much control, and then it comes. A quick, silent release, eyes clenched, an obliterated chunk of time. Over in a second. Did that really happen? Wipe hands on the Kleenex stuck in your pocket, get out, out of the dank and into the sun, get on with the day, on with your life. For God's sake.

And out into the light I march, stomach scooped hollow. And what rushes right in to fill the pit is punishment. A thrashing in the chest, the mad, criminal heart. Like day follows night, shame rises up and it's old hat, it's an old, surly friend come pounding, stubborn and loud, to announce he's here and plans to move in. To crash in your living room for the foreseeable future.

9

IN THE SPRING of 1988 I moved into Henry's place. A sweet and nervous leap of faith. A month later (the Gypsy life) I was hired to "Make 'em Laugh" as Cosmo in a Salt Lake City production of *Singin' in the Rain.* I wanted to live up to the brilliant Donald O'Connor so I decided to incorporate the back flips off the wall during the big number. One night, midflip, I freaked and landed on my knee, then promptly in the hospital for surgery, and, knowing I couldn't negotiate Manhattan on crutches, I ended up on my back in my old bed in Denver to recuperate.

Sprawled in a postoperative stupor and looking for the bright side, I decided that this stretch of time at home was meant to be a blessing. Since I'd left for Stanford ten years before, I'd hardly been back, and here, I figured, was a rare opportunity to slow down and reconnect with family and friends. Carpe diem.

Mom set up a convalescent bed in the dining room so I wouldn't have to use the stairs. She organized meals and got me to physical therapy in the mornings, and Dad picked me up most days and took me to lunch. My little sister, Carolyn, and my brother, David, would stop in and shuttle me places. Here we were, all of a sudden, finding one another older and mellower.

Dad's marriage, it seemed, had deepened. He'd quit drinking. His wit was readier and wryer than ever and his kindness, his wish to help, was as clear as his sober eyes. The love I saw there was lucid, not the glazed kind I remembered from dinners past, the kind lit up by vodka and birthday candles. Mom was working hard at her job, excelling at bridge, and becoming a keen lover of films. We saw movies together, went for dinner. Discussed the plots and themes and cinematography.

Henry came for a couple of weeks to visit. With great care, Mom prepared our room. She'd done a lot of work through the years to comprehend and accept her son's homosexuality. And, besides, during the few trips she'd made East, she'd grown very fond of Henry.

Crutches under my arms, I proudly showed him around my boyhood town and, one evening, even took him up to the Rockies, into Estes Park, where we spent a night in the Stanley Hotel, the prototype, supposedly, for Stephen King's ghostly resort in *The Shining.* We couldn't help but laugh after the gawky guy at the counter gave us a ghoulish stare when we asked for a queen instead of twin beds. *Redrum, Redrum,* Henry intoned all the way up the tiny, squeaking elevator.

One afternoon I brought Henry, unannounced, to the *Denver Catholic Register,* where my father was then writing. Dad mumbled hello, staring at the keys of his typewriter. He never got up from his chair. Henry stood in the doorway, struggling, suddenly, through a fit of coughing. I died a thousand deaths as we stood there for two excruciating, wordless minutes before I croaked out an irritated and hasty goodbye. "Some things will never change," I said to Henry as he helped me hobble back to the car.

"That wasn't a great idea," he said.

"I know. Sorry."

But, even with the barriers and tensions that remained, there was a truce, a quiet acceptance, which reigned over the family reunion.

My old pals from high school, Mike and Kelly and Dave and Steph, came by and got to know Henry. And in the weeks after Henry left to play Trofimov in a production of *The Cherry Orchard* in D.C., friends continued to stop in and take me to dinner, once, to a Sting concert. Here was a beautiful Colorado summer, chums nearby, workmen's compensation footing the bill, family taking good care. A gift.

So why, I kept asking, did I feel so intensely troubled? The smell of the night air (so distinct in Colorado), the clouds moving over Mount Meeker, rendered me black with an inexplicable despair. Everything I laid eyes on—the green street sign on Flamingo, the gold leaf dome of the state capitol, the ash tree in our front yard— caused sudden bursts of remorse. As if Denver was booby-trapped with forgotten devices, triggered by sight, that sent shrapnel flying. Flying straight for the heart. Suddenly, I was once again confronting serious thoughts (the kind that had begun to recede after I left Stanford and headed toward New York) of suicide. *Christ, get a grip,* I thought. Was it the Vicodin? Postsurgery blues? Or was it just that, without the rush of Manhattan, without the push of the next performance, I was suffering from none other than time. From too much of it on my hands.

I needed a project. I borrowed Mom's old IBM Selectric. We set it up at the dining room table and, acting on advice I'd received from my newfound friend, an old and wonderful actor, Morgan Farley (a cousin in Los Angeles who Aunt Marion had told me about), I began to type out, as neatly as I could, every line that Hamlet utters. "Memorize the great parts," Morgan had counseled. "Get ready, don't wait for the bastards to call you."

> *O that this too too sullied flesh would melt,*
> *Thaw and resolve itself into a dew!*

I punched out the script, studied the words, popping Vicodin along the way more for the buzz than the pain in the knee. A couple of afternoons into the Dane's drama, I found I kept stopping to scribble bits of text in the margins, odd fragments floating by, asking to be pinned down. *What happened when you were twelve? Tell the truth.* It was irritating and strange and it was messing up my neat columns of iambic pentameter.

> *Thus conscience does make cowards of us all;*
> *And thus the native hue of resolution*
> *Is sicklied . . .*
> You had a lover. You had sex.

The pen, as if on its own, would get to my hand and dash things off.

What do you mean, lover? Molester, more like. And so what?

Soon the words moved off the typing paper and onto a yellow legal pad and off it went, or I went, as if dictated to. My heart pounded, my groin swelled as I wrote because with the spilling of ink came an instant response. An instant erection, powerful, Pavlovian. I described a fence, a field, a truck, a man, a loft, a sleeping bag. Images of a ranch, horses eating hay, ghostly and beautiful. A lost fable unfolding. It went on most afternoons for several weeks. At the top of each page I began to place a capital *C,* with a circle around it. It stood for a name I could not yet spell out. I hid the scribbled pages in a peach-colored folder that I stuck under the typewriter. I'd take them out and add sentences each day.

I'm in mourning here. For what happened, I think. Every smell, every site in Colorado reminds me of him. Of our bodies together. It was the force of flesh, I guess, muscle scooping up a naive altar boy, wasn't it? What happened was dishonorable. Evil? But wasn't there something honorable too? Holy? An awakening? Pleasure. It was unbelievably erotic. Or am I just remembering it that way? Wasn't it awful? How much happened to me? How much did I make it happen? The questions are like a purgatory. A fire I'm stuck in. It was some kind of exchange. My little body for his big attention. He had a way of stroking my mind as well as my penis. Con artist. His penis was huge, frightening. I had never seen a man erect like that. The size, the will of the thing, shocking. A thrill, a terror.

I was so little. It was like entering an adult race too soon and tearing muscles I'd need later to move well through the world. To find my own way. Or, maybe, it just strengthened me. What doesn't destroy you . . . right?

At school a nun guided my fingers over the frets of a guitar. On week-ends he slid his lips down my chest. I am two different people, aren't I? The altar boy and the slut. One's in hiding.

Henry knows one and not the other.

How can I hate the part of me that partook? Then, I hate myself. I hate myself.

Nothing I can do or become will ever be as vivid as this black crime in my soul.

Where do you put the ache, the anger, so it makes movement? Not statis?

At the end of that summer, I packed the secret pages away in my luggage. When I returned to New York I put them in a drawer and forgot about them.

10

MEN.

The letters are yellow, painted on a sign above the second-floor hallway near the end of the aisle marked FICTION.

But I'm not thinking about that. About *MEN*.

It's my day off from the play and I'm looking for a classic. A good solid read. The deep comfort of sinking into the era and into the lives of others. I'm thinking George Eliot. Or Tolstoy. Or Stegner. And maybe I'll find a good new novel for Henry. A gift. I wander among the shelves, cracking open books, reading first sentences, catching the whiff of ink on new paper. I come across the Eliot I've always meant to tackle, *Middlemarch,* study the first words— *Who that cares much to know the history of man, and how the mysterious mixture behaves under the varying experiments of Time*—and then, a force in a tight pair of jeans and a black turtleneck arrives to peruse the titles. A fat leather belt announces itself, the tip of it dangling toward the young man's thigh. And, as best as I can describe it through the haze of the stubborn shame, it's like this:

A body has arrived to take mine away.

And *away* is what I crave.

Suddenly, I am nearly shaking. Every pore of my skin alert to his presence, while George Eliot is obliterated. I hold myself motionless, as aloof as possible, trying to hide the waves of desire breaking off of me. My body screams as I feign silence, as I pray for discipline to close the door on this man and not the book in my hand. I glance over. His slip of a grin, the twitch of his brow, vocabulary from a language it seems I've studied now for years. A kind of Homo-Esperanto, spoken worldwide by a particular subsection of the tribe. I reshelve *Middlemarch.* My breath has gone shallow and quick like it does when you're ill. Or breathless with anticipation. *Whose body is this?* I wonder, as I step back, try to take stock. What's that my old therapist, the one I saw now and again for a year, what's that he used to say about insanity? Repeating the same behavior again and again and expecting a different result.

It always leaves you feeling horrid. Stop. You're losing control.

So? Is control such a great thing?

He steps past me, deeper into the alphabet of FICTION. I move away and turn the corner toward SELF-HELP. Testing things. Is he really following, interested? He finds me again, gives me a quick look. He's got bad skin, a sweet smile. He brushes his crotch. I do too and it's off we go, in our electrified stupor, to the nearby park to see what's up.

Book, gift, never purchased. An hour, a chunk of eternity, gone.

Next evening, I'm playing on Broadway again. "Doctor Stage," an actor friend of mine calls it, "because, no matter what ails you, you always feel better after work than when you came in." When we reach the finale, I look out at the audience as we take hands and make our company bow, *happy you're here,* our bending bodies say, *so glad to be of service.* The chorus swells and I'm belting my F-sharp, it is tucked tightly inside the last, huge chord. Six months running and our harmony still gives me gooseflesh. The surge of music, a thousand people clapping, the lights at full tilt, it's a golden moment eight times a week. A giant house full of joy. It happens every night except Monday, this musical story, this miraculous curtain call, and I know I'll never get over how lucky I feel that this is my job, that I get to tell stories for a living. Up to the dressing room I go. Out of costume. The stage manager announces the call for next day's understudy rehearsal, drops off the actors' valuables that had been locked up for the evening. "Goodnight, folks. Good show!" come the last words over the loudspeaker. Down three flights of steps, I hand Josh the doorman the key to my dressing room. He slaps me five.

And out into the night I am flying home on my bicycle when I see a young man standing on a corner of Ninth Avenue. I slow down, smacked by a longing that's been crouching quietly under my ribs. He's swarthy, cute. Instantly, I perceive that he is interested. It's there in the air, coming at me. A libidinous vibe. I come to a stop near the curb and offer him a quick smile.

"What the fuck do you want!" he blurts out.

"I . . . I . . . thought maybe you could sell me a joint," I lie.

"Get the fuck out of here, faggot!"

He steps over suddenly and kicks the front wheel of my bike. Hard. The handlebars jerk out of my grip. I regain my hold and start pedaling. He decides to give chase. Runs and kicks my back tire. I nearly fall. "Get the fuck out of here," he screams. "You're lucky I don't have a fucking gun."

My legs are pumping, my heart exploding with shame, fear. I take a right and head toward the river, then left for a block, and stop to collapse against a mailbox. The street is silent, seemingly safe.

After a while, I pedal slowly home, wondering what I was thinking. He was a guy standing on the corner, minding his own business. How is it that I can long for something so badly that the longing makes me trust any possible path for attaining it? All this want inside, but just what the actual want is, I don't know. It's somehow not about sex, I think. But something to do with danger, destruction.

How many times now have I walked into a park alone, late at night, telling myself with each step to turn around. Get out. A part of me arguing: *But there's sanctity in everything, isn't there? Even behind a bush in a park with a stranger. There's something to be learned.*

Once, a guy gripped me by the belt of my just-opened jeans and told me in a suddenly menacing voice that I'd better disappear or I might get hurt. "Give me ten bucks and I'll get you out of here safe," he growled. And like a light switching on in a dark and empty room, I saw how stupid, how unconscious, my act. And back on the lighted avenue, ten dollars poorer, it floats through my addled brain that there is something suicidal in what I'm doing. Something angry. My bottomless search is a curse I don't understand. Why do I do this? What is this fierce longing for a connection that, if stumbled upon, crumbles to nothing?

I I

I'M LATE, HE'S already in bed.

The lamp in our room is turned low. Henry's lying face up on his side of the bed. Eyes closed, perfectly silent. His hands are folded carefully over his chest, one on top of the other, a body laid to rest. His sweet, Slavic head is sunk into the pillow. He looks like a great leader lying in state. Lenin, perhaps, who, like my dear Henry, was bald and brainy. My breath stops as I get a disturbing, momentary glimpse of what he might look like in death. My God, I think, he is too still. But as I stand in the door of our room and stare, I see that a certain, deep quality of life emanates from him. I also see the gray wires that flow from the tiny speakers in his ears to the new CD player and I breathe again. He's awake, I can tell, and listening, even as he drifts toward sleep.

I wonder what he's playing. His tastes are refined and wide. He listens to composers I've heard of but whose names I could never spell or pronounce, whose music I rarely recognize. Henry's played piano since he was a boy. Music is a constant for him, a staple, a passion. I know how important it is for him to simply stop all else and listen. He's that way with the people he loves too. He listens. He's lost now, I imagine, in chord progressions, compositional elements that elude me. (Though he insists I'd hear so much more if I *stopped* . . . "You treat music as if it's underscoring for all your activities," he often tells me.) I look at his powerful shoulders under his T-shirt. They're broad like those of his father, and his Polish grandfather, who was once a wrestler in the circus. I watch his chest, thanks be to God, rise and fall with breath.

I move gingerly toward the closet to begin hanging up my clothes. I can't help it, I speak. "What are you listening to?" I watch a ripple move across his tranquil face. I see how my voice has dipped into his world. My voice, which is so much a part of this earth. My voice, which has come, after our years together, to sound like his. I'm sorry for having disturbed his singular space, but I want his attention. I want him to kiss me. To look at me.

"Janáček," he says quietly. His voice is soft, floating in ether, floating elsewhere, like him. He seems to me, in moments like this, not of the earth. "Piano works," he whispers, his eyes still closed. I hear his desire to stay where he is inside the sound and the meaning that comes with it. I hear the echo of patience it takes for him to pop up from within and speak. I can see that he's receiving something. A message from the composer? Voices from beyond? I wonder what Janáček would think at witnessing such concentration. If the composer walked in I'd say, "Look at that guy on the bed, he's a brilliant man (whose maternal grandparents were Czech, by the way), and he's drinking in *your* work. You are gone from here, but talking to him still. Isn't that something?"

So much of Henry is a mystery to me, I think. How deeply he loves certain things, loves me, and how far from me he can seem. And I think how much I love that too.

I skitter across the room and deposit my backpack near the desk. I put my wallet on the bureau and strip to my underwear. I glance in the bedroom mirror, taking stock again of how my thirties are treating me. The slight, new folds above the hips, the circles under the eyes, the slightly leathery look of the face. I check the curves of my chest to see if the weights I lifted at the Y that afternoon have had any effect. I see how aroused I remain under the cotton of my Calvin Kleins. I think of the phone calls I could make, the mail I should answer. Maybe I'll stay up a while. I look to my lover, think of being naked with him. Of being wanted. Wanting. The litany of endless desires skating across my brain.

Henry's repose is stillness itself.

I sit on the edge of the bed, ready to ask him about his day. To insist. But he looks so calm.

I go to wash my face, take a final pee.

I come back. He's still there, still. I crawl in next to him and one of his hands levitates, moves over, and rests on my chest for a moment. After a while, he turns and pulls the headphones out of the stereo and piano music floods the room. His hands have returned gracefully to his chest.

"Beautiful playing," I say. "Who's the pianist?"

"Firkusny," he whispers.

I press my little toe against his and tap along in rhythm to what must be, I think, Firkusny's left hand.

"Did you buy soy milk?" I ask.

"Yeah. I got two."

"Thanks . . . any messages?"

"Just Michael. He got us tickets to his show Sunday night."

"Oh. Good."

There's more I could ask but I remain silent. I listen. I scooch my hip over so that it touches his, tucks into the curve there like perfect sense. Bones, continents, linked.

"What's this piece called?"

"'Auf verwachsenem Pfade' . . . 'On the Overgrown Path' . . . I think."

"Sounds sad," I say, and give Henry a quick, light peck on the cheek. He responds, his eyes still closed, by puckering his lips and offering a delicate kiss to the air. I know it's meant for me, this bubble of him coming up from the deep. I feel how it's linked to the countless kisses of so many kinds we've shared before. I know he's glad. I'm where he wants me. Close. We listen to the delicate piano for a time, toe to toe, hip to hip.

Henry says, "Oh, I got this today. Listen. . . ." He reaches for the remote, the fancy clicker that goes with the new player. The one I got him for his birthday. He loves it because he can stay still and choose exactly what he wants, three CDs at a time. It's a big success, this present. A happy gift coming from happy, steady gigs: me in another musical, Henry performing in another Shakespeare in the Park. "Listen . . . to this adagio section," he says. "Ravel. Concerto in G Major. Listen."

I do. I listen and it is unspeakably beautiful. From the very first gentle notes of piano to the entrance of strings and clarinet, I am lifted and caressed. I am floating home, at first, to Denver, over the mountains. The places I walked as a boy. And then, suddenly, I'm thinking of my Great Aunt Virginia, who just died at ninety-five. She loved music with a passion similar to Henry's. "It saves my life, it does," she used to say. "Makes me right with the world when nothing else can." She lived alone in London and told me how walking along the Thames toward the Royal Festival Hall and stopping for tea before a concert, how this was heaven on earth for her. She must have known this piece, this gorgeous Ravel. *How did he compose a thing of such beauty?* It's as if his very soul is soaring through our little apartment. Henry's toe presses against mine and my eyes well up and I promise myself to remember this—the depth of my gratefulness. To remember living this moment of contentment. When the noise, the galaxy of desires, skittering across my day, calmed to this very one: to be with Henry as he offers a piece of music to me. To lie, to listen with Henry, as we hold our separate thoughts is, for now, completely, utterly, enough.

He taps me on the shoulder twice. That's code for me to turn on my side so we can spoon. I sink into the warm, music-filled sweetness of him. The adagio ends.

"Wow," I whisper.

"I knew you'd like this. It's sweet. Like you."

"Oh God, I'm not . . ."

"*Shhhhhh.*" He switches off the music. I press close, as close as I can, and we drift into our separate sleeps.

12

AND WHAT WOULD I tell him if I was able? That sometimes I wake in the morning with such madness in my heart, with nothing else on my mind but where, how, I can sneak off and find some kind of fix. A thrill I can only get elsewhere, not here in our sweet bedroom with the clean flannel sheets, under his favorite portrait of Buster Keaton. Not in the warmth of us, of our home, but in the wilderness of some other place, some stranger.

This would be, this is, the hardest thing to speak of. It terrifies me. To speak would change everything, I think. He would see me for what I am and leave. And I would not blame him.

I think sometimes of my first-ever boyfriend back at acting school in San Francisco. An ardent, elegant boy named Bill. We were crazy for each other, and one night when he found out that I'd gone off to a bathhouse with our ballet teacher, he confronted me, slapped me across the face, and yelled: "You are nothing but an anxiety-ridden slut!" My cheek stung for days. My heart for months. Stung with anger and with what I felt was the truth of it. Stings still when I recall my inability to, at the very least, speak honestly. When I think of how fearful and confused I am around matters sexual. It seems to me that I have no integrity, that I simply own the kind of desire that sullies.

The thing to give up here, to sacrifice, is the secrets.

To converse, to draw close. To make sacred. This is what I want to do. But I am terrified to speak. *How will Henry and I ever make it?* I wonder. *Survive* me?

13

I WAS SITTING at a piano, sharing the bench with Ricky. We were in a cozy old apartment in Philadelphia. It was an autumn morning in the early 1990s. Ricky was the composer of a new musical in which I was performing, an ambitious saga about the birth of the United States. He was teaching me a love song hot off his press, and during a break, as will happen, the subject of sex came up. He talked of an early experience, how painfully shy he'd been in high school and college. At one point, surprising myself because I seldom thought and had only rarely spoken of it, I tossed off what felt to be a bit of a joke. "Well, hell, I had an affair with an older guy when I was twelve. It went on for nearly three years. One of those Catholic stories, you know?"

"You're kidding," Ricky said.

"No."

"That's kind of *major*. Don't you think? I mean, that's like . . . *abuse*."

"Nah," I said, swiping a hand toward Ricky's furrowed face. "No."

My *no* came out rather more sharply than I'd meant. I was aware of how much I hated, how defensive I felt about, that word: *abuse*. How it was necessarily and frighteningly tethered to words like *crime* and *perpetrator* and, worst of all, *victim*. God, I wanted nothing to do with that. I didn't want to be anywhere near that loser word, that kind of sad-sack story.

"I mean, the guy wasn't violent or evil," I told Ricky. "And . . . ya know . . . I got over it. It happened. No big deal."

I spoke these words, I remember, with simple conviction. Ricky cocked his head and fiddled with his glasses. "I think you don't realize how major that is. I mean, Marty, you were twelve. Maybe you've convinced yourself it's nothing, but I think it matters in ways you don't even know."

"Ricky, look, I struggle with things. I have hang-ups, probably, around sex. I mean, God knows . . . I was raised Catholic. But look. I'm OK."

"But this is more than that. You were a kid."

I dismissed his words, but his eyes, I remember, slammed into my gut, and somewhere at the bottom of my diaphragm a portal popped open. I felt how I wanted to kick it closed, this little trap-door, but something was in the way, the tip of an iceberg, the foot of someone wanting to sell me on the past. On how much it matters. But I didn't want to waste one nickel, one bit of the now on what was then. I sat up and snatched my sheet music, suggesting we get back to work, back to singing.

That night, I was onstage playing an eighteenth-century Scotsman who had traveled alone to the New World to search out a place, the means of survival, for his beloved wife and children back home. In the play he sang his epistles to his faraway love, and each one began: *My dearest life.* Ricky had set these words to the most haunting and beautiful melody. During that evening's preview performance, I kept choking up whenever I sang them. When I got back to the apartment afterward, I telephoned Henry. When he answered, I said, "My dearest life."

"What's that?"

"A tune in the play."

"Are you all right?" he asked.

"I don't know. Had a teary show. Miss you."

"You're cute."

"You're cuter."

After I hung up and hit the pillow, Henry's voice wouldn't leave me. Nor would the song. I kept humming the notes. The interval between *my* and *dear* was a sixth. And then *life* landed on the fifth of the chord, pure and simple and restful. Perfect harmony. It suited wonderfully the character of John, the strong and loyal Scotsman. A man of such integrity. Perfect for Henry, too, I thought.

My dearest life.

It matters, he'd said. What does that mean? Ricky's music, his stubborn words, wouldn't leave me. A sad and sour feeling came over me. I was thinking of the pack of scribbled pages I'd stuck in a drawer. The ones with the circled *C.* And I was wondering about the ugly, persistent depressions. And all the stuff that was hidden.

My dearest life.

I picked up the novel I was reading. The bookmark was blue and ragged. It came from an old store called the Book Barn. I stared for a long time at the etching of the barn, the little window drawn over the hayloft. *Christ,* I thought, *if you start digging into this, you'll never get to the bottom.*

Several weeks later when I was back in New York, Ricky phoned. He wanted to tell me about a men's group run by a pair of doctors at St. Luke's Hospital. An eight-week course based on Mike Lew's groundbreaking book. *Victims No Longer: Men Recovering from Incest and Other Sexual Child Abuse.*

"Thanks," I said to Ricky. *Jesus, no way,* I whispered to myself as I hung up the phone.

We met, seven guys and two mellow doctors, for eight consecutive Thursday nights. We sat in a circle under fluorescent lights. An easel with poster paper and colored markers stood at the front of the class.

Loss of Childhood.

Men and Feelings.

Incest.

Survival Strategies.

I could barely look at the lingo on the board. Mostly I kept my eyes on the red carpet, on the ring of snowy boots that were jiggling on the feet of seven young men. The docs' voices gently dovetailed. They were good at this stuff, but mostly what I heard was my own voice telling me how my case was different.

By the end of the third meeting I couldn't avoid it any longer. It was my turn to say something about my "story." I'd listened to the others through the noise of my squirming brain. There'd been a drunk uncle, a violent father, a coach, a neighbor. Harrowing. My heart went out to them, poor guys. Now I leaned forward, my hands clasped between my knees, and tried to explain the basics about a Catholic summer camp and a counselor. About three years of furtive encounters. "And, look. I'm the one," I blurted. "I went back, I partook. He was a kind of a . . . I don't know. Like a friend. It wasn't destructive. I don't think. It happened. Life goes on."

The doctors nodded calmly. OK. No judgment here.

One of them, the younger, shorter one, began to discuss the particular difficulty men have at revealing experiences of abuse. The sense of threat to one's masculinity, the struggle with sexual identity. The shame of feeling complicit. The denial. I stared at the carpet.

The taller, dark-haired doctor chimed in. "I understand what you've said. That you don't see what went on in your early adolescence as necessarily harmful. But, can you consider for a moment the particular violence, the trauma, inherent in a sexual act between an adult and a child. That inequality of power. Consider what it is for the natural bond of trust between a boy and an authority figure—a camp counselor, for instance—to be suddenly broken."

I began to say that, yes, I could see that, I could consider it, but that *violence* seemed such an extreme word. And then, trying to explain what Bob and I were to each other, I fell silent.

"Consider," the doctor went on, "the capability of a twelve-year-old to partake. The brain of a boy that age is not fully developed. By a long shot." I felt an odd lift in my chest. Like something, someone, being let off a hook. "And certainly not capable of absorbing the enormity of a sexual violation—in your case, a chronic violation that, as Mike Lew points out so clearly, is traumatizing."

At the end of the meeting that night, after I'd put on my parka and folded my chair away, I stepped over to say goodnight to the doctors. The younger one said, "You know, Marty, it's the job of a kid to fall in love. And it's the job of the adult to have boundaries." Simple enough.

I walked across the Columbia campus that night to get to the Number 1 train. I stopped to sit on the steps of the library, next to the statue of Alma Mater. Soul Mother with her bronze arms outstretched as if welcoming one and all to crawl up into her cold lap. Ten at night might as well have been noon. Students rushing everywhere. They looked twelve, for God's sake. A young Asian woman loaded with books passed me on the steps. She had on a red plaid skirt, very Catholic-school.

An image took hold of me:

A boy, a little kid, balancing on the rear axle of a tractor.
Staring at the back of the head of the man driving.
A rubber band is there, attached to the man's glasses.
It cuts into the skull, across the tangled, greasy hair.

And I knew it. Absolutely knew that this kid was in trouble. I felt how every nerve of his body was scrambling to hide, to make sense of, what had just happened. How he'd woken with his underpants missing, his innards going haywire. I could see him perched there on the tractor, fine boned, numb. I knew the exact place. I knew the date, the exact morning. I knew the kid. It's like his skin was folded inside of mine, pushing hard to get out.

And I thought: *It matters. It does.*

I went to my dog-eared Webster's that night: *Trauma.*

A wound to living tissue caused by an extrinsic agent.

A disordered psychic or behavioral state resulting from mental or emotional stress or injury.

The following Thursday there was a long and colorful list on the board. *Frequent Issues Faced by Survivors of Sexual Abuse.* Among them were compulsive sexual activity, anger, extreme anxiety, suicidal thoughts. That night the doctors launched into a description of

PTSD (post-traumatic stress disorder). I was back to staring at the
floor, back to my profound discomfort of things (of me) being reduced to lists. To some sorry syndrome.

What a load of psychobabble crap, came a familiar iteration (my father's? An old highschool priest's? my own?) ringing in my head.
I could certainly accept how this syndrome might apply to those
who'd survived the horror of war, but not to those who'd stumbled
into the vagaries of early sex. As I struggled to listen, the doctors
came to a word that seized me. *Compartmentalize.* Compartments.
It made me think of Max, the guy on the old TV show *Get Smart,*
and his silly secret compartments. "It's very common for a victim
(that fucking word) to have a public self and an entirely hidden other
self. A split. A fragmentation. This is a prevalent condition among
survivors of trauma. Compartmentalizing things as a way to survive. It can become a pattern. A way of life."

And I thought:

That's really true.

And I thought:

*Yeah, the brain takes a box with a very tight lid and stashes the stuff
away.*

And I thought:

Stuck in my compartment are countless unspeakable items.

- A sexually active altar boy
- One molesting camp counselor
- The counselor's naked girlfriend
- One lying little cuss
- One unfaithful lover

So many items tucked away tight:

- One San Francisco dance professor. Remember? He was
sixty, for God's sake. You, nineteen. He offered attention, free
classes. You gave out. Secret rent boy, feeling trapped.
- One brief and frightening transgression with an underage
boy in a Coney Island men's room. Never forgotten.
- One massage advertisement. Remember? Placed by you,

way back, your early days in New York. *Student with a swimmer's body, trained hands.* You rang the doors of Upper East Side gentlemen. Seventy bucks a pop. You got to be, wanted to be, the young, adored one. Never told anyone. Little hustler killing time, soul going bankrupt while you scrambled for rent.

Ad infinitum. The secrets.

How often have I said to Henry when he tells me that he loves me, "If you really knew me, you wouldn't."

"Why do you always say that?" he'd ask, irritated, and I'd shrug, continuing to wash the dishes or fold the sheets, feeling the corrosion seep from my secret compartment and stick itself, like a dark wedge, between us.

Somewhere near the end of the eight-week course, I'd begun to talk more with Henry about why I was attending these Thursday-night meetings. I didn't use the word *survivor*, another tag I hated. Like I was in some club of fellows who'd made it through a shipwreck. I did, though, begin to mention this man Bob as one might talk of a creepy junior high school teacher or the distant memory of a groping priest. I'd begun to speak more seriously about how I felt this counselor had left a mark. That I had stuff to figure out. "I'm thirty-two years old," I said to Henry, "and for some reason this is bubbling up bad and I realize I feel so much shame about it. About who I am."

One night, I was reading Mike Lew's book in bed. Henry was next to me. We'd had a good day. Saw an Italian film at Lincoln Center that got us talking about Italy, about planning another trip. We'd been there two summers before and it'd been glorious. Especially Venice. Henry's crazy for Venice. As I lay there, I was making my way slowly through chapters like, "Is Recovery Possible?" "Breaking Secrecy," "Sex, Trust, and Caring," and, at some point, I tossed the book on the floor.

"This shit gives me the creeps," I said. "It's all so pathetic and I hate the cutesy little photo on the front cover. I mean, it's a little boy in culottes holding a kitten, for God's sake. Have you seen that?"

Henry stopped reading and turned to me. "I think it's brave that you're looking at all this stuff."

Suddenly my heart was trying to somersault its way through my ribs.

"Henry?"

"Yeah?"

"You know how I always say to you that if you really knew me, you wouldn't love me? And how much that bugs you and how you always ask me what I mean and tell me not to say that?"

"Yeah?"

"Well, I want to explain to you what I mean. I'm struggling with being . . . I'm really compulsive."

"Yeah?"

"I mean, compulsive about sex. I go into parks or men's rooms and stuff and look for anonymous sex. It's like a craziness. An addiction thing, I guess. It has to do maybe with all of this. With when I was a kid or some screwed-up Catholic thing in me. I don't know. I'm getting better, I think."

He was silent.

"I'm sorry. I know it's weird. I love you. It doesn't have to do with you. It's this problem, my problem. It's not totally out of control . . . I'm not fucking anyone . . . I don't understand it."

He was silent.

"Do you hate me right now? Do you need me to go away?"

"No. I don't want you to go away. What do you mean, 'compulsive'? What do you do?"

I explained, as calmly as my pounding heart would allow, that the form my compulsivity took was, at least from a sexually transmitting point of view, guarded. That I'd maintained at least that much sanity and was determined to stop. When as much as we could handle for the moment was said and done, Henry looked at me and said, "Promise me you'll be safe. For *us*."

He let one hand drift over and rest near my shoulder. I lay still, looking at him for a long time. In silence, I asked, *Even like this? Even like this you love me?*

Everything in his presence said: *Yes.*

When those two months were over, I thanked the good doctors (and, wherever he was, Mike Lew) and walked away thinking, *Please, God, that had to have been enough digging.* Case closed.

14

IN THE FALL of 1992, my old high school friend and former New York roommate, Jodi, purchased a used Toyota in our hometown, Denver. She needed to drive it to Los Angeles, where she lived, and called to ask if I wanted to fly out and take a western road trip. Mesa Verde, Four Corners, Grand Canyon. A rare chance to catch up. Henry was starting a new play; I was unemployed (or currently unenjoyed, as we'd taken to calling it). The timing was good.

As we worked our way over Wolf Creek Pass and cut through the canyons of the eastern slope, Jodi began to discuss her thoughts on alcoholism. "Do you think you have a problem?" I asked. She nodded. Said she'd made a decision to join AA. "Wow," I said. "Good for you." She'd brought six cassettes on the 12 steps and, as we approached Utah, asked if I'd mind listening. I didn't know much about the famous program and she was so bravely gung ho that I silenced my cynic and told her sure, play them.

By the time we reached the spooky formations of Zion National Park, the disembodied voice on the stereo was walking us through the final stages out of addiction and into spiritual awakening. Tunneling through the vast walls of red rock and under the otherworldly arches, surrender to a "higher power" seemed only natural. At a Zion café that night, over my cabernet and her coffee, Jodi and I watched a bloodred sunset as she laid it all out about the depressions and the cocktails and I poured forth about the anxiety and the secret sex. We'd been confidants since senior year of high school and, though we didn't see each other often, we always cut to the chase.

"Sex addiction. That's harsh," she said, running a hand through her thick, black hair.

"I wouldn't call it that. No, no. Not addiction. It's an occasional obsession...like, when I'm really depressed or out of work it'll come over me. It's getting better, or it gets better, sometimes, and then it's not, I'm ashamed to say." I took a gulp of water, then of cabernet. "My old therapist used to call it 'acting out.' It's like the illicit and the erotic got fused in me, somehow, in this crushing way. I mean, sex is a gift, right? A joy, no matter how much they bashed it in Catholic school. But I experience it sometimes as this curse. Hen and I have talked about it. I told him I'm getting healthier. I promised. I've got stuff to figure out."

I watched Jodi rip open a packet of brown sugar, sprinkle some in her coffee. "Thank God you've got Henry," she said. "After this last breakup I feel like I'll be alone forever. Not even a cocktail for company."

"You'll meet someone."

"It's good you guys talk."

"It's hard, but we've talked about it. To a point. Some things are private. There's a difference, though, between *private* and *secret*. Privacy has to do with respect, I think, with not needing to share with him every psychosexual drama or personal struggle that passes through my life, my brain. But secrecy is something different, it eats away at things. I hate the sense that there's a hidden, *bad* me. That I'm going to ruin everything. It's juvenile."

A young woman with an amazingly long ponytail refilled Jodi's coffee.

"When did this start, with the alcohol?" I asked.

"I don't know, exactly. I just suddenly realized I could never stop at two. Or three." She wrapped her hands around her mug. "How's your wine?"

I raised my glass, she her cup. We gazed out the large window at all the crazy, jagged forms of rock. Huge creatures, frozen in time.

"Beautiful," I said. "It's so eerie."

"Yeah, like in a disaster movie." She smiled.

When we arrived in LA, Jodi suggested that I come with her to a meeting. *What the hell,* I thought. *Maybe I'll learn something about my Irish heritage.* We walked to an old church not far from her apartment in West Hollywood. She led the way up a stairwell to a second-floor room. Three tall windows, gleaming with the California light, faced west. Several rows of folding chairs were arranged in a semicircle, but most folks were still standing, grouped around one of several pillars along the center of the room or gathered near the table with the coffee urn. Moms and Dads, it seemed, and bikers with helmets and gay guys with boyfriends. Big and small and black and white and everything in between. The cheery hubbub was not at all the image I'd had in my head, of a somber room with men in dark suits, faces taut with remorse. We sat in the back row. The meeting began with individual hellos. I was startled when it came to Jodi and she ended with the actual words, "and I'm an alcoholic." I mumbled my name and pointed. "I'm with her."

Material was read that I recognized from the tapes, stuff about lives becoming unmanageable and turning our will over to God *as we understood God.* I bounced between hearing the stuff as some morose admission of defeat and as the wisest words in the world. Saint Anselm's proof kept running through my mind: *God is that than which nothing greater can be thought.* In any case, I was busy judging as folks began to raise their hands and talk. A ruddy-faced guy, jacket and tie, said he needed to speak. He'd been sober and was approaching, he said, the one-year mark from when he'd fallen off the wagon and forgot to pick up the kids, lied to his wife. He was struggling today with the shame of it and wanted a drink in the worst way. His candor was remarkable, disarming. It was as if, as he spoke, he was peeling off a mask, a mid-forties business-guy mask, and written there across the wrinkles and scars of his suddenly soft and one and only face was the simple truth. It cost him. It took courage to speak, that was clear. People near me were nodding. His words seemed to yank everybody into the present, to galvanize the room. There were many others, then, who spoke off the cuff and from the heart. I gathered that this is what happened at these meetings. It was one of the most sane and impressive things I'd ever witnessed.

When the final prayer was over (reminiscent of the "Go in Peace" I'd heard for years at Mass), Jodi informed me that there'd be another meeting following. Same 12 steps, different addiction. "Maybe you should check it out," she suggested. "It's to do with sex." I shrugged, my cheeks already burning with her mere mention of it. She gave me a hug and went on her way.

The chairs remained in their same semicircle, the coffeepot, the blackboard, the same. But now there was a new group, generally younger, not quite as many people. I took the very last seat in the very last row and acquainted myself with the silver doorknob that led out to the street.

I found the hellos harrowing. The calmness with which people were saying, "Hi, I'm a sex addict," was unnerving. The voices were cavalier, but the designation sounded so dire, so collapsed-in-the-alley-with-a-needle-in-your-arm. When it came to me, I muttered my name and something about "first time."

The sun by now had set and the windows gone dark. I stared out to where a street lamp illuminated two palm trees. The fronds shimmered sickly under fluorescent light. My stomach churned. How did I get here? Washed up at the end of a continent, end of the line. Land of Manson and Moonies and me and God knows what. I glanced at the doorknob.

As in the previous meeting, there were readings about the group and its purpose. About admitting powerlessness, in this case over sexual behavior. A young woman began reciting from a list of characteristics common to the group. She read one and passed the booklet to the next person. It talked, among other things, about using sex as a drug, as a way to avoid feelings such as anxiety, how we'd compartmentalized it rather than integrated sex into our lives in a healthy way. I watched the pamphlet move from lap to lap, stunned that such an accurate inventory of my secret struggle existed in the world, that it had been written without me.

A slim guy with a wool sweater and Levis took a seat front and center. He was the main speaker for that evening. He crossed one leg over the other, leaned forward so that his bearded chin was in his hand and his elbow upon his knee, and he began, quietly, to tell his story. He'd been an altar boy at a parish in the South. A man there, a deacon, seduced him when he was thirteen. First sex he ever had. It was a shock, a crazy jolt, a kind of high. He described how, after his initial fear and confusion, he felt weirdly flattered by this man. Adored, even. But that, over time, it became nothing but destructive. He began to feel like an *object.* I was so struck by the word, the articulation of that idea. He explained how he felt stuck. But how he was hooked into it. The pleasure of being touched like that.

"The most awful part," he said, "was the secrecy and the guilt. It went on until I went to high school. I never told a soul."

He was scratching his beard as he spoke, looking down at his boots. He had the gentle manner of someone who'd been through hell, and I couldn't keep my eyes off him. It was as if all my life I'd had an appointment to hear this guy. He talked of his sexual confusion and depression and how he'd fallen in love and married, had two kids. How, in his late twenties and thirties he started sneaking off to have sex in arcades with men. Porn places. He said he didn't know why. That his feet took him there, like they were wired, and he never told anyone. Was sure he never would.

"But I got AIDS," he said. "I had to tell my wife, had to get help. My kids think I have leukemia. I don't want them to know, they're too young. Maybe that's wrong, but I'm doing the best I can. One day at a time. I'm sober now, for more than two years.

Life, my health, is good right now. I'm so grateful for the help of this program. Thank you."

He was smiling as he finished. Shrugged his shoulders. My throat had clamped shut. The room, my chair, my chest, felt electrified. *Pay attention,* I was telling myself. *Look at the consequences of what happened when this man was young.* I felt livid about what that deacon had dared to do, and I was astonished at the direct connection this man made between what happened when he was a kid and what came to pass in his adult life. I thought I understood the connection; I believed it. I felt for him a compassion and a fury that I could not seem to find for myself. And this baffled me.

A woman talked of losing her job because of the seemingly uncontrollable obsessions she experienced in relation to coworkers. She clutched a ring of keys as she spoke of her determination to turn it over, turn it around, ask for help. A young man talked of the fortune he'd spent on female prostitutes. In a hoarse voice, hands clasped, he told of the experience of having been abused by his mother. His sense of how this sexualized him in a way that he was only just beginning to understand. He talked of his progress and how, one day at a time, following his plan for sobriety, he hadn't called a prostitute for seventy-three days. Creating a specific plan, I learned, with a mentor, was one of the tools used here. For most, a sexually sober life wasn't about abstention but about mindfulness and balance.

When the meeting was over I found myself asking for literature and schedules. And I realized I couldn't leave without saying something to the bearded man. I walked over to where he was sitting speaking with friends.

"Thanks for that."

He stood and took my hand. "Welcome," he said.

It astonished me that humans had figured out a way, found the guts, to come together and talk of healing from this compulsion. (It would be months before I could use the dreaded word *addiction*.)

My heart sank at seeing so clearly that I belonged here, even as I felt enormous relief, a wild wave of hope, at finding these concepts, this fellowship.

As soon as I returned to Jodi's that night, I called Henry. I sat cross-legged in an armchair and spoke in a torrent. I told him all about the evening. The men and women who'd talked. The plans, the sponsors, the steps. The few times Henry and I had circled the subject of compulsion, it had been so difficult, fraught with my shame, a slow pulling of teeth. But the context of my discovering the group gave the subject a sudden space and light.

"It's amazing to find this," I said. "There are a lot of meetings in New York too."

"That's good. That's good, I'm glad," he kept saying.

"Are you all right, me talking about all of this?"

"Yes, yes. Just hurry home."

I felt as if Henry was curled right there in the chair with me. Our two heads leaning together, talking out the dark and tangled mess. The demons and the hope. Nearly eight years now we'd been together, and in so many ways we were closer than ever. We'd weathered rough patches of doubt and distance. Two ex-Catholics often reticent to articulate feelings. But hard days had always grown into good ones, and here we were still together. Phone to my ear, I felt him listening the way he does, the way I tried to when he talked of his own very different demons and depressions. *This is it,* I thought. *This is the work of love. The drawing close.*

"I'm getting better, you know," I told him. "Promise."

Though I often hated it, wished to God it wasn't necessary, for some years to come I got myself to those good and god-awful meetings. Grateful or grumpy, depending on the day, I would sit in circles of folding chairs and listen and talk about one day at a time and let-ting go, letting God. The phrases (like the meetings) were inspir-ing, vapid, life-saving, exasperating. There were moments when I wanted to scream at myself, at every one in the room, *How did we manage to make such a lovely thing as sex so complicated?* It was as if we'd become the embodiment of Buddha's second Noble Truth: *The cause of all suffering is desire.* At times I felt like we were products, prisoners, of a culture gone haywire, a society fraught and frightened about sex. As if we'd gotten all twisted up by the voices of politicians and prelates and priests who'd unleashed their Western brand of shame (not to mention their legions of sad offenders) onto our bodies. Enough navel-gazing. Lighten up. *Let's get out of here and play! Let's move to Bali!*

I had a million theories, a million methods, to distance myself from the matter at hand—health. Whatever the complicated truth of how we'd come to be who we are, and however absurd or frustrating the meetings seemed at times, I knew this work was important and good because, in the end, it had to do with awareness. It's a deadly experience to have an addiction living you rather than you living your blessed, precious life. It's a drag to use something as magnificent as sex to drug yourself. And here was one way of shedding much needed light, of untying the knots of a compulsion that wanted to yank you its own direction, usurp your day. For me, the opportunity to talk about this stuff was a way toward reclaiming, rediscovering sexuality as an utmost expression of presence and consciousness. Not a crazy loop of learned behavior, of disappearance, not a numbed-out habit of turning humans into soulless matter, but as an act of divine communion. As fun and life affirming. Whether gay or straight, monogamous or not, it was about being free and responsible enough, it seemed to me, to make your own *conscious* choices. The gratitude I felt that I was able to turn my feet toward a meeting and not down an alley, was enormous. Grace of this group, my compulsions began to lift for wonderful stretches of well-being. I grew more alive in my work, with my friends and family and certainly with Henry. Health brings with it peace.

But I would find, as time went on, that I had things to say and work to do that I couldn't seem to get to in these 12-step rooms, and I would eventually drift away from attending meetings.

I couldn't shake the feeling that I was walking over the rumble of something unresolved. Something stronger and smarter than me that still had a hold on things. I wasn't really free. Not from the compulsions, not from the depressions, not from the grip of it. But the grip of what, exactly? I couldn't name it. It was a kind of shadow, a yearning, a riddle. I thought there must be a key. A code. And if I prayed hard enough, one day I'd crack it and everything would tumble, restfully, into place. I tried to look for the key in the present, inside the good life around me.

I remained embarrassed, reticent, when things about Bob would pop out of my mouth or, more often, onto the pages of one of my countless journals. When I spoke or wrote of it I'd think: *There it is.* I've stumbled again upon that boring story of the boy and his counselor. That lame excuse for being a lousy adult. Enough of that. *Old news.* Get back to life. Get back to work. Get back to *here*. Have a good rehearsal. A good audition. Get home to Henry. You're thirty-three years old, for chrissakes. Live in the now.

Funny, though, how much energy it takes in the present, to continually dismiss the past. To stomp over what you've so stubbornly buried. I moved through the days wondering if I'd ever arrive at the point where I could pull together the pieces of this puzzle that were waiting, but refusing, to come together to make a whole picture, a whole life.

15

IT'S EASTER AGAIN; 1993. Spring is ready to burst after a long winter of forgetting. I'm on a visit to Denver. Mom still lives in the old house. She hasn't retired and moved to New Mexico yet. I'm sleeping over the squeaky springs of my childhood bed. I yearn for this—to come home. It beckons. I arrive and find it unbearable.

It's a bright, April afternoon. I'm sitting on the edge of my mother's bed, staring at the phone. I've just finished talking with my old high school friend Dave. We've made plans to go see a film later that evening—a comedy. We both agreed that it'd be good to laugh. The house is empty, Mom at work, brother and sisters grown and moved away. Midafternoon, suburban silence. Deadly. Not even a lawn mower . . . too early in the season. I sit, frozen, staring at the pale yellow rotary-dial phone, trying to take measure of the storm inside my chest, wondering just what name to give it on this particular day—high anxiety? Deep depression? Plain old self-pity? Why, why is it so hard to come home? What is this thing clawing its way up the back of my throat, banging at the underside of my sternum? It's like some body within my body—wanting out. Badly. A living thing pressing up, trying to push the stone aside to say: *Here, look at me. Deal.* A gigantic nap seems the next best move. And it is then, gazing at the carefully painted-to-look-like-an-antique nightstand, that the idea shoots through me. An electric current. A dangerous fancy.

Call him.

It's never actually occurred to me before. Not in this concrete way. And now it blossoms through my brain like a hit from a bong and my heart beats out a furious protest: *Absolutely not. What the fuck are you thinking. Why open that crazy door? Past is past. Period.*

"I don't know," I whisper, "aren't you the least bit curious if he's alive? If he's out of prison? Where he might be . . . if he even fucking remembers you?"

NO.

OK. Calm down. Just an idea.

I walk to the kitchen and sit at the table and I think, once again, of Passover dinner the night before.

I was the gentile guest, the beloved goy, at Jodi's parents' home. I'd even won the game of finding the hidden matzo—the afikomen—before the seder began. Jodi's dad beamed as he handed me five bucks for discovering the cracker behind a photo on the windowsill. He patted me on the back. *Ah, if only you were straight,* his twinkling eyes seemed to say, *if only you were Jewish, if only Jodi and you cared to, you'd make a great son-in-law.* There was a lot of warmth there among the if-onlys.

I sat at the table next to the place left empty for the prophet Elijah and directly across from Jodi's young cousin, Zack. Blue blazer, blond hair, sharp red tie. Handsome devil. He was twelve and rather sullen. His parents, Jodi had whispered to me in the kitchen, were in the midst of a nasty divorce, and the split, it seemed to me, was written all across his adorable face. So there I was to the left of absent Elijah, not far from the bitter herbs, athwart the handsome cousin. There I was, thirty-three facing twelve, and the equation rose up within me like an explosion: *This was nearly the math with me and Bob, but now I'm the larger sum.*

I'd quite forgotten what twelve looked like. I kept glancing at the boy, the way tufts of his hair poked up over the Passover Haggadah as he bent his face to read. He turned the pages backwards; I did, too, that's how it worked in Hebrew—as if we were playing with the sequence of things, moving in reverse to uncover the lessons. I kept looking up, stealing peeks, thinking how it's the details that kill me, that bring on the rush of tenderness. The fuzz across his lip and down the back of his fine neck. The two tiny pimples next to his right nostril. The way, when he stood, he jammed his hands in his pockets and leaned into his left hip, cool, casual little man. The way a quick blush moved over his smooth cheeks when I'd asked him about school, what subjects he liked. "French," he mumbled. "Français, moi aussi," I'd said, glad for the connection, the chance to show off. "J'adore la langue française." His lips were deep red and tough-sweet, on-the-cusp-of-becoming. That's it. That's what gets me. This particular age, this particular bursting beauty. The just-about-to-become-a-man part of it. I am touched by it. Attracted. Moved. I want to tousle his hair. I want to hear again the soprano of his voice with the raspy air wrapped around it. Is this akin to the affection a parent feels sitting on the edge of the bed in the minutes before their child falls asleep? Or is this more like how it starts with coaches and counselors and priests and lonely neighbors? Does it begin with this unbearable tenderness? This longing to help the boy, to reach out? And is the fondness you are feeling a fondness for the boy in front of you or, really, some yearning that has to do with the lonesome kid within? Are you really just reaching, wanting, to offer tenderness to the boy you once were... before? Back there? Is this a reaching that could transform itself into manipulation, exploitation? To violation? Could you turn beauty here into prey?

At one point, after Zack read the Four Questions (*Why is this night different from all other nights?*), I reached across the table and squeezed his arm. A rush of affection moved through me even as my own internal secret service erupted inside my head, guns drawn and voices screaming: *Drop your hands, asshole!* And, withdrawing my fingers gently from his shoulder, I felt like guilt sitting across from innocence. *What is this chaos?* I wondered.

Mr. B. asked me to read a passage.

Blessed are You, Lord our God, Ruler of the Universe, who has kept us in this life, sustained us and enabled us to reach this festive season....

What would it take for a scoutmaster or a camp counselor to cross the line? To get this kid in the sack? Imagine the kind of planning it would take to create that situation. Imagine the blind need, the insanity to touch this child sexually, to cross that boundary, that moral precipice.

To reach the season of our freedom in remembrance ...

But that's it! I thought. I could never, ever, in a million years do that. I would never wish that turmoil on a young person. On any person. No way. Look into the eyes of that boy and see. *See.*

Blessed are You, Lord our God, Ruler of the Universe...

What did Bob *see* when he looked at me? Did he look at me with tenderness, a kind of caring? Was he even capable of that? He was sick, wasn't he? Something was wrong with him, had happened to him, how else to explain? It wasn't me he saw or loved or was drawn to. It was an image in his own head that turned me into a thing. He took what he wanted, gave what little he could. Why do these things happen? What makes us reach across and take what we want at the expense of another? In one way or another, it rests in all of us, doesn't it? The capability to harm.

And it was then, all this stuff roiling in my head, somewhere around the recitation of the Ten Plagues, as we dripped red wine for each disaster, that I excused myself and went to the bathroom off Jodi's old bedroom to have a cry. *That's twelve,* I kept thinking. *Look how little he is, how tender. He is to be cherished, protected.* And in the midst of this sorrow I was grateful, because for a moment I grasped the trespass, understood what had been lost. The thing *that matters.* My tears felt like a layer melting away, getting me closer to the thing worth being angry about. The thing worth examining.

And this was clear. Looking across at twelve, I understood that I was different from Bob. I was not and could not ever be *that.* A predator. And I understood that my care for that beautiful boy across the table was something good.

All the way home from Passover dinner my thoughts, my tears, kept tumbling. *Who knows Twelve? Twelve are the tribes of Israel... Who knows Twelve?* We'd sung from the Haggadah at the end of the meal. I'd forgotten. Twelve hit me like a thirty-ton truck. I was so glad to shake Zack's firm little hand when I left Jodi's house. "I wish you all the best, young man. You deserve it. You're a champ." The way he dropped his head and blushed touched me no end.

I'm on the edge of Mom's bed again. I'm holding a Mountain Bell phone book. I talk to my pounding chest: *Look, it's not possible that he'll be in here, this will all be over in a second, just looking, calm down.* I open the pages and begin to run my fingers down columns of names beginning with *C.* I keep repeating it, the hard consonant, as if it's something caught in my throat. I hate to see that my hand is shaking. It makes me feel foolish and weak. *This'll be over in a sec...*

It appears.

It's the same size, the same black print as every other name on the page, but it seems to be lit from within. To shimmer.

It's his parents, not him. I recognize the address. I'd been there once or twice with Bob when we were on our way to the mountains. My index finger rests there under the letters. *So they're alive,* I think. *Or one of them is, anyway. Mother? Father?* I'm astonished that they're actually listed. Wouldn't they opt to hide, to be out of print? Don't they know that they have a son who went to jail for molesting children? It strikes me as rather brave, or perhaps as a kind of defiance... or denial?

C——. A Germanic-sounding name. Or, maybe, Russian? Who knows? I never asked about his family. So many things I never knew about him. Where did he grow up? What sort of childhood did he have? What happened to him? Did he ever live at this address?

I place a hand on my chest. *Calm down. Just looking,* I think, even as my eyes, my arm, act on their own. Dialing. Four digits, then hanging up. Pause. Five numbers, then hanging up. *Crazy, this is crazy.* I walk out of Mom's room, down the hall, and into the kitchen. Drink a glass of water, gaze out at the quiet street. The old ash tree is in bloom. Sunny. Everyone at work, at school. I walk back and dial again. It rings. My God—a voice.

"Hello?"

His mother.

In the silence before she repeats her greeting, her face comes back to me instantly. Pale, wrinkled skin, ivory-colored glasses, a bun of white hair—a grandmotherly mother. "Hello?" she says again. It's a kind, tremulous voice, just as I remember.

"Yes, hi. Hello . . . you probably don't remember me. My name is Marty Moran and I lived in Denver years ago and your son was a . . . a close friend of mine and I moved away a long time ago and lost track of him. I always wondered what happened to him. He had such an influence on my life." I feel myself playing the part, good boy, all snake oil and charm. But what I've said feels as full of truth as it does deceit. "He was a good friend and I always wanted to get back in touch." *Back in touch . . . Christ, does she get a lot of these calls? Maybe she's about to tell me he's dead or, at least, dead to her.* There's a long pause. She's about to hang up, I think, and I ask, "Is he around town still? Might I reach him?"

She asks me to repeat my name.

"Well . . . Marty, how good of you to try and contact Bob. Where do you live now?"

"New York."

"Oh, far from the West. What brought you all the way out there, may I ask?"

"The theater. I ended up becoming an actor."

"Oh, that must make for an interesting life."

"Sometimes, yes."

"I think I do remember you, you were in the spelling bee weren't you? All those years ago? You did very well."

"Yes, that's me."

"Yes . . . I remember. Bob was proud of you."

"Oh, really?"

"Yes.... well...he cared. He tried to do good for a lot of people."

Fuck, he's dead, I think, realizing that I harbor a belief he's someone who would have been gravely ill. Or murdered. Then she says,

"You know, he's had a rather rough time of it. Some hard years. But I think things are better for him now. More positive. *(He's alive!)* That's the thing, you know, we've got to try and see things positively."

"I find that, too."

"You know, I've become a member of a wonderful church that helped me see things in a brighter light. Do you have a church you go to in New York?"

"Not formally, no. Not at the moment."

"It's amazing the way a bit of faith can go a long way in opening our eyes to the wonder of being."

"Do you have an address for Bob?"

I picture the space between us going red, somehow, with her suspicion. It's as if I have a fish on the line and I have to make just the right tug to hook it.

"Well," she finally says, "I think I could give you his phone number."

I find it interesting that she doesn't want to give me his location. As if she's promised him she won't do that. Is she afraid I'll hunt him down? Or send someone to get him? She reads out the number. I don't recognize the area code. I scribble it on the back of a housepainter's business card that's sitting on my mother's nightstand.

"Thanks."

"Good luck, all blessings to you in New York. Goodbye."

"Bye."

I stare at the ten figures for a long time. I can't believe it. A series of numbers, a map that could lead back to him. Finally, after several attempts, I manage to dial. My heart is furious, hoping for an answering machine.

"Hello."

Fatigued, nasal, cavalier. The sound of him is astonishing. Something within me thrashes, leaps through my skin, as if a particular vibration had been trapped and waiting in my body for years, waiting for just the right frequency to erupt: *That's him!*

"Hello," I say. "You may not remember me. It's been twenty years. I'm Marty Moran. I knew you when I was a boy."

"Of course I remember you. I remember you well." He sounds very calm and it occurs to me, instantly, that this is the tone of someone I would know now to avoid. Unctuous, that's the word. He sounds unctuous. "You were a great kid," he says. "Sure, I remember you." The mountain, the myth I've made of him is shrinking to the size of my inner ear. A lonely hum, a little man.

"Where are you?" I ask.

"A small town in California . . . a nowhere kind of place. I'm glad you caught me. I've been away for a long time in the hospital with a back injury. You know . . . the kind of work I do has always been very physical and, well, my body isn't what it used to be. I'm fallen apart."

Oh, he's smooth, I think. He jabbers as if I'm an old friend, chats like the con man he's always been. "Where are you?" he asks.

"I live in New York."

"What do you do there?"

"I'm an actor."

"I always knew you were special. Such a talented kid."

"You say that to all the boys?"

I can't believe I've said this. That I've made this stab at something *real* and dangerous and I can feel us both waiting now to see where this is headed. The pause continues and then he simply says,

"No."

He's been through this before. I can feel it. I can almost sense the chorus of kids-become-men who've called him. I don't rush to fill the silence. I feel myself reaching down for strength, for directness, and I say, "That was quite a time in my life, you know? A lot happened when I knew you."

"Yes."

"Bob. We had sex."

"Sex wasn't the only part of our relationship."

"Do you have any idea how much I think of you? Of what happened?"

"It does no good to dwell on the past. I've made my peace with God. I hope you do too."

I can feel the door closing. No remorse there, nothing to talk about. My stomach is tied in knots. I want to say just the thing, explode with a genuine anger that might pry things open, lead us to a heart-to-heart or some kind of all-out fight. But I'm stunned by his sureness, his self-righteousness. I can think of nothing to say. After more silence he says, "Write to me if you can. I'd sure like to know about your life, how and what you're doing. Here's my address."

Obedient boy, I scribble it under his phone number and stick the card in my wallet. When I hang up the phone I feel, at first, some strange glimmer of relief. A kind of triumph. I walk around the house thinking, *At least I did it. I called the bastard, I heard his voice, I whittled the whole thing down to size. The size of a tired old laborer in a ramshackle house. Write him? He's not worth it, I'll never write him. Forget it. The end. Ever after, amen.*

I walk to the kitchen and look out the window, past the mountain ash. The tree is thick, four times the size it was when I was a kid. As I stare toward the orange disk of the late-afternoon sun, whatever flicker of relief I feel gets swallowed into a wave of dread. My body, source of endless trouble, screams, *Go! Get Some!* My knees are practically shaking with it. And that's it. I'm off, a madman. I get into the car and drive straight to a place I know on Colfax Avenue, where I can touch a stranger until I am senseless with it.

16

I'M LATE. HE'S already in bed.

The lamp is turned low. Henry is lying faceup, his hands folded carefully over his chest. Eyes closed. I see the gray wires flowing from the speakers in his ears. He's awake and listening. I watch his chest rise and fall with his breath.

I put down my pack, place my wallet on the bureau.

"What you listening to?" I ask.

"Mozart."

I move to the closet to hang up my clothes, go to wash my face, brush my teeth. I come back and crawl in next to him. One of his hands moves over and rests on my stomach. He scoots over so that our hips touch. "How was your audition?" he asks.

"It went OK. I think I might get a callback."

"If they're smart."

"Did you hear anything about the movie?" I ask.

"Just that I'm still up for it."

"The air conditioner folks come tomorrow, between eleven and one."

"I've got yoga."

"I'll be here. If they even come. They're so screwy. God, I'm anxious."

Henry switches off the music, turns and wraps his arms around me.

"What about?" he asks.

"Everything. Work, money . . . you know. *Me.*"

His lips find mine. I understand his kiss with every nerve in my body. I reach over and switch off the light.

"I love you," he whispers.

"I'm so glad you do."

We kiss again. It's like picking up on a conversation we've been having for a very long time. And tonight, suddenly, there's a need to speak of everything and I will not disappear. *I'm right here,* I tell him, with every inch of my skin. We press close and closer. Desire and safety, all at once. That's what hits me, each time it happens. Hits me so hard. This much desire wrapped inside this much sanctuary. And it's unspeakably sweet to move across this sanctum. The one I know so well.

When all is said and done, I sink into the music-filled sweetness of him. And we drift, together, toward our separate sleeps.

Grace.

It is the word that comes to me as I lay there with him.

I'm never sure exactly what it means, but I try to think of all the ways it's defined.

Mercy.

Divine assistance.

Charm, courtesy, and kindness.

A reprieve.

God, yes, a reprieve, that's right. His arms around me, a reprieve.

The Catholics, of whom I suppose I will always be one, speak of grace as something God gives us to become partakers of the divine nature of eternal life.

It's a prayer before a meal.

It's a musical trill.

Well, that's it. I'm in the arms of music. A passport to the infinite, as Winnie used to say. Can a person be that for us?

This one thing I know. I am at rest where I belong.

Lucky.

17

THIRTY-SIX AND a half years old and one spring evening a man ten years my junior slid in under the radar.

The lousy word, *cheating,* always makes me think of my French teacher, Ms. Palmer, the one and only lady amid all the Jesuits back at Regis High. She caught me one desperate day with irregular verbs written on a card underneath my shoe and with her jet-black eyes suddenly towering over me said, "Looking for answers in all the wrong places, aren't you Mr. Moran?" I felt I might die for shame. She didn't send me to JUG. Said she was sure it was a rare indiscretion.

Now the rules, the promises I'd broken, were my own.

I paced the living room, out of breath, telling Henry there was a terrible puzzle. A twisted riddle in my chest. That my body was plunging down a dark chute. "What are you talking about?" he asked. "You're making no sense."

"I'm *seeing* this boy," I said. "I'm losing my marbles."

He turned to me with the simple force that is his integrity, the part of him I'm convinced is rooted right to the center of the earth, and with nothing but a look nearly knocked me to the floor. "Stop," he said. "*Enough.*" I thought my chest would cave in.

It wasn't any kind of bliss or new love, this affair. That, I suppose, would have been a conversation of another order. No, this had all the familiar numbing qualities of my age-old compulsion. But worse was that it came after a long period of relative calm and that it wasn't my usual MO—the quick, anonymous fix. One encounter with this guy turned into a few. And that morphed into a month and then another marked with secret trysts. It was obsession of a new intensity. My anxiety screamed, *Shame,* it screamed, *Who do you think you are?* It shrieked, *You don't deserve a good life.*

With Henry's help and some health insurance, I got myself back into therapy. Recommended by our good friend Brooks, she was the first female shrink I'd ever gone to. I call her Carolyn now, all these years later, but when I first walked into her West Side office in the fall of 1996, I called her simply Doctor, and prayed it would be over quick.

She sat in a comfy swivel chair. I chose the blue couch near the window. Her hair was beautifully coifed. Blond. She had gold earrings, a smart black pantsuit. A New York gal. I stared out at tugboats on the Hudson, wanting to be anywhere but sitting in the middle, once again, of my own sorry-assed trouble. I told her the only thing I knew was that my life had got away again. That whatever was good about it had to do with Henry and I was fucking it up. I struggle with addiction, I remember telling her, but I wonder what it is I'm actually addicted to. Chaos? Sometimes I think it's the adrenaline of chaos. I rambled for a session or two about passion. That maybe that's what was at the bottom of this affair. That I wanted to feel twenty again, you know, one of those midlife crises. What is passion? I kept asking. How does any couple keep it alive?

She nodded, sipped from her bottle of Poland Spring. "There's all kinds of passion," she said. "Intellectual. Artistic."

"Sex is at the top of my list."

"It is certainly a kind of passion to choose to be together, to choose one another continually for over a decade, as you and Henry have done."

I veered into lengthy complaints about my unreachable theater agent, my frustrating career, another fight I'd had with Henry about my chronic lateness or his cranky depressions. She'd cross her legs, sip her water, nod. All patience, all ears, and I kept thinking,

*I'm some kind of a broken record spinning in a miserable groove, paying
someone to listen. Stop.* And I did. I shut up. I began sitting for long
periods of uncomfortable silence. I couldn't think of one useful
thing to say, I told her, couldn't think what any of this yakking had
to do with getting healthier. She nodded, tried breathing exercises,
meditation bells. On the day I came in to quit, I simply blurted
out, "What I can't stand is when I wake up with it. I open my eyes
and it's already there."

"What?"

"Anxiety. The anxiety. It rules my life." She suggested drugs and
I told her that frightened me but I'd think about it. "You know
those stories?" I asked her, "about the witch hunts? How they'd pile
rocks on someone until they admitted knowing the devil or whatever? I wake up and it's as if there are stones on my chest and I'm
supposed to admit something but I'm not sure what, beyond the
fact that I'm a shit. I can't breathe, it's as if the day has already gotten away, I'm behind on everything and I could never accomplish
enough to make up for the crushing thing I've done wrong. Maybe
it's just the old original sin."

"Are the Catholic voices still that strong in your head?"

"I swallowed that stuff whole."

"You're in charge of your life now."

"But I'm not in charge. Look what brought me here."

I looked out the window. There was a boat with an *M* pulling
a barge upstream. I knew it stood for Moran, the name of the tug
company, and it looked to be hauling garbage. I couldn't help but
smile at the obvious metaphor.

"What's funny?" Carolyn asked.

"I am some kind of bore."

"It's your life we're talking about. What makes the anxiety so
bad some days?"

"Shame."

We sat in silence. I hated the silence. The waste of money, the
crazy white noise in my noggin. She was as calm as could be, made

a note in my folder. And then, on this day I was meant to quit, I decided to tell her about a stupid, as I thought of it, recurring dream. She nodded when I'd asked, "That's a classic therapy thing to try, right?"

So I proceeded to describe the dream I'd never before put into words, of a murder, in my old neighborhood. A little girl down the street has been killed. Maybe it's a little girl. I'm not sure, but I'm involved, somehow. The corpse has been hidden for some time, buried in our backyard or, sometimes, near Cherry Creek. But there's blood bubbling up through the weeds now and the police are on their way. I am absolutely terrified. I didn't pull the trigger on—or stab?—the dead person, but I helped hide the body and the FBI dogs are circling and the whole time I'm trying to figure out, remember, who the victim is. We are all—the neighbors, the detectives—about to see the face, and I know then they'll come get me but just before they unearth the body, I wake up. I wake up sure that the story is real. I mean *really*, in real life. And I lie in bed trying to grasp it, to convince myself I didn't murder somebody along the way. I get up and try to do the usual things. Make coffee. Kiss Henry. I try to hang on to the relief that it was just a dream, but there is this nasty anxiety. I mean the fierce kind that has no nameable cause. And I feel like I've got to get out of my skin, that the day is lost to angst. I end up swimming a million laps or acting out or scribbling for hours in my notebook.

I noticed that Carolyn was making notes inside my folder. I thought I must be on to something.

"What do you think it means?" I asked.

She looked back at me, her brown eyes the picture of calm. "What do you think?"

"Well, tell me what the textbook might say."

"No textbook here."

"Give me some Jung or something."

She smiled. She waited. And I told her that I once heard that every character in a dream is actually you. Yourself. She asked me to venture a guess. Could I be the faceless corpse? And for the hell of it I said, "Yes, it's me." And when I said it, heat rose instantly in my chest.

"Who's the murderer?" she asked.

I took another stab.

"Me."

"Who's the authority that wants to punish you?"

I realized that my heart was racing.

"Me," I said, and I felt something shift beneath my sternum. As if two bones were trading places and suddenly I was afraid I might cry.

"Why do you want to punish yourself?"

"This is all so simplistic, ridiculous."

"Look, we're just exploring." She took a deep, deliberate breath. Exhaled slowly. I understood that she was encouraging me to do the same.

I came back the next week. We kept talking. I told her I'd gone back into meetings. How much I hated that this stuff still plagued me. "I've read all the literature," I told her. "I've let go and let God, what the hell is wrong with me?"

"It takes time."

"I sexualize everything, everyone, I guess. But that's true for a lot of men, isn't it? Especially with gay guys, don't you think?"

"Not necessarily . . . no. I take it from what you've relayed that that's not necessarily true for Henry, for instance."

I stared out the window, at the ice forming on the edges of the Hudson.

"I've been at this a long time."

"At what?" she asks.

"Sex that's hidden, fraught. Christ, I've been at it since I was twelve."

"What happened when you were twelve?"

Reluctantly, I give her a thumbnail sketch. I'm surprised that all these weeks have gone by without my actually talking of it specifically. I tell her I feel like a walking cliché, "another altar boy diddled, blah, blah, blah."

"Do you have a picture of yourself around that time that you could bring in?"

That sounds silly, I tell her. Absolutely maudlin.

"Will you bring a picture of you as a boy next week?"

Utterly embarrassed, I toted my kid picture to her office the next week. I kept thinking of any number of people, my father, folks at work, who'd scoff at this. The way *I* was scoffing. I was dreading that she would ask me to talk to it or hold it or some stupid thing. The photo I grabbed was one that had followed me around for years. A picture of me standing in a kayak at the edge of a pond. It had been stuck in the bottom of drawers at my various apartments. Tucked in manila folders or between album covers as I moved around California and on to New York. It had come out of hiding one day not long after Henry and I met. I gave it to him as a gift because he'd seen it and thought it cute. He framed it and hung it up. I don't recall telling him much of anything about it but that it was at camp in the mountains when I was twelve.

Carolyn asked me to put it down and talk about the time at which it was taken and, strangely, the shift was almost instant. I don't know if it was the photo or being fed up but it was as though a switch got flipped and my body just gave up the ghost. The reversal was powerful, as if the mechanism, the energy, dedicated to burying swapped suddenly to unearthing. My constant reluctance to speak of it, to seriously consider the connection between then and now, lifted. I began to talk forthrightly, for what felt like the first time in my life, about the paper route and George, the troubled parents and, more than anything, about the counselor. The words tumbled.

After a few weeks of this I blurted out, "I think I'll lose my mind if I say or hear his name one more fucking time. Bob, Bob, blah, blah. I'm wasting time on him. I don't want him in this room or in my life!"

"There's a reason you're talking so much about it, trust your intuition."

"But why do I come back again to this man?"

"You circle around a story, you come back to it at different points in your life and each time you've spiraled deeper. You're coming at it with more experience, more reflection, till you get nearer the bottom of it."

"But what's the bottom?"

Carolyn tilted her head, smiled.

"There is no bottom, right? Why don't I want to kill him? When I think about the time before I met him, I remember feeling, at the most interior part of myself, really alone and really frightened. About being different, I guess. Being a gay boy, probably. I felt such a sense of doom in that culture. He exploited that and, at the same time, opened something up to me. It was chaos because he was sad and sick. Confused. But he was also a clue somehow. I was drowning in some ways and he was . . . a life preserver."

I looked up at her and repeated *life preserver*. She nodded. She looked at me as though what I'd said was perfectly reasonable. "After all of this, I just called him a preserver," I said.

"It's the paradox. He was destructive. He was a life force. And you reached for that force. In that way he was a life preserver."

"But he was a criminal."

"Yes."

"What he did was wrong."

"Yes."

"In a way I loved him."

"Contradiction is part of the legacy of this. It's part of what grips so tightly. What he did was violent, no question. But that does not erase the fact that he had qualities that you instinctively knew you needed. Wanted. Reached for. Learned from."

We sat in silence.

"Why do you think you're crying?" she asked.

"Because this is it, the first moment it feels like the rocks are lifting from my chest. Talking about it this way is just a . . . huge relief. A light. I'm the most rabid judge of myself. Punishing myself for going back, for being with him, for admitting my desire. It's almost as if it's the punishment I'm attached to, addicted to. The sense of condemning myself, that kid with the oar, for wanting the attention, the touch, and now I just want to give the kid a fucking break. It's life! He was living his life. He was smart and good and doing his best. He wasn't a bad little shit." I leaned forward on the couch, put my head between my knees. "God, the grip of this is unbelievable."

"What happens when you're a child grips your nervous system."

"What exactly is the grip? Am I trying to re-create the jolt of what happened then? The mother of all orgasms?" I sat back up. "Why do I repeat certain behavior? Why am I talking about it?"

"To get to the other side of it."

"What's the other side? Understanding? Freedom? I've been writing about it like a crazy person. It's the only thing that eases the anxiety. To write and write."

"You once said that your anxiety is like fuel."

"The push, yes. The drive. I feel I have to tell about this. Tell the truth. That I'm *supposed* to. That that's what's meant to be."

"Perhaps it's part of what you're called to do."

"My Great Aunt Marion used to say that. She talked about having a calling. God, if she could see me now in this fucking mess."

"I imagine she'd be very proud."

And I saw Marion's wrinkled face. Saw her countless letters stacked in my drawer. I put my head in my hands. I couldn't stop the tears.

18

SPRING; 1997. MOM called. She'd finally done it, she said. She'd sold the house. Our old house on Glencoe. Moving to New Mexico. Life is change, I told her. Good luck.

I hung up and couldn't stop thinking about it. The rooms, the basement, the backyard. Nostalgia. Forget it. But I realized I wanted to see the old place before it changed hands. I suddenly thought of our house as an archaeological site about to be closed. The cigarette burns on the porcelain sink in Dad's old bathroom. The four-o'clocks under the master-bedroom window. I wanted one more look. And what I wanted to see more than anything, I realized, was the hole in the banister of the basement steps. In all these years I'd never looked for it. Never thought to. *Did that actually happen?* I wondered. *Did I pull down a .22 rifle and try to put a bullet in my head in the months after Bob?* I'd spent so long forgetting, I began to doubt what was truth and what wasn't.

Henry and I were performing together in a long-running musical that spring—*Titanic,* sinking eight times a week. Mondays were the day off and, on the one day, I flew from New York to Denver and back again. Mom thought me crazy but agreed to pick me up at the airport. I helped her and my little sister pack a few boxes. When they went out to run errands I wandered the site. I touched the burn marks on the sink, sat on the back porch. I walked the basement stairs, toward my old bedroom. I ran my hands along the banister until my fingers came across the hole, splintered and hidden, cutting clean through the bottom half of the wood. I supposed no one had ever noticed it. Or the gouge in the wall made by the same bullet. I sat down on the steps and reached up again to touch the splintered wood. Proof.

On my way back to New York, I pulled the old housepainter's business card out of my wallet. The one I'd hidden away years before. The one that managed to stay stuck from wallet to wallet. It was wrinkled and frayed, but still legible on the back was his address and the California phone number.

"I woke up early from a dream this morning," I told Carolyn. "It punched me in the stomach."

"What was it?" she asked.

I remembered it vividly as I told it to her. I still do, though I had the dream but this one time. In it, I was riding in the truck. Bob's truck. We came to a stop in the middle of a meadow to watch the elk bend their necks and pull grass from the ground. There were hundreds of them, wild and beautiful, surrounded by purple-colored peaks. Bob went to put his hand on my nape. I could see, as you do in dreams, his callused palm reach over my head and toward my back. But there was an arm tucked snugly around my shoulder. The steady arm of a quiet man gazing out over the clearing. It was my father. He was sitting in the truck and he'd been there all along. And Bob put his hand away and none of it ever happened.

I woke with the most profound sense of regret, I told Carolyn. She asked me why, and I said I felt a fierce longing for my father. A terrible sadness that he hadn't been there. That I blamed him.

"For what?" she asked.

"For not protecting me!" I blurted.

She nodded, and we sat with that for some time. I was shaken by the admission, the words, that had leapt from my mouth. I felt what I'd said to be absolutely true. And then, not true. Did I really want my father (or mother) to have saved me from the way things happened? The way things are. The way I turned out? I can't lay that at their feet. I said to Carolyn, "I'm not sure what the truth is. I feel I want to have been protected, but from what? From knowledge? From what would be my own life? This is who I am. The blame, the regret feels . . . useless."

Then she said, "Remember when you suggested that everyone in your dream may actually be you?"

"Including the man with the steady arm," I said, my voice suddenly breaking. I had the greatest desire to go to sleep right there on Carolyn's blue couch. "This stuff is bottomless," I said to her.

"It's complex," she said.

"What are we doing here, do you think, on earth?"

She smiled her calm smile.

"Sometimes," I said to her one snowy day, "I think about finding him. Facing him, if he's still alive. I've started so many letters to him, never finished, never sent."

"What do you think you'd want from a meeting?"

"I'm not sure. It's this feeling that I want to lay eyes on him, bring him down to scale. To see the evidence of the story, maybe? To show him I'm a person. See if he remembers me? If I mattered? If he's sorry? Maybe it's having a chance to say something I couldn't then, a way to put my arm around twelve. You know?"

"You'll know when the time is right, if you're meant to find him. When you have more clarity about what you want to say and how to do it while taking care of yourself. Give some thought to what you would want from such a meeting."

I thought about it, off and on, for four more years.

19

I REMEMBER THE muddy snowdrifts melting along the curbs of Cabrini Boulevard. The winter of 2002 was warming to an end. I recall I was to meet Henry later that day at the fountain at Lincoln Center to go to a movie. I was planning a trip west, I remember, to see Dad in Vegas, friends in Los Angeles. A trip I managed to make about once a year. But why it happened after all this time on this particular day in this particular year that I finally wrote him a letter, I do not know. Maybe it was watching the painful Catholic sex abuse scandal explode in Boston and erupt across the country. Maybe that was a catalyst. Perhaps it was the writing I'd been doing and my own revelation that thirty years to the day since I'd met him was fast approaching. Perhaps, without my knowing, something had shifted inside and I was ready. I struggled still with anxiety and compulsions but in so many ways my life was flourishing. I was working steadily, Henry and I were happy. Bob would pop, now and again, into my head. A jab, a nuisance. *I wonder if he's alive? What would it be like to see him? Would that put an end to it? To thinking about him?*

The letter to him felt like a whim, though I'm sure that fate played its part. It was as if I suddenly recalled I had a dentist appointment and I dug from my wallet the crumpled little business card. The card I had never misplaced. Heart pounding (will it ever be thus?) I walked to the phone in the bedroom and dialed him. I got the recorded voice of an operator. *I'm sorry, the number you have reached is no longer in service.* I checked information, nothing, no sign of him. He's gone, I figured. Moved or since died. Lost. I'd waited too long. I'm not meant to find him. Just as well. I had never come to any conclusion about what I wanted from such a meeting, anyway. What in the world would I say to him? I was about to toss the useless card into the trash but instead ripped a page from a notebook and scribbled.

Bob,

　　It has been many years since we spoke, many years since you gave me this address. I don't know where you are now. I hope you are well. If this finds you I wanted you to know that I will be traveling in Southern California in early April. If it's possible, I would like to see you. Enclosed is my number.

　　Sincerely, Martin Moran.

I addressed and sealed the envelope and wrote in large letters, *Please Forward.* And on my way out the door to an audition I slipped it, hurriedly (absentmindedly, it seemed), into the small box in the lobby of our building. As the flap snapped closed I thought, well, at least you finally tried. By the time I was halfway down the block moving toward the A train, I'd forgotten the letter.

Until the moment, a few weeks later, driving down the Hollywood Freeway, when my cell phoned bleeped and I pressed voicemail. It was then that I recalled I'd actually sent the note. *My God,* I thought, as I listened to the tired words of an old man—"I would dearly love to see you." *My God. It's him.*

20

APRIL 4, 2002. We have just stepped outside the Veterans Hospital. I've finally clicked on the tape recorder; I feel it buzzing, proof in my pocket that this whole thing is happening. There's not a cloud in the sky and we move to the shade of a palm tree—me on a bench, Bob in his wheelchair. I am so aware of the face-off, of all my grown-up effort, my thousands in therapy, for this: to be frank. As I am about to speak, a little brown sparrow arrives, flutters close to Bob's head, and disappears. Then he says,

"I must have read your letter a dozen times to try and see . . ."

"What I wanted?"

He nods, then looks down at his hands clasped tightly in his lap. "To try and see your state of mind, I guess. I fix up old cars for a living. Can't work much anymore." He gestures toward the bandage on his partly amputated foot. "Lost my lease." His right hand becomes a fist now, which he's squeezing around his left index finger. It makes me think of a little boy who's got to pee bad. He looks up and says, "I mean, if you're thinking of suing me, I don't have anything."

His lips lift with a hint of a grin, his eyes saying: *your move,* and I wonder if he's joking. But then I think, no, he's worried. It's all over the papers, isn't it? Younger men like me, nailing older ones like him, seeking answers, damages.

"Look, I'm not here for that," I tell him.

He unclasps his hands. "It was my fault," he says, grabbing the arms of his wheelchair. "When you called me all those years ago, I didn't have words. Mentally . . . I still don't have the words . . . mentally it's like I was the same age as you. But, I have to take it on my shoulders."

This strikes me as a sentence from his psychiatrist.

"It was your fault. You were the adult and I was a child and I did not have consent to give." I feel a sudden heat beneath my sternum, like the breath of the twelve-year-old I'm here to represent, as if he's in there saying: *Yeah, that's good. Say that, get me off the hook, please.* "I . . . I wanted to help you. You were such a gentle soul," Bob says.

"Soul?" I say. "My soul? You went for me the very first chance you had. Didn't even wait for a second date." He seems (chooses?) not to hear this remark.

"Mentally you were way ahead of the other boys. You were special."

"Now *that* I hate. What does that mean, *special?* How many specials can you have, Bob?"

He holds up a hand and says, "There were others, I admit. But not like you. You were so curious about things but you were afraid and . . ."

"Afraid? What do you mean?"

"Well," he says, "you were kind of wimpy."

"Oh, come on. Don't say that to me!"

"No, I mean you were shy and I wanted to teach you about the land and animals and help you gain confidence. And you did."

I want to disown it but it flashes through me that with this guy: I rafted a river, I watched a calf being born, cleared a field, conquered a glacier, learned a Hereford from a Holstein, a spruce from a cedar.

"I watched you grow to be a young man."

"Yeah, you did, didn't you."

"There were lots of levels to what we shared," he says, dropping his head again.

The brown sparrow is back, circling the crown of Bob's head as if tracing a halo. As if it might land. Bob is slumping there, his silver head shimmering in the California sun, completely unaware, it seems, of the bird, and I wonder, in some Catholic way, if the creature bears a message from On High. *Be gentle,* the fluttering spirit seems to say, *I've come to bless him to whom you speak.* Then I tell myself: *Marty, stop it. The bird's scoping for food, or nesting material.*

"Who was it that sent you to prison? A camper?"

He nods. "Yeah, the boy's family ... and the archdiocese. They hounded me. It got the attention off the priests who'd been fooling around at St. Malo. I was a scapegoat."

I have the sense that he's lying or exaggerating and I ask, "I heard you got ten years, Canyon City? Is that true?"

He shrugs and gives a little nod.

"Must have been awful."

"You can't imagine. It made my eighteen months in Nam look like a walk in the park."

Just then, a black guy sits down on the bench next to me, same hospital uniform as Bob, smoking a cigarette. Bob lets out a rude growl, says, "Let's go," and wheels himself down to the shade at the next bench, where he launches into a monologue about the good parent he's tried to be to his daughter who's all grown up and doing great. He speaks then of Karen, their breakup and troubles. After a time I try to interrupt, to get back to the "us" of this but, "Just let me finish," he says, raising his hand sharply and somehow this, more than anything else, lets me know I really don't like the guy. My candy-striper quotient evaporates and I say,

"Hey, I had sex with both of you ... several times. Remember? You, me, and Karen. One morning there was blood in the bed. I thought something terrible had happened until you explained it was her period."

This shuts him up.

Then he says, "It was an awkward attempt, I guess, at helping you be more, you know ... a man. I knew you were worried about ..."

"Being gay?"

He nods.

"You know, Bob, you used to tell me that homosexuals were peo-ple without love. Interesting thinking."

"I wasn't thinking."

"Have you ever figured you might be gay?"

He brings his hands to his face and says, "I've had to climb so many walls in this life, I suppose there are some things I never could really look at."

"Imagine, Bob, what our friendship might have been if . . ."

"If what?"

"If you hadn't crossed the line. Do you *know* what it does? Did? The utter chaos when you walk back into Mass, or your sixth-grade classroom, and you're standing there in your muddy boots, listen-ing to your teacher, thinking, *Wow, this thing's happened. I'm gonna be a man. But it's happened all wrong, I'm broken, broke the rules, I can't belong here.* And God only knows where you turn because even the mountains and the statues look at you differently and because no one speaks of such things in our Catholic world with all our se-crets and our terror of the body. And crazily enough, Bob, then the *only* place to find five minutes of relief, five seconds of what felt like forgiveness, was back in your arms, again and again." He looks away and I tell him, "You know, I grew up to be insanely sexually com-pulsive. I mean, back alleys, bathhouses, hurtful, crazy secrets from my family, my lover, you name it. And it has a lot to do, I think, with all that happened between us. I mean, Bob, I was twelve."

He shakes his head and looks down at his tangled fingers, and I wonder if I could ever convey to him how that was too young to get shot up with desire. And suddenly I'm thinking of the picture of the boy I saw on page twenty-eight of *Time* magazine, when I was standing with my dad in the checkout line a few days earlier in Vegas. The photo of the boy who didn't make it. And I want to ask Bob what he thinks of that. And I'm wondering if he remem-bers the photograph he took of a fine-boned boy standing in a kayak near the edge of a pond, where we went, just the two of us, three weekends after it first happened. I wonder if he remembers how small I was, holding up an oar, wearing the life jacket he gave me lest I drown.

And all at once, I just want to make clear to this man in the wheelchair how much he's haunted me, of the terror that lives in me still of repeating, in some way, his trespass. I wonder if I could describe for him how there isn't a time I don't squeeze with crazy joy and affection my gorgeous eleven-year-old nephew and think to myself: *Oh, God, careful, careful now.* I want him to know how I know this child is sacred, and to respect this child, a moral imperative. A certainty. This I know in my body, in this world, now: That *here is the Face of God.* But I don't have the words or the will to say any of this to the wounded vet sitting at my side, and all that finally comes out is,

"You know, Bob, I almost didn't make it."

He glances at me, then off to the hospital roofs. "I guess," he says, "on the one hand I wanted to build you up, but on the other, I was tearing you down."

"OK," I say. It's funny but I'm hearing Sister Agatha's words from way back when. About the angel and the devil, about the tangle inside. And I am looking at this man, this wreck of a man, I'm looking at *his* face and I can see it. I can see that some part of him means, meant, to be good. And at a time I was lost—my father drinking, my mom gearing for divorce—in he clomped and, in some way his love, and my love for him, helped me. Stranger things have happened in these Disturbed Regions.

"I'm sorry you went through all of this," he says. And I don't know if *sorry* was the sound I was after, but suddenly it's all enough and I stand to go.

"Will you be here in the hospital long?" I ask.

"Another month, at least. I'd sure like to hear from you."

"Oh, well, you've got my info, right?" It comes out really cold like a: "We'll do lunch," because underneath my thought is, *You've had enough of me for this lifetime.*

He backs up his wheelchair a foot or two. "I hope," he says, looking down at the grass, "I hope you don't hate me."

"Bob," I say, and my words just spill, "whatever else there might have been, there was kindness too. You were kind and I don't hate you."

He hunches forward as if hit in the gut and takes the wheels of his chair. "Once," he says, "we were shopping, you were riding in the cart and you grabbed a box of cereal off the shelf and said: 'Let's get this, Dad.'" He looks up at me. "Do you remember that?" I say nothing, thinking, *God, that cannot be true,* even as an image floats through my mind—a Friday night, a fluorescent aisle. "You don't remember, do you?"

"No."

"Maybe it was just a slip that you said *Dad,* but I nearly fell through the floor. It was one of the happiest moments of my life."

And my hand moves to his shoulder—whoosh—just like that. And I squeeze the loose flesh. God, there it is, I think, *touch.* Anybody watching from the windows of the hospital might think the two of us a sweet sight.

He extends his hand to shake and we do, like two gentlemen.

"Sometimes I wonder who I might be if I'd never met you."

"I can understand that," he says, his face going hard.

I pull away and move down the sunny sidewalk toward the stairs that lead to the parking lot. I can feel his eyes on me. I think he's waiting for me to turn, to give some kind of sign. When I reach the door of my rent-a-car I spin around and, sure enough, he's positioning his wheelchair right at the edge of the steps where he can watch me go. He's silhouetted against the white brick and I am just amazed that he's there. That he gave me this stab at the past. And, without permission, my hand flies into the air and waves, jauntily. Ever the boy from Christ the King. And when Bob raises his arm to wave back I'm filled with the strangest, strongest feeling that this very goodbye was contained in the first moment I ever laid eyes on him.

21

I SIT ON the grass of the Getty and wait for Jodi. The elevators rising from the subterranean parking garage open and close continually, disgorging and gobbling up museum guests. Between glances for her I scribble in my notebook.

4 April 02. 2:05 PM. I just left him. I want to feel something momentous, that everything is different for having done it . . .

I take in the sky. Clear blue. A breeze laced with the brine of the Pacific moves by me. I hear my name. She's already waving, strutting in my direction. She has on dark slacks and a purple blouse that sets off her short black hair. She's got the swagger of a girl who seems to trust the world. I recall how she moved just this way in high school, but with a Marlboro dangling from her lips.

"Hey, Mart."

"Hey." I stand and we hug.

"Ya good?" she asks.

"Yeah, fine."

Without speaking we move to the tram, ride up the hill, and then stroll straight toward the center of the gardens, which overlook the ocean. It smells of sea and sage. We pass by a guide saying, "Here on your left—the bright yellow, those are called sticks of fire, and on the right, angels' trumpets." The path loops through the fire and the trumpets and takes us around to a thick collection of cacti.

"God, this place is stunning," I say.

"I knew you'd like it." She points. "Succulents galore."

I turn away and I get into the car thinking, *That's it. I came, I met him, I did it. I was frank. This will put an end to all of it. Right? That's why I've come.* But the grip of it, of him, it's still there. I start the car and I back away wondering what in the world you have to do to get free of it. In another thirty years, I'll be seventy, he'll be dead. *Enough.*

And a thought came to me. Something Sister Christine said all those years ago. That with the really rough things it would always come down to grace. *A gift from the beyond that moves us toward our own salvation.* And as I crawled out into the thick Los Angeles traffic, what I kept hearing in my head was this prayer, a plea repeating: *OK, grace, please, to let it go, let him be, for heaven's sakes. Let him rest.* I mean Bob, of course. But then, I realize I'm really talking about someone else. The twelve-year-old. The sweet kid caught in a photo, still talking his way out. And I'm not sure how in the world to let him rest. Not yet, anyway.

"Maybe there's peyote in here."

"I doubt it."

"It'd be a good day, wouldn't it? To smoke a joint, eat some shrooms, float away."

"Those days are over," she says.

"I know. The very thought of pot makes me crave a Xanax."

We pass a shrub with purple blossoms. "Matches your shirt," I say.

She takes my arm and steers us toward a bench.

"So?" she asks.

"I don't know where to start."

"Start with how he looked."

"Awful, really. So small. A wreck. Missing part of a foot. Sitting in a wheelchair."

"Karma. His worst punishment is being himself."

"It feels so foolish, embarrassing really—this lifelong obsession over a loser."

"Did you let him have it?"

"I let him have something. I said what I wanted to say, I think. At least he had to face me as a grown person. That felt right. But it was all oddly rational, calm. I kept hearing myself and I sounded so reasonable. There weren't any fireworks."

"Is he out of your system?"

"God." I laugh. "Don't know. I drove away with this feeling that it was really me, not him, I needed to forgive. That he's actually, almost, beside the point. I don't want to be stuck back there anymore. With him. With blame."

Enormous, billowy clouds are moving swiftly past the high stone walls of the Getty galleries. The stones and the clouds match, they're the same brilliant white, and each time I glance up at them I have the wild sensation that Jodi and I are moving as fast as the wind, that we're sailing.

"Did he apologize?"

"Not really. He kept trying to justify, explain."

"What a shit," she cries.

"There you go again, getting angry on my behalf."

"Anger's a good thing. Tells me what I care to fight for and what I love. I can't let go of the fact that he hurt you. My best friend."

"I love you for that."

She bumps my shoulder with hers.

"I wish I had a cigarette," I tell her.

A group of schoolkids marches past our bench. The teacher is a man, his voice low and firm as he calls out to his charges. "Isaac, stay with the others," he says. All the boys have yarmulkes, the girls, lovely skirts and white stockings.

Jodi takes my arm again and we walk.

"You think you'll ever see him again?"

"Oh God, no. But, then again, who knows?" We hike along a path circling a fountain. Pennies and nickels glimmer in the water. "He said that I called him 'Dad' once."

"OK. That's . . . strange."

"I know. I don't know if it's true, but it sure makes me wonder just what primordial thing was, is, rumbling under all of this."

Jodi's phone rings. She slips it out of her pocket. We sit on a ledge surrounded by bougainvillea. It's her sitter, checking in. They chat briefly.

"Everything OK?" I ask.

"Logan's down for a nap. That's good. I'll turn this off."

The Pacific is in clear view beyond the hills. A haze that had been there earlier has lifted. I can see a tall spinnaker moving south along the coast. We continue down the trail through countless flowers and come to a verse etched in stone.

Ever	*Ever*
Present	*Changing*
Never	*Never*
Twice the	*Less than*
Same	*Whole*

Robert Irwin, December 1997

My toes point to EVER PRESENT. Hers to EVER CHANGING. I burst out laughing.

"What?"

"I don't know. That's either totally Hallmark or completely profound. Today, I can't tell which."

"He's talking plants," Jodi says.

"Mortals too, maybe."

"He's the artist who landscaped this place. Gorgeous."

"Yeah, Eden."

We move up the staircase for the Gallery of Ancient Art and stop on a balcony overlooking the garden.

"If only I hadn't gone to the ranch," I say.

"What do you mean?"

"You know. If only Eve hadn't taken the bite. If only my parents had done something different. If only I weren't raised Catholic—"

"What are you talking about? You've always been Jewish."

"I mean, you have to let go of the if-only's, you know? This is who we are, what is. I've spent so much time thinking that what happened when I was twelve split me into pieces. Maybe pieces is a part of being whole? Maybe it's tangling with evil that helps us to know good."

Jodi looks out over the banister, her eyes following the Hebrew school kids.

"Marty, you're forever letting that man off the hook, distancing yourself from the breach of it. The truth of what he did."

"I hear you."

The kids have pencils and paper and are kneeling over the beds, learning the names, it seems, of the various blossoms. We watch them and I wonder how I can explain this feeling I have that somewhere in the middle of the whole tangled mess, the whole story, there has always been something sacred. Something good that was doing its best to grow. And I want to describe this picture I have in my head of waving goodbye to Bob and thinking how possible it is, how amazingly possible, that what harms us might come to restore us. I take Jodi's hand. She's still surveying the garden and the students.

"It's exquisite here," I say.

"Yes."

"You know what it is?"

"What?"

"It's letting go of the sense that the past should have been any different or better."

"That's tricky. Are you hungry?"

"I am."

We climb up the many steps toward the entrance plaza and cafés.

"What are those hills?" I ask Jodi.

"Santa Monica."

"Saint Monica. She was the mother of Augustine."

"God, you Catholics are everywhere."

"Especially him, he was all over the map. Fabulous sinner, famous saint."

We reach the terrace that leads to the restaurant. The view is spectacular.

"Have you called Henry?" Jodi asks.

"He's in rehearsal today. I'm going to call him tonight."

"God, where are you going to start?"

I turn, blinded by the sun, its rays fractured and shimmering across the Pacific.

"By telling him how much I love him."

We step inside, and a smartly dressed man leads us to a corner table. It is strangely hushed. Green carpet, gracious service, the tinkling of silver against plates. The smell of good food fills the air. We take our seats. On three sides of the spacious room, north, south, and west, walls of glass give way to the mountains and to the bright sky of an April afternoon. The light splashes across the white tablecloths. Across all the couples and families and children gathered, talking softly, eating lunch on a hill overlooking the sea.

Afterword to the Anchor Edition

New York City, Fall 2005

ONE EVENING at a store in Seattle last summer, I was reading aloud from the book. I'd chosen two chapters—one sober, one humorous—hoping to offer a balanced performance. I'd barely finished the last sentence when a hand shot into the air and waved with the urgency of a second grader dying to give an answer. It belonged to a middle-aged woman with auburn hair, three rows back, who, I'd not failed to notice, was scribbling in a notebook the entire time I'd been reading. "Yes?" I asked.

"Who did you write this book for?"

Her forehead was furrowed, her pen poised above the notepad. I wanted so badly just then to put my head down on the little podium and go to sleep. I was several weeks into the book tour, had been performing my play for quite some time, prided myself on answering post-show queries fully, graciously. I couldn't say why this particular question unhinged me. I looked around the cozy bookstore trying to compose myself, to dig up a genuine response. *Myself and strangers,* isn't that what Gertrude Stein had said. I looked back at the woman, and we locked eyes. Much more loudly than I'd meant, I blurted, "You!" And curtly asked for the next question.

A young man who identified himself as a Franciscan priest asked me to discuss the differences between the play and the memoir. I told him that the play was crafted to create a communal experience of the complexity of the subject. Its eighty-minute span meant that choosing what to leave out, the "telling omission," was important, whereas the book allowed a more complete and, in some ways, intimate rendering of the story, of my adult life and the road toward healing.

"Are you still a Catholic?" someone else asked.

"I don't often go into a church but the church is in me. My anger at the destructive messages I received as a child, at a duplicitous institution, as well as my deep affection for the souls who guided me along the way, gave rise to this work. To the man I am. Ever the paradox."

I suddenly turned back to the woman in the third row. "You know Ms, ah, ma'am, regarding your question, I'm sorry. I didn't mean to be so short with you. Let me try to respond more to it."

Looking down at the cover of the book, at the little kid in the kayak, I slowly explained how private the writing had been. How secret. That for so long the idea of telling the world what happened seemed unthinkable. That writing about something that caused so much anguish was to gain a kind of authority over the past. How, at some point along the way, the desire to offer the story to others became more and more powerful, that I began to believe it might be of use. And that it might give voice to some as yet unexpressed aspects of a really troublesome subject. "I don't know," I ultimately said. "I guess, I wrote it for . . . possibly, for you. For me and for you."

She said thanks, wrote something in her notebook.

I now realize what unhinged me about that moment. When she spoke what I registered wasn't her question but this: *What makes you think anyone would want to know this? Sit down, keep quiet.* What my body felt was the slap of my own judgment, a jolt of the shame still stuck to my ribs. My own ancient fear that there's something unsightly, unmanly, dangerous, about telling. The work of hiding the truth of one's past can be such a long, deep habit, a habit that doesn't die easily. God knows, it has killed people. What's locked in the body takes a long time to rise to the head, let alone get expressed in some way to the world.

In the space of just these last few weeks the morning papers have reported an avalanche: scores of men and women struggling to overcome the angst and terror of "going public." Men nearly my age, spilling forth for the first time about the abuse they experienced as boys. A group of fourteen in Los Angeles, two brothers in San Francisco, and several people in my hometown of Denver. In each case heartbreaking destruction had been covered up in some way. Secrets held tight since 1968, 1972, 1974. In Los Angeles alone there are 560 sex abuse cases filed and pending. And that's just the Catholics.

It's been nearly two decades since I scribbled on a scrap of yellow paper: *What happened when you were twelve? Tell the truth.*

All the time I was at work on the book I remember thinking: Oh God, what if the Maryknoll nuns were to read this? Or, how uncomfortable, how embarrassing it would be when, if, my colleagues, my friends, read it. Or when the taciturn Irishmen of my beloved family lay eyes on it . . . they'll . . .

They'll what?

"Your book is an open door to someone like me," said a man, taking my hand at a Salt Lake bookstore. "You've lifted such a burden from my shoulders."

An assessment from my hometown newspaper: Why isn't Mr. Moran more angry? Is he in denial? Why doesn't he use Bob's real last name? Is he still protecting his perpetrator after all these years?

A woman cried out to me as I walked into the lobby after a performance of the play in Seattle: "It's all about reverence for children."

An e-mail that reached my computer screen: "I heard you on the radio. When will you people stop exploiting your salacious stories?"

A hug from my mom: "Darlin', you've honored your memories beautifully."

An invitation from a prosecutor in the Manhattan District Attorney's Office: "Would you come speak to the staff about all this, about what's between the black and white?"

"Did you ever wonder what happened to Bob when he was a kid?" asked a man in D.C. "Yes, and I regret not ever asking him," I replied.

Michael Berg, the peace activist whose son Nicholas was murdered in Iraq, wrote to me about breaking the cycle of revenge, about the radical challenges of forgiveness. "I cannot accomplish my goal," he wrote, "with hatred in my heart."

A comment from a neighbor on the street: "Congratulations on your book. I can't bring myself to finish it. It's just too . . . too sad."

Winnie, my old singing teacher (still teaching full-time), called a few days after she'd received the book: "I've read it." She was laughing on the other end of the line. "Marty . . . it's enchanting."

"Enchanting?" I said.

"Yes, full of wonder. And I predict it will make you rich."

That's when *I* laughed. Big time.

One night I sat in a West Coast pub with three Jesuit priests. After a reading they'd asked if they could buy me a beer. They discussed, to my shock, how they'd like to try in some way to add the book to the social sciences curriculum at their Catholic University. "You know our founder St. Ignatius Loyola's fundamental statement was always, "'Finding God in all things.'"

"That's the tricky part," one of them said.

One night in Colorado, a man approached me outside the theater where I was performing. His name was Dave. I hadn't seen him in more than thirty years. He was one of Bob's boys. He'd been initiated, I'd come to learn, shortly after I was; he'd been through hell. Putting his arms around me, he wet my cheeks with his tears, and whispered into my ear, "We made it." He introduced me to his wife. Showed me pictures of his two kids. As he walked away I wondered, as I had so many times—fist in the gut: What if I'd spoken up way back then? Would he and others have been spared this?

A woman in Portland: "Did that guy Bob make you gay?"

And everywhere and always the query: *Are you over it now?*

A few weeks ago I received a letter from Sister Grace, one of the nuns at the Maryknoll Cloister. I saw the elegant cursive, the return address, and immediately felt a wave of guilt. Though I had once mentioned to them, a long time ago, that I was at work on a book, I'd never shared anything about the subject matter. Nor that they were part of the story! Why hadn't I? Why hadn't I sent them a copy? Oh Lord, still, the shame. The fear that it would be "too much." The sexual trespass, the frank descriptions of my compulsions, my betrayals, as an adult. My embarrassment still so vivid. It turned out they'd read a review in the *National Catholic Reporter* and ordered two copies. A few lines into the letter I began to cry.

"... your story is a call for complete transparency—a call which you heard on some level of your being. . . . I find it remarkable to hear in the enormous suffering of obsession, the distinct echo of Love's Passion for Love. . . ."

That night I read the letter to Henry. We both welled up at its eloquence and generosity. "Now, there's the genius of the church," Henry said.

In June, twelve days after the book's release, my father died. I was in the middle of Sunset Boulevard trying to make a left-hand turn into the parking lot of a West Hollywood store—Book Soup. I was due to give a reading there in twenty minutes. My cell phone rang: It was my sister Carolyn, her voice breaking with the news.

He'd never seen the play or read the book. He never said it outright but I understood that it was something he felt he could not bear. I'd shown him the jacket and the dedication page where his name is written along with Mom's and Henry's. In his way he let me know that he was proud. He grinned and grumbled, giving me a slight punch in the arm, "Finally," he said, "my name on a book."

I went ahead with the reading that night. "Do it for Dad," my sister had said. The room at Book Soup was beautiful, embracing us with wall-to-wall, ceiling-to-floor volumes. I started to speak and found myself talking of Dad.

When I was little, I told those before me, I used to get up to pee late at night and now and again I'd see my Dad curled on the basement floor, smoking a cigarette, staring up at the many shelves of books he'd been collecting since his high school days. Mostly

Modern Library editions. The ones with the little man holding a torch high, leaping across the binding. One night I sat down on the floor next to Dad.

"What are you doing?" I asked.

"Looking for a good read," he said.

He stared. We were quiet. Then he said, "If there's one thing I can tell you to do in this life, it's read. Read, read, read. Stories are a Godsend."

The kids are back at school, careening around the playground across the street. Henry is in the other room warming up his voice. He opens soon in a new musical. The headlines in all of today's papers are about a subway terror alert: *Bombs in Baby Carriages.* The kids out there seem completely unaware of the warning, spinning around on the tarmac like molecules delighted at their existence.

For so many years I sat at this desk, my story seeking its way into sentences, into meaning. Now it's out there in ink, its own agent. As I write I glance, again and again, through the window at the chaotic playground, through the faint outline of my own reflection in the glass. As I look out there at the bobbing heads I feel an abiding wish, a kind of prayer.

That we not move through this life in isolation. That compassion and understanding render the secrets unnecessary. That we blessed beings learn to converse about the truth of the way it is, no matter how hard or complex. That we are able to speak about the subjects that all of us share and need to face. How do we love and care for our children, our world? How do we begin to listen, without judgment, to the stories that make up our lives? How do we lift the veil of indifference to each other's presence, each other's human plight?

"Who did you write this book for?"

I keep looking out the window.

"You," I say, full of wondering. And hope.

Acknowledgments

THANKS ETERNAL. To the whole gang at Beacon Press who originally and lovingly ushered this work into hardcover. My editor Amy Caldwell contributed in countless ways to its creation, as did author Cynthia Huntington. Much gratitude to Alice van Straalen and the team at Anchor Books for guiding *The Tricky Part* into paperback. For their guidance and steadfast support I want to thank Michael Klein, my agent Malaga Baldi, Seth Barrish, Dr. Carolyn Tricomi, Jodi Binstock, Melissa Dobson, Catherine Coray, Randolyn Zinn, James Lecesne, Liz Rosenberg, Ellen McLaughlin, Chris Moran and the Gordon guys, Robin Hemley, Reverend Cynthia Heller, Eve Ensler, Elatia Harris, David and Stephanie Fine, Ricky Ian Gordon, Michael and Kelly Schreiber, Marie Howe, Nick Flynn, Jan Crain, the Barrow Group, Paul and Karen Kandel, Sundance Institute, Bill Davis, the Fine Arts Work Center, Jeff Nathanson, Dave Johnson, Winnie Hartman, Sister Theodore Farley, Maggie Black, the Moran family, Ken Weiner, the Rockies, the Maryknoll Sisters, the New York Foundation for the Arts, Phil Baker, Ted Sperling, Dr. Mark Groshek, Steven J. Stone, Dame Judith Blazer, David Pearl, Victoria Clark, Melanie Braverman, James B. Freydberg, David Schechter, Marin Mazzie, David Costabile, Barry and Deb Schwartz, Brian D'Arcy James, Lisa Loosemore, Theresa McCarthy, SCA, Larry Green, Jessica Molaskey, Bill Buell, Amy Ryder, Suzette Sheets, Jason Danieley, Mark Adams, Richard McCann, Marc Vietor, Michael Hayden, Mark Schlegel, Steve David, Genine Lentine, Alexa Fogel, and Henry Stram. ETERNAL THANKS.

Some Resources

Darkness Into Light
www.darkness2light.org
Darkness to Light
7 Radcliffe Street
Suite 200
Charleston, SC 29403
1-866-FOR LIGHT /
1-866-367-5444

MaleSurvivor
www.malesurvivor.org
MaleSurvivor
PMB 103
5505 Connecticut Avenue, NW
Washington, DC 20015-2601
1-800-738-4181

Canada
MaleSurvivor
c/o BCSMSSA
1252 Burrard St., #202
Vancouver, B. C.
V6Z 1Z1
tel: 604-822-6482

Morris Center
www.ascasupport.org
P.O. Box 14477
San Francisco, CA 94114
415-928-4576

**National Clearinghouse on
Child Abuse
and Neglect Information**
Children's Bureau Administration on
Children, Youth and Families
370 L'Enfant Promenade SW
Washington, D.C. 20447
tel: 800-394-3366 or 703-385-7565
fax: 703-385-3206
Website: nccanch.acf.hhs.gov

Next Step Counseling
www.nextstepcounseling.org
A site by Mike Lew and
Thom Harrigan with a guide to
multiple resources.

Recovery Canada
www.vansondesign.com/RecoveryCanada/
2-558 Upper Gage Avenue
Suite 250
Hamilton, ON
L8V 4J6
tel: 905-389-3178
fax: 905-383-3200

Recovery from Sexual Compulsion
www.sca-recovery.org
SCA
P.O. Box 1585, Old Chelsea Station
New York, NY 10011
1-800-977-HEAL

Shepherd's Counseling Services
2601 Broadway East
Seattle, WA 98102
206-323-7131
www.shepherdscounselingservices.org

Stop It Now!
http://www.stopitnow.org/
A national nonprofit organization for child sexual abuse
prevention.
351 Pleasant Street, Suite B319
Northampton, MA 01060
helpline: 1-888-PREVENT (1-888-773-8368)
tel: (413) 587-3500 fax: (413) 587-3505
e-mail info@stopitnow.org

Survivors Network of Those Abused by Priests
www.snapnetwork.org
Survivors Network of Those Abused by Priests
P.O. Box 6416
Chicago, IL 60680-6416
1-877-SNAPHEALS
(1-877-762-7432)

Wings Foundation
www.wingsfound.org
WINGS Foundation, Inc.
8725 West 14th Avenue, Suite 150
Lakewood, CO 80215
1-800-373-8660